I'm deeply honored that you chose to pick up my book among so many others! I hope these pages offer you something valuable. Your support keeps me inspired to write more. Happy Reading!

M.R. Raghu

M R Raghu, CFA FRM FCMA

Foreword by
Navneet Munot, MD & CEO HDFC Asset Management

As the market expands and deepens, drawing in greater number of investors each year, there is a need to demystify the complexities and nuances of investing in Indian equites for the lay investor. This is where MR Raghu's book stands out. It is no mean task to lay it all out in a simple, non-intimidating and easy to read style and language. Drawing on his extensive experience, Raghu offers a practical guide and a compass for navigating the equities market without falling prey to fear and greed. Various frameworks together with sections on dealing with situations that investors inevitably face are presented in a compelling blend of theoretical foundations and practical insights.

– Sanjeev Varma,
IT & Telecom professional and passionate hobbyist investor

Raghu has dealt with the subject of investing at many levels. Whether he deals with the big picture or with the multitude of investment choices or the various investment strategies, he writes from a perspective of practicality. The book takes investors into how they can be better practitioners. The wide scope of the book makes it a one stop shop to learn almost everything early-stage investors must learn. It also takes the investor into his growth needs, what he must know before he grows and what he must not do after he grows. A very useful practitioner's handbook.

– Shyam Shekhar,
Investor & Portfolio Manager

Copyright © M.R. Raghu 2024
All Rights Reserved.

ISBN

Hardcase 979-8-89556-935-1
Paperback 979-8-89475-623-3

*This book is dedicated to V4 (our family WhatsApp group including
my wife, daughter and son).*

Contents

List of Figures

List of Tables

Acknowledgement

While weightlifting as a sport is a one-man/woman activity, I realised that writing a book needs more than two hands to lift! The biggest challenge starts with the flow, and I am truly grateful to several experts in the field who provided valuable suggestions to make the flow meaningful.

I sincerely thank Navneet Munot, CFA, for writing foreword to the book. Navneet is the CEO and MD of HDFC Mutual Fund and is a consummate investment professional, having observed the Indian capital market landscape for a very long-time. As he rightly pointed out, there are many topics in the book that can lend themselves to deeper evaluation for interested investors.

I would like to thank Pattabhi Ram for holding my hand from the beginning, for thinking together about the flow, for reviewing the work, and for explaining the publishing aspects. Pattabhi is a CA and a respected teacher. Having authored several books himself, he is best positioned to have provided me the needed fillip.

I also thank Dr Abhijit Phadnis for a thorough technical review of the book draft, which resulted in significant changes to the book's architecture. Abhijit is an acclaimed speaker on capital market topics and has published several videos for the wider benefit of investors. He has coached many professionals in his long and illustrious career.

Madhusudhan Chandarasekaran, CFA, offered his generous time to go over the initial draft and provided excellent technical inputs.

I thank Sanjeev Varma, a long-time friend who provided some great comments on the initial draft. Sanjeev is a keen follower of the Indian stock market and has practiced as a consultant to global organizations, providing business improvement programs.

I also took the privilege of requesting my former colleague Rajesh Dheenathayalan, CFA, to provide his commentary and views, which he willingly provided. Many of my present colleagues at Marmore helped me with this project, and I would like to thank all of them, especially Ajay Samuel, Jeniv Lasrado, and Boojitha who helped design the book cover.

Thanks are also due immensely to G Srivatsan who provided copyediting support.

Nothing is complete without family support, which includes my wife, Dr J Hemalatha, our daughter Shruthi Lalitha, and our son Shravan Ram.

Foreword

There are few books on investing in Indian equities written by professional practitioners. MR Raghu's "Blueprint for Billions: Mastering India's Equity Market" fills this important gap. The book is well organised and has a comprehensive and methodical approach. Raghu brings together a bouquet of insightful ideas—many of which are unconventional—that the reader should understand and also try.

One of the book's most notable strengths is its ability to provide both top-down and bottom-up views on India. This dual perspective is useful for a holistic understanding of the complex dynamics at play. For example, Raghu's discussion on "Decoding the Economic Web" and his observations on India's bond market and its potential evolution, among others, showcase his practical experience and understanding of the subject. The principle of "getting the macro right before the micro right" is sound and well-articulated, offering a foundation for investors to build upon. That "demography is destiny" is a powerful reminder of the long-term trends shaping the Indian markets. Raghu's consideration of dollar returns adds an important dimension for international investors to consider. His piece on interest rates, the concept of PIP (persistence in performance), and the 4D perspective for evaluating managers are valuable additions that can be directly applied in practice.

Bottom-up insights that the book offers are as important, if not more, as compared to the top-down perspectives. Raghu's coverage of active investing, his critical appreciation of the pulls and pressures in identifying winning stocks and the framework for researching equities are useful conceptual guardrails. While the book offers an excellent view of investing in Indian equities, the readers may want to delve deeper into specific areas. For instance, reading up more on value investing and how emerging markets evolve into developed markets over time could bring more value. Asset allocation is another important area – readers may want to use the topics covered in this book as important starting points.

In summary, MR Raghu's book offers a wealth of knowledge and practical advice that is both relevant and insightful. While there are areas for refinement, the book stands as a significant contribution to the literature on Indian equity investment. I am confident that future editions will build on this solid foundation, incorporating more advanced strategies and deeper analyses. I highly recommend this book to anyone desirous of learning about the Indian equity market.

– Navneet Munot, CEO & MD, HDFC AMC

Preface

I have been a keen follower of Indian capital markets for over 30 years and an investor, too. While my career path took me to the Middle East, where I had the opportunity to specialise in Middle Eastern economies, including capital and energy markets, given my geographic disposition, I continue to observe the Indian equity market and slowly developed an interest in managing my personal portfolio.

This book is a humble attempt to synthesise my learnings and experience to present market anlaysts, professional and high-net-worth investors with key viewpoints about investing in Indian equity markets. Some ideas border on conventional wisdom, but there are many unconventional ones, too. While the broader issues remain the same over the years, it is just a matter of a new perspective, which is what I am attempting in this maiden book of mine. I attempted to diagnose certain parts of the Indian equity landscape and shed some fresh light using critical data points and analysis.

The Indian capital market is at a tipping point now, where the equity market is ranked as the 5th largest in the world (market cap \$5 trillion), while the Bombay Stock Exchange enjoys the distinction of hosting the largest number of listed companies globally. Retail investors are active participants, with a 45% share of the market turnover at the National Stock Exchange. Though we can take pride in the fact that more than 5,000 companies are listed on the stock exchange, that represents barely 1% of total active registered companies, implying huge opportunities as we move forward. Even among the listed space, only about 5% of the companies enjoy mutual fund investments.

Table : 1 India's Equity Growth

Metric	Time Stamp	Data	Notes
Market Capitilization	May-24	$5 trillion	$2 Trillion in July 2017
Top Companies		Reliance, TCS, HDFC Bank, ICICI Bank, & Bharti Airtel	
Nifty cagr	2013-2023	13.40%	
AUM of Domestic Mutual Funds	Apr-24	Rs. 57 Trillion	Rs.9.45 Trillion April 2014
AUM of FPI's	Apr-24	Rs.72 Trillion	Rs. 16 Trillion April 2014
Liquidity	FY24	Rs.81,721 crores	Rs. 17,818 crores FY15
Holdings in NSE-listed companies	Mar-24	Promoters (40.7%), FPI's (17.9%), Government (11.2%), Individual Investors (9.5%) & Others (11.8%)	
Source: NSE & FXEMPIRE			

From a capital market perspective, unlike the US or China, India's bond market is not as well-developed as the stock market. For example, India's corporate bond outstanding as a percentage of GDP is a mere 17%, compared to South Korea's 80%. Even here, we notice a skew where the primary issuance of corporate bonds is mostly from banks and NBFCs. This low share means that many transactions happen in the private placement market with flexible and easy-to-structure terms, along with less disclosure and compliance standards. Retail investor participation in India for bonds is still very nascent.

There are events that can produce severe market impact, such as the Great Financial Crisis (2008), COVID-19, or the Russia-Ukraine War. We can call them *high-intensity low-frequency* events. We then have events like elections, budget presentations, sudden foreign investment inflows/outflows, etc., which we can call *low-intensity high-frequency* events. As investors, we must contend with both, having to make investment decisions around these events. Both scenarios call for a good understanding of macroeconomics. Therefore, investing in Indian equities or any market would involve a deep understanding of key macro events.

Figure : 1 Investing in Indian Equities

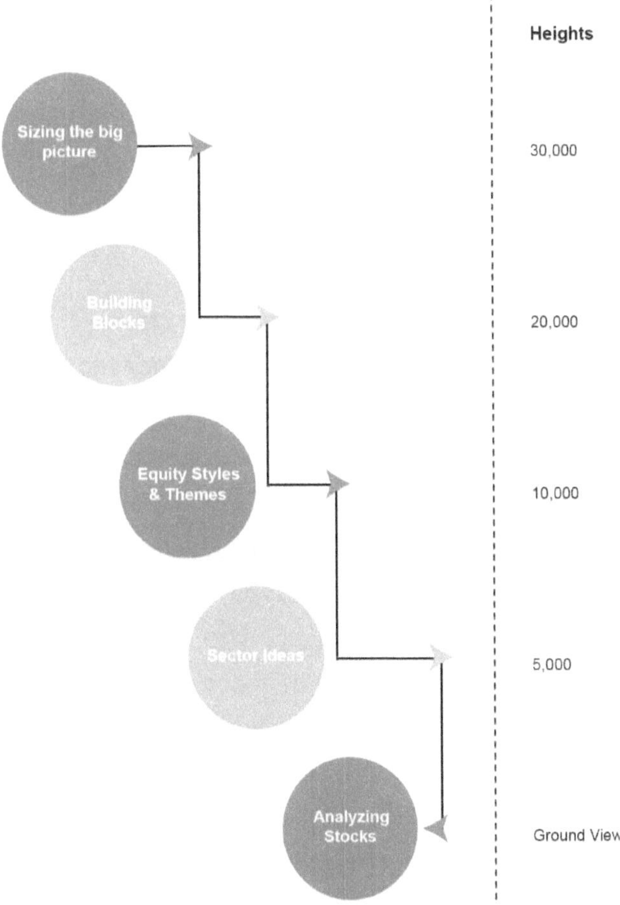

There are so many moving parts in the economy, and one must not only keep pace with most of them but relate that to how well they will trend in the future and affect markets. Most media analyses are rear-view mirror assessments that labour at length to explain what happened. But the key question is, "What next?" **Section 1** is all about sizing up the big picture and how investors should practice taking a 30,000 feet view, like a plane. The economic web of a nation is a complex interaction of many aspects, and decoding this economic web is central to understanding the role of the big picture. The big picture view focuses on broader economic issues like growth, inflation, liquidity, etc., and extraordinary scenarios (such as war) and how they can affect foreign flows and the currency. Remember, as the plane takes off, things appear clearer and clearer and vice versa.

The knowledge and perspectives gained through big-picture observation should lead to an understanding of building blocks that can help in formulating a credible investment strategy in what I call a gradual descent to the 20,000 feet level. This includes fund management, alpha generation, and market timing, which is the aim of **Section 2**. Globally, there has been a strong trend towards asset allocation strategies with the help of Exchange Traded Funds (ETFs). Understanding building blocks like mutual funds that offer these products will be a key building block. For those inclined to source alpha from mutual fund investing, the challenge is to identify managers who can beat the benchmark. While history can be a guide here, it may not repeat itself. The key element of asset allocation is shifting from equity to bonds and vice versa, which implies market timing. While textbooks say that one cannot time the markets, nevertheless, the predominant source of alpha remains market timing, primarily aimed at avoiding periods of steep market declines, technically called drawdowns. However, market timing looks elegant in retrospect but may be highly challenging to implement in practice. For investors aiming to capture long-term returns, plain beta is still a sure bet. The Indian stock market has indeed produced great long-term returns measured by the performance of Nifty 50 or Sensex. However, an investor's performance can vary significantly based on their entry and exit. More than the market performance, investor performance counts.

The book gets into investment styles and themes, which is like descending to the 10,000 feet level. **Section 3** focuses on this extensively by researching various equity investment styles, including size-based approaches, concentrated portfolios, core/satellite approaches, contrarian investing, value investing, momentum investing, dividend investing, and active vs. passive investing. As they say, there are various ways to nirvana, and hence, different styles bring with them different outcomes. Sometimes, it is also a question of which style suits your character. The section also looks at some off-beat themes like multi-baggers, penny stocks and IPOs.

The market lens can also be looked at from key sectors that move the needle, including a debate between banks and non-banks. We have global multinationals that have a wide presence in India for several years. We also have several Indian companies (especially information technology companies) whose main target clients happen to be global companies. This two-way engagement provides a fascinating framework for researching companies. Regulations now allow investing in international stocks, though there are limits to it. There are cyclically driven sectors like energy, which dance according to oil prices. India is a major importer and consumer of oil, and this can have wide implications for the economy in general and for oil-based stocks in particular. **Section 4** takes a detailed look at key sectors and how they influence investment outcomes, which is now closer to the ground at the 5,000 feet level.

The climax is, of course, stock selection or touchdown to the ground. At this stage, the noise level increases disproportionately and is a far cry from the clear view one can have from a height of 30,000 feet (the macro). There are good companies and bad companies, but there are also good stocks and bad stocks. The relationship need not be linear as some good companies can be bad stocks (due to exorbitant valuation) while some bad companies can be good stocks due to market excesses on the downside. **Section 5** provides a template to analyse stocks with a case study.

There are companies that survived Nifty successfully for many decades, but many of them fell by the wayside. Stocks that continue to be in the index always receive investor flows, both domestic and foreign. What lessons do we take through this simple observation that can hold the key to stock selection? The average age of companies in the index has been falling globally and in India. Hence, tools that can analyse the ability of stocks to sustain in the index or even predict future inclusions can produce handsome alpha opportunities. **Section 6** presents various index stories, including scenarios on how Sensex will unfold and how Nifty Top 10 will look in the future.

The aspect of equity investment is incomplete without assessing volatility and risk. Risk and return are the two sides of the same coin, which means one should labour about risk as much as trying to spot the next winner. While investors are primed to structure their strategy on returns, risk-based investing can produce better outcomes. Stock market outcomes are more about avoiding losers than embracing winners. However, we need to constantly study major risk failures (both global and desi) and draw lessons to pursue this strategy. **Section 7** deals with managing risk and volatility.

Institutional investing is different from retail investing. Retail investors suffer many emotions and, therefore, biases while making investing decisions. Appreciating the impact inflation can have on one's investment is key and will shape asset allocation for retail investors. However, not all of them are trained to navigate the investment world.

Hence, help from credible and independent financial planners can be the key. One must have heard several times about the need to start early and let the power of compounding do the magic. Investing cannot be a one-time activity. Producing capital at regular intervals (either through business or through salary) and deploying it consistently is key to investing. If we run dry of capital, the impact is far reduced. The focus of investors, therefore, is to generate this capital so that the power of compounding can do the rest. **Section 8** focusses on retail investing from various angles including SIPs.

Section-9 argues that investing is more about managing emotions as much as analysis. Soft aspects like psychology, networking and conflict of interest are most dominant but least understood or researched. Emotional investing is often done by investors, be it high-net-worth or institutions. Hence, an honest assessment about mistakes made, lessons learnt and processes that should be set in motion not to repeat them becomes critical.

Section-10 provides some research tips for aspiring equity researchers. The tips are a result of multi-decade experience and observations of the marketplace.

Section 11 summarizes key takeaways.

Sizing the Big Picture

(30,000 feet view)

01

Introduction

Sizing the big picture is essentially to see where the country is headed ten or twenty years from now in terms of various economic metrics. India, as an emerging market, is piped for strong growth in the next several decades and this provides opportunities for investors if they get various aspects of the big picture right. The forecast for big numbers looks very promising as we can notice from the table below:

Table:2 INDIA – Now and in the Near Future			
	2023	**2030**	**2050**
GDP	$3.5T	$7 T	$35 T[1]
Airports (No's)	148	230	330[2]
No of Demat A/c (Crs.)	11.6	30	93.8[3]
No of Tax Filings (Crs.)	6.7	16	100[4]
GST Tax Collection (lakh/Crs.)	18	42	180[5]
India Population (Crs.)	141.7		167[6]
Adult Population (Crs.)	94.0		125
% of Adult Population	66%		75%
Source: Complete Circle Wealth, EY, United Nations Population Estimate, EY			

1   https://www.ey.com/en_in/tax/economy-watch/indian-economy-by-twenty-fifty-in-pursuit-to-achieve-the-thirty-trillion-dollar-mark
2   Vision 2040 suggests 100 new airports per decade. Extrapolating the data to 2050
3   Assuming India will reach Developed Market average by 2050
4   Assuming 80% of adults will file taxes by 2050
5   Assuming GST collection will grow at the same rate as the broader economy
6   https://www.ndtv.com/india-news/indias-population-expected-to-rise-till-2050-and-then-decline-un-3961880

The current market cap represents an increase of nearly 80 times since 1994 in rupee terms and 30 times in dollar terms, and is more than the size of the banking system in India. One in every three households relates to the stock market either directly or indirectly. While the market cap is expected to touch $7.5 trillion by 2030, it is expected to surpass $20 trillion by 2050. Post COVID, retail investor interest in the stock market has increased exponentially. We have over 150 million demat accounts, and it is increasing at a rate of 3 million a month[7]!

It is quite common to see the reference to "market" in many analyses, implying that it is a homogeneous concept that one can visualise as a person. But the term "market" refers to interactions of millions of views every second and is as heterogeneous as it gets. It does well to simplify all of this into one term and keep referring to it as "the market", especially when it is also reflected as an index. Looking at the term "market" in retrospect is easy and intuitive, but such visualisation hardly serves any futuristic purpose as there is no one entity or person called "Mr. Market". If everyone is buying, the market is bullish; vice versa applies. However, the market incorporates several data—both structured and unstructured. People buy or sell in anticipation, and when millions of such anticipations collide through stock prices, it becomes almost impossible to unify them elegantly into one form.

Technically, the market is composed of buyers and sellers in a zero-sum game where each buy transaction is matched by a sell transaction. But beyond this simple logic lies the interactions of so many stakeholders that primarily define the price discovery function of the so-called market. Hence, it keeps changing every second, and the game is to correctly anticipate the change. Here again, it is a

---

7   https://economictimes.indiatimes.com/markets/stocks/news/politics-may-be-fluid-but-economics-is-still-solid-time-to-be-somewhat-greedy/articleshow/110717534.cms

zero-sum game where one correct anticipation is always matched by another incorrect anticipation. The news flow that primarily defines the day-to-day market movement also suffers from significant lags where public availability of such news comes with a delay, mostly found in standard reporting formats of the stock exchange, which can be boring to read. But many other things also influence market movements, including the resignation of a CEO, the arrest of a director, a sexual harassment case filed by an employee, etc. Unstructured data plays a larger role than financial statement analysis, especially when the game is about anticipation. In multiple-choice questions, among the four or five options presented, there will be a "none of the above"—an option often ignored. Human minds are trained to think and believe that every problem has a solution, and the trick is to find them within the choices given, excluding "none of the above". Given the range of unstructured data that influences corporate behaviour, sometimes the smart thing to do is to opt for "none of the above", which then pushes one to find more answers than restricting to the one given.

Managers routinely miss the waves as the past cannot enable us to see the future. Business cycles are crystal clear in the rear-view mirror, but imagining the wave pattern 6 months or 1 year in advance is a task not many managers would love, as it is akin to walking in a dark forest blindfolded.

In our long history of the market, we have seen many companies come into the prime index and silently exit as well. The average age of stocks in the index has been decreasing over the years. Companies that were once darlings just vanish from the scene, all within a decade for several reasons (including mergers). Market leadership can sometimes be a burden with a cost to pay, while the number two or three will silently be making better margins. In addition, there are several investing myths that one must contend with in everyday investing life, and one can imagine the size of the problem getting bigger.

In this setting, one must get the macro right before getting the micro right. The 30,000 feet views from an aircraft are always elegant, clear, beautiful, and inspiring. As one gets to the ground, the noise level increases, and the traffic with pollution catches up. The big picture reading can enable a manager to get the broader direction right, narrow down the options, and gain better visibility. There are several economic influences, including geo-political factors, and navigating the stars with these variables at play is the biggest challenge for any investor. Big-picture observation can be time-consuming, all-encompassing, and not easily reducible to logical conclusions. However, like yoga, if one starts practising them bit by bit, there are significant rewards.

02

Big Picture Themes

a. Decoding the Economic Web

Understanding and decoding an economy is as difficult as understanding the human body, since both have significant moving parts that interact often in not so direct a manner. In the famous Economy-Industry-Company (EIC) framework that we are all familiar with, we often jump to the I and C as they are more manageable than the E. However, that does not take away the importance of the economic view. Macro research, as it is fondly called, is turning out to be more of an art than science given the multiple parameters one must consider before deciding on future directions. Even multilateral agencies like IMF and World Bank, with an army of economists, struggle with forecasts, as can be seen from the frequent revisions. It just goes to show the huge task at hand.

As a keen follower and commentator on the economy for several decades, I have tried to bring all of it into the form of a framework for ease of understanding. At the heart is the economic system, primarily influenced by what I call the six pillars: GDP, Demographics, Credit, Inflation, Trade, and Employment. However, I must admit that this is a simplification exercise at best, and I could have easily missed many other aspects of the economic system.

I will now explain their importance, with the caveat that the order of presentation does not imply their order of importance.

Figure : 2 Economic web

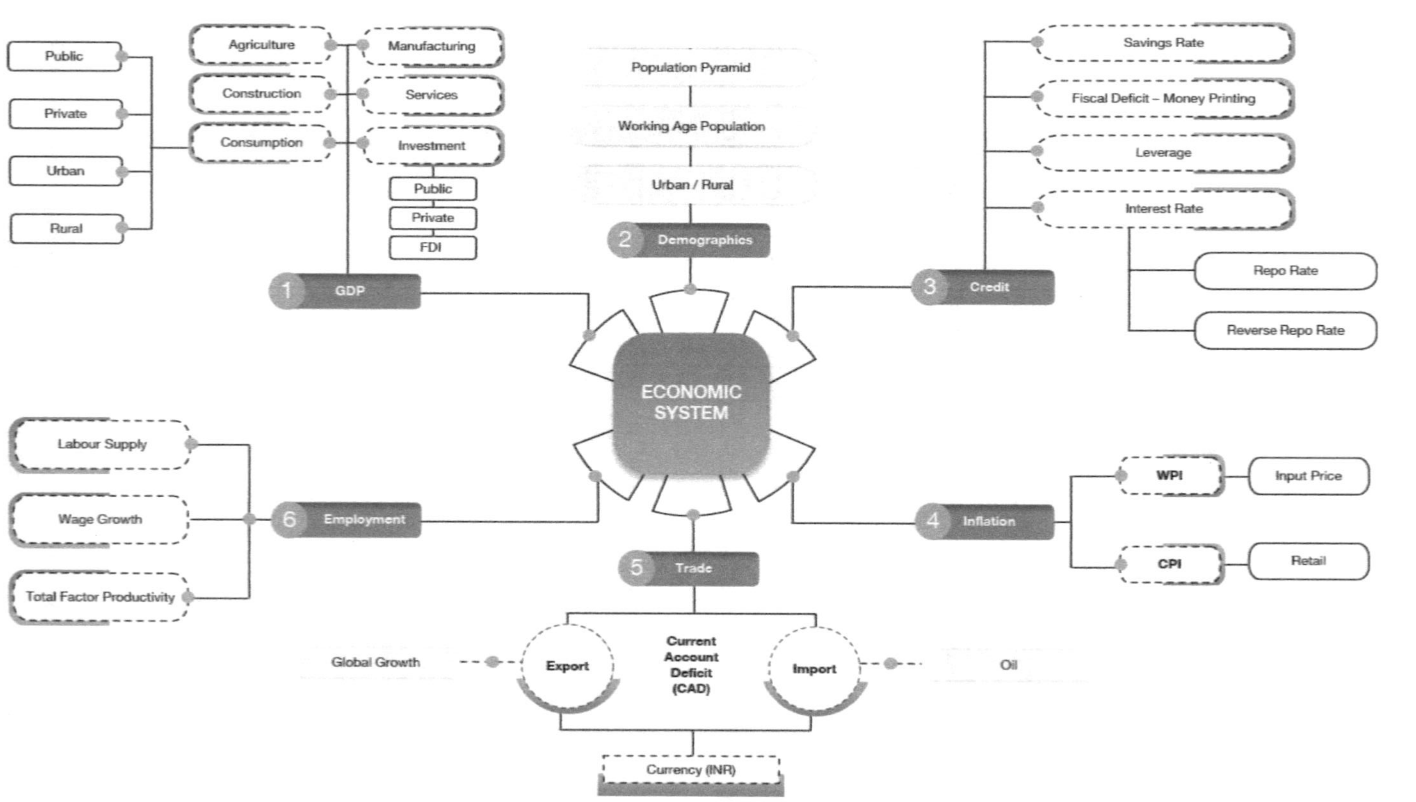

Pillar 1: GDP

Gross Domestic Product (GDP) is the primary measure by which an economy is measured both at current prices and at constant prices (called the real GDP and is adjusted for inflation). Also, GDP can be measured by aggregating all production or through expenditure. The latter is a measure of several mixes which can contain some proxy components as well.

There are many forecasts as to how big our Indian economy will get from the current $3.5 trillion. It is likely to reach $30-$40 trillion by 2050 based on the real GDP growth that is expected. At the cumulative level, India's real GDP growth averaged 5.7% during the period 2012-2022, with a high of 8.3% in 2015 and a low of − 5.8% in 2020 (thanks to COVID-19). More than the overall GDP, what may be of interest is the GDP per capita, which currently hovers around $2,850 (compared to $13,000 for China and $58,000 for advanced economies). If the anticipated growth rate materialises, our per capita can increase to $15,000.

The GDP can ideally be imagined as a pie that gets bigger and bigger over time due to growth, and this growth primarily accrues due to population growth that triggers more consumption. If one is trying to project GDP growth, the exercise must start with projecting growth at a segment level and then aggregating it up. The GDP is mainly comprised of agriculture, manufacturing, construction, and services. Most of the developing nations start heavy on agriculture (primary sector) and then graduate to manufacturing (secondary sector) before dominating the services (tertiary sector) aspect. Developed economies like the OECD countries derive the bulk of their GDP from the tertiary sector, while some developing economies like India are also getting there.

The cumulative growth of GDP is a function of the growth of each of these segments within the GDP. Since India's independence, India's grand vision has been to propel manufacturing, but the services sector has grown swiftly. Manufacturing accounts for roughly 18% of the share, while services share is close to 55%. The service sector will continue to be the key driver of our export engine. The idea that we could exploit our labour, infrastructure, large domestic market, and industrial development largely proved inconsequential compared to the strides we achieved in the service sector. If we must highlight one thing that holds our manufacturing aspirations, it should be our poor logistics, which led to spiralling costs and losing cost competitiveness. Also, while India prides itself on an adequate supply of labour, the skill set requires steps to improve the value added per employee, which is half of some of the East Asian countries. India is now exploring the idea of a central intelligence agency for manufacturing. The idea is to develop key performance indicators on metrics such as value added, export performance, technological prowess, supply chain effectiveness, labour productivity and access to the global market.

There is another way of viewing GDP, which is the consumption/ investment lens, which can be viewed as two sides of the same coin. On the investment side, the main driver is always government investment, as the government possesses a greater ability to invest through borrowings. Private investment will be contingent on opportunities and cost of capital, and during periods when both are not favourable, private investment tends to lag public investments. Also, public investment can be counter-cyclical in that the government can provide the needed investment push during tough times when the economy needs investment backing. Private investments tend to be more pro-cyclical. India's share of investment (also called investment rate or Gross Capital Formation) hovers around 30% of GDP. Investments are mainly fuelled by foreign direct investment and domestic savings. Investments are mainly channelled into infrastructure that enjoys a strong multiplier effect than consumption. It is learnt that the multiplier effect can be three times as much money spent on infrastructure as it has a transformation effect as it tends to impact multiple industries along the way.

The other side of the equation is consumption, which again can be viewed as public and private consumption. Many leading economies in the world including the US are dependent on consumption growth to propel GDP growth. In India, the split between urban and rural consumption also plays a significant role. An attended study here could be demographics that provides a framework for broader population growth but more importantly the rural-urban migration that can shape the consumption trajectory.

Pillar 2: Demographics

Demography is destiny[8]. The structure of the population of a country (called demography) influences the future trajectory of an economy. While a mature economy will suffer from an ageing population that needs social support (be it pension or healthcare) as seen in Japan or Europe today, a young demography like India is likely to reap what is termed as "demographic dividends". The momentum that the demographic structure implies can be felt for generations.

India is the largest populated country in the world (ahead of China) with about 1.4 billion people and 330 million households. The median age, at 28.4 years, implies that India is a young demography being touted as a demographic dividend. This should offer relatively cheap labour and mobilise savings to fund higher investment. However, as the population pyramid indicates, the young cohort will decline over the years. We can observe in the pyramid the distribution of population across age groups. It is interesting to note that under-5 children peaked in 2004, and under-15s peaked in 2009. A visual inspection of the

---

8   Auguste Compte 19th Century philosopher

pyramid indicates that the current bulge in the middle will slowly move higher, implying that as a nation, we will age.

There are many critical metrics to follow within demographic studies. Life expectancy has significantly improved from 53 years to 70 years. The fertility rate, at 2.1, is claimed to be "replacement level fertility" by demographers. There is rapid movement of people from rural areas to urban areas. The urban population, at about 500 million, implies an urbanisation rate of 35%. By 2047, India's population aged 60 and over will almost triple from current levels. Even then, India will have fewer older people than the US or Europe. The dependency ratio[9] has fallen from a high of 73% in the 1990s to about 47% and is likely to further decrease to 30% by 2050. This ratio has been on the rise in Europe and the US. The middle-class in India is also growing, which opens opportunities in banking, insurance, real estate, and asset management.

Demographics is the elephant in the room. The age factor, the urban/rural divide, the fertility rate, and the dependency ratio all influence several industries from FMCG to healthcare. Hence, this elephant in the room is a key component of sizing the big picture.

Pillar: 3 Credit

Credit aspects of the economic system analyse the role of money and the cost associated with it. Hence, the key aspect of credit is interest rates, which are again influenced by the demand and supply of money. However, the Reserve Bank of India (RBI) has a crucial role to play in shaping this, though I cannot say that they set it. RBI, through its monetary policy actions, set the benchmark interest rates mainly through what are called repo rates and reverse repo rates. The repo rate is the rate at which RBI lends money to commercial banks, which in turn lends it

---

9   (Elderly+Children/Total Population)

to borrowers. A reverse repo is the rate at which RBI borrows money from commercial banks. Both these actions influence the money that is available to banks to finally provide loans to borrowers. However, the cost of money is also influenced by the amount of savings undertaken by the people of a country at what is called a savings rate.

Banks provide an intermediation function between savers and borrowers. The difference between deposit rates and loan rates is termed net interest income and net interest margin. Banks can mop up more deposits by increasing the deposit rates but will be forced to increase their lending rate to preserve their net interest margin. If business conditions dictate, they may choose to reduce their margin. Borrowers will trigger the leverage function in the economy, and hence, leverage becomes a key aspect of money creation and growth. In all of this, the government has a peculiar role to play in the form of monetising budget deficits. Emerging markets like India typically run a deficit budget (meaning expenditure is higher than income), and usually, the deficit is met through borrowings and, in extreme situations, money printing (given the god-given power to do so!). However, if the deficit runs at unreasonable levels for a long-time, it will result in steep inflation as more money needs to be printed to pay for expenses, which will lead to erosion in currency value. India's fiscal deficit is higher than the emerging market average. A high deficit leads to high debt. India's public debt as a % of GDP is at 84% of GDP, while the EM average is about 60%. While this looks bad per se, most of the debt is internal (as opposed to external debt) and hence creates lesser concern. Another angle to consider here is the local currency vs. foreign currency debt. India's debt is mostly denominated in Indian Rupees, and hence, any global adversity will have a lesser impact, very similar to Japan (whose debt/GDP ratio is well over 200%).

There are various sources of funding or credit available to a borrower (be it retail or corporate). They are mainly from banks, stock market and bond market. Bank credit remains the most consistent source of funding while stock market funding happens during boom years. However, bond market funding remains muted due to the absence of a mature debt market.

At the broadest level, the role of credit in the economy is measured by the credit/GDP ratio, which is presently about 50% for India, far below the world average of 150%. The health of banks determines credit growth, which is the lifeblood of the bank. In periods where banks face high levels of non-performing assets (like the period between 2014 and 2021), credit growth will fall. India's credit growth should accelerate from the current sub-10% levels to, say, 13% to 15% to achieve its ambition of catching up with others. The higher levels of credit growth expectations are based on the belief that bank cleaning up is largely done since NPAs have declined considerably with improved regulatory oversight. While credit for the broader economy is reasonably well-oiled, there are areas where it is yet to make a difference. The increasing demand-supply credit gap for Micro, Small, and Medium Enterprises (MSME) can be cited as a classic example.

Apart from GDP growth, credit growth is therefore considered to be a key metric for macro analysis. A stronger economy will aid stronger credit growth and vice versa.

Pillar: 4 Inflation

India's inflation averaged 5.9% for the period 2012-2022. Inflation simply means a price rise for the same volume of goods and services. Goods and services experience price increases, and hence, analysis should always factor adjustment to inflation. Imprudent money supply/printing or wasteful government expenditures such as freebies could drain resources, widen deficits and lead to inflation, which ultimately bites the consumer/individual investor. There are many examples in the world (Argentina) where it is common to see inflation at over 100%.

Once inflation gets out of control, it is very difficult to get the genie back in the bottle.

Other things being equal, high inflation will need high nominal growth to make wealth. While inflation provides pricing power, it can also mask inefficiency. From an economic system point of view, inflation can be broken down into Wholesale Price Index (WPI) and Consumer Price Index (CPI). The WPI is influenced by input prices and signifies inflation at a business level. The CPI is influenced by the prices of goods generally consumed by the public in their day-to-day living, including food, housing, and transport. CPI is more followed than WPI.

Inflation is also critical while measuring GDP in that nominal GDP adjusted for inflation becomes real GDP, a measure mostly used for economic analysis. However, instead of using CPI or WPI, another measure called GDP deflator is normally used to derive real GDP from nominal GDP. While CPI is hard data, GDP deflator is not hard data but a derived number. In today's world, inflation is a serious problem for both developed and developing countries thanks to supply—chain—induced bottlenecks. A classic tool to temper down inflation is interest rates. By increasing interest rates, we can dampen demand and, hence, dampen price rises and vice versa.

Pillar: 5 Trade & Currency

A country's trade is shaped by its exports and imports. A country with more exports relative to its imports enjoys a trade surplus and vice versa. In India's case, our imports are shaped by our dependence on oil (mostly imported) and other goods that are used for either internal consumption or re-exports. Our exports are primarily driven by service exports. Since our imports tend to be more than the exports, technically, we run a balance of payment deficit on the current account. A high deficit in trade will depreciate the value of the currency if the quality of the trade deficit remains the same. Hence, coordination between the government that regulates the trade and RBI that regulates the currency is crucial. The 1990 economic crisis is a good example of India facing a huge trade deficit and falling currency due to geo-political developments (the fall of the Eastern Bloc and the Iraq-Kuwait war). The subsequent reforms initiated were aimed at acquiescing to IMF and World Bank demands for opening the economy. The long and hard lesson India as a nation learnt in that episode points to the need for stable and sustainable economic management as a key pillar.

India's exports also depend on global growth and positioning India as an export hub, which is yet to materialise. Some South Asian countries like China, Singapore, and Korea have the world's export leadership, and the same applies to many developed markets. Tariffs are normally imposed by the government to protect its home market from cheap imports, especially for countries like India, which has a vast consumer base thanks to its status as the most populated country on earth.

India's share of global exports has steadily increased after stagnating for a long-time. Our global export share was 1.8% during the period 2010-2020 and has now improved to 2.6%, which is just a shade lower than South Korea's 2.7%. India's share of imports has also risen from 2.5% in 2019 to 2.7% in 2022. A key aspect of increasing the trade quotient is trade deals (Free Trade Agreements, as they are called). In 2023, India signed FTAs with Australia and the UAE. Such deals give preferential and concessional access to respective markets. Vietnam has perfected this art and bestows preferential access to nearly 80% of the global GDP. In relative terms, India's number is somewhere close to 25%.

Trade has a strong impact on the currency's value. Managing the current account deficit (CAD), which is nothing but a savings-investment gap, will have implications for the currency. A sharp fall in the Indian rupee can trigger inflation and financial stability concerns. For e.g., the rupee fell almost 20% between May and September 2013 when the taper tantrum happened. A sharp fall in the currency can hurt foreign investors whose dollar-based returns can suffer.

The performance of the Indian rupee is a key topic for both domestic players and foreign investors. For the domestic players, any trade engagement (imports or exports) opens the Rupee door. A CFO of such a company can either have export earnings coming into his company (if he is a software exporter, say), or he might have raised a $ denominated debt for his expansion plans. Either way, the performance of rupee becomes crucial for local companies that are engaged with foreign shores in one way or another. From a foreign investor's point of view, the performance of one's portfolio is always measured in dollar terms, and hence, any appreciation or deprecation of the rupee will show up materially in terms of portfolio performance. A look at the table below clearly shows the difference between the performances of the Nifty index (domestic) vs the MSCI India USD index. The USD return has trailed behind the domestic return in a significant way due to currency deprecation. Foreign fund managers need to factor that as an additional risk when deciding to invest in India.

Table : 3 Nifty USD Returns					
	Name	1Y	3Y	5Y	10Y
1	Nifty 50 Total Return	32.2%	16.8%	15.3%	14.2%
2	MSCI India USD TR	39.9%	12.9%	11.9%	9.9%
Source: Refinitive; Data as of Q1 2024					

In general, emerging market currencies weaken over time due to various factors. For instance, the Indian rupee weakened against the USD by 3.7% annually during the last 10 years. This does not mean that Rupee will consistently depreciate year after year. There may be periods when it can appreciate, but in general, the direction is one of falling Rupee against major international currencies. A strong economy will lead to a strong currency and vice versa. Foreign investment happens at two levels: FDI and FPI. Foreign Direct Investment (FDI) is less volatile, more enduring, and can be a seal of international approval for a country's progress. These are generally done by multilateral agencies mainly oriented towards infrastructure building, which is generally long-term in nature. On the other hand, Foreign Portfolio Investments (FPI) are highly volatile and hence not enduring. However, these are also signs of global approvals where inflows exceed outflows. During times of market strength and confidence, inflows tend to beat outflows and vice versa. Technically, the rupee depreciates against the dollar when people sell the rupee and buy dollars. In addition, when people sell rupees and buy dollars, it results in negative capital flows and leads to downward pressure on the currency (and vice versa). A key lesson that India learnt during the 2013 taper tantrum is the need to have adequate foreign exchange reserves to manage crises. One measures the sufficiency of reserves by how many months of imports it can cover. Eight months is the sweet spot, and the rupee normally depreciates if it falls below that threshold. India's foreign exchange reserves have now risen to about 10 months of imports.

Pillar: 6 Employment & Labour

The biggest economic challenge for any government is to create meaningful jobs for its working-age population (new entrants to the labour market). A strong GDP growth will spur investments that will create the needed jobs. However, there are other factors at play as well, including the supply of labour (depending on the demographic composition), wage growth that defines the affordability of labour from an employer perspective, and labour factor productivity that shapes the quality of labour. The mere creation of jobs without an attendant increase in productivity can be economically inefficient in the long-run and may create unnecessary additional inflation.

Most of the Indians rely on employment as the main source of income (more than capital or land). Also, most of the employment tends to be unorganised and informal. In the total scheme of things, the informal sector comprising own-account workers (like tea shops), casual workers and unpaid family workers (those who support a mom-and-pop store run by a father or mother) constitute nearly 75%.

India's cheap labour has enabled it to foray into industries like automotive, IT Services, and BPO, which resulted in an increase in the middle-class population with associated economic benefits. India's working-age population will exceed 1 billion shortly and this is roughly about 70% of the total population. India will also be the largest contributor to the global workforce for the foreseeable future. The current and increasing labour shortage among developed economies is truly a great opportunity for India.

While we have about 300 million people entering the labour market annually, we also have about 150 million retiring or exiting the labour market annually. In effect, jobs must be provided for nearly 150 million people annually. A key metric to measure employment is the Labour Force Participation Rate (LFPR), which currently is about 55% overall and 33% for women. This is surprising given the fact that we notice greater female education. Hence, while we can boast of a growing working-age population, the low LFPR may impede growth, especially that of women.

Another key dimension of employment and labour is the unemployment rate which is now placed at around 5% but what is concerning is that youth unemployment is higher at 8%.

India has the twin challenge of providing employment to new entrants to job market as well as increase the productivity of labour to achieve higher value add and income prosperity. The demographic dividend is likely to peak in about 20 years and may exhaust completely in 30-35 years. Policy reforms oriented towards employment should kick in well before we move from a developing nation to a developed nation.

Connecting the Pillars-Macro Stability

A country is measured by its macroeconomic stability. Often, emerging or developing nations encounter economic issues that can weaken macro stability. The resultant price will be increasing deficit, inflation, debt, and currency fall. On the other hand, with prudent management of the economy, where deficits are kept within reasonable levels and where investments are directed to produce better multipliers, one can notice those economies enjoying better credit ratings and can be attractive destinations for foreign capital. Hence, the cost of having weak macro stability will be clearly visible and can lead to public outcry and suffering. However, the benefits of good macro settings will mostly be intangible. Central banks use interest rates to manage inflation and exchange rates to manage capital flows, striving to maintain both internal and external balance. Creating enough fiscal space during good times is recommended but not always possible unless it is a commodity-selling economy like the Gulf. Managing the twin deficits (fiscal and current account) is central to achieving macro stability. It is possible that governments can choose to face increasing deficits through money printing, which can lead to inflation, whose typical economic response is to increase interest rates. High deficits may also lead to high bond yields.

b. Estimating Interest Rates-Key To Everything!

"Investors looking for double-digit returns from fixed-income portfolios over the next year may consider an allocation to long-duration funds, as these capture the maximum impact of a decline in interest rates."

"Fund managers expect the Reserve Bank of India to reduce interest rates by 50 to 75 basis points in the latter half of 2024, following global rate cuts. This could potentially lead to capital appreciation in long-duration funds and yield double-digit returns."

"The real rate—the repo rate (6.5%) minus estimated one year forward consumer price inflation (4.5%)—stands at 200 basis points, exceeding the RBI's targeted real rate of 150 basis points. This leaves room for a potential 50 basis points rate cut. If the US economy slows down, rate cuts could range between 75 to 100 basis points to support GDP growth."

These excerpts from business newspapers focus on the Reserve Bank of India's anticipated actions, which are contingent on expectations regarding the Federal Reserve's policies. Economic analysis heavily involves forecasting interest rates, a task fraught with complexity; accuracy in this area can yield substantial financial rewards.

Implicit in interest rate determination is the concept of the time value of money. Put simply, longer durations entail higher rates due to prolonged exposure to risk. Hence, the yield curve[10] reflects this relationship between the cost of money and time. The yield curve normally slopes upwards; when they do not, they are termed inverted yield curves[11].

---

10   A group of interest rates from the very short term (say overnight) to very long-term say 30 years.

11   Meaning short-term rates are higher than long-term rates.

Table : 4 Bond Yields and Spread

Residual Maturity	Yield	Spread vs Bond					Spread vs Central Bank Rate (6.50%)
		3 months	1 year	2 years	5 years	10 years	
30 years	7.129%	8.9 bp	5.4 bp	11.8 bp	8.4 bp	7.6 bp	62.9 bp
10 years	7.053%	1.3 bp	-2.2 bp	4.2 bp	0.8 bp		55.3 bp
5 years	7.045%	0.5 bp	-3.0 bp	3.4 bp			54.5 bp
2 years	7.011%	-2.9 bp	-6.4 bp				51.1 bp
1 year	7.075%	3.5 bp					57.5 bp
3 months	7.040%						54.0 bp

Source: worldgovernmentbonds.com

In the enclosed table, we can see that 30-year government bonds have a yield of 7.129% while that of 3 months is at 7.040%, with other tenors in between. What is even more valuable is the spread or difference between different tenors (10 year minus 2 years being the most popular).

Table : 5 10Y-2Y Bond Spread

India 10 Years / India 2 Years Government Bond spread: historic value range for every yea

In case of domestic spread, a long term bond should grant a higher return than a shorter one.
A green candlestick means that spread variation is positive in the year.
A red candlestick means that spread variation is negative in the year.

Year	Spread	Change	Min	Range	Max
2024 Feb 21	4.2 bp	-6.9 bp	2.5 bp Feb 16 2024		18.4 bp Jan 7 2024
2023 Dec 31	9.6 bp	-27.6 bp	-7.2 bp Oct 5 2023		44.6 bp Jan 22 2023
2022 Dec 31	37.2 bp	-108.6 bp	24.6 bp Oct 13 2022		198.9 bp Apr 17 2022
2021 Dec 31	145.8 bp	-57.1 bp	116.0 bp Dec 24 2021		202.9 bp Jan 3 2021
2020 Dec 31	202.9 bp	+130.3 bp	51.2 bp Feb 3 2020		208.0 bp Dec 20 2020
2019 Dec 31	77.8 bp	+39.6 bp	21.7 bp Jul 16 2019		109.9 bp Oct 28 2019
2018 Dec 31	35.6 bp	19.9 bp	10.7 bp Sep 17 2018		87.0 bp Mar 5 2018
2017 Dec 31	54.0 bp	+40.4 bp	0.9 bp Jun 22 2017		57.2 bp Dec 20 2017
2016 Dec 31	13.6 bp	25.8 bp	13.6 bp Dec 30 2016		54.2 bp Feb 2 2016
2015 Dec 31	32.4 bp	+40.1 bp	-21.9 bp Mar 5 2015		42.4 bp Dec 14 2015

Current Spread: 4.2bp
Last update: 21 Feb 2024 6:15 GMT+0

Source: worldgovernmentbonds.com

A look at the spread evolution of 10y-2y shows that the difference need not be positive always. The candle sticks indicate both positive and negative spreads. The spread has historically remained at a range between a positive number of 130 bps (or basis points) and a negative number of 108 bps since 2015.

While market pricing determines the yield (like stock price), the central bank (RBI in this case) has a guiding role in terms of setting the pace and direction in what is called monetary policy setting. The RBI takes up this task through the Money Policy Committee (MPC), which has several policymakers who decide the policy rate through intense deliberations. The MPC sets the "Repo Rate" – the rate at which RBI lends money to banks and, in turn, decides the loan and deposit pricing of banks. By implication, reverse repo is the rate at which banks lend to RBI. RBI has adopted what is called a flexible inflation targeting (FIT) framework since 2016. Central banks worldwide believe that price stability (read as inflation control) will lead to financial stability, which will further rapid growth. A stable and low inflation can help everyone, from households to corporations, to plan their affairs, be it spending plans or project financing. Stability is at the core of innovation, productivity, and sustainable growth. RBI targets inflation to be under 4% with a margin of +/-2%. Considering this, RBI will provide forward guidance on inflation and growth for investors to develop their expectations.

After the global financial crisis in 2008, the Federal Reserve of the US reduced the interest rates to 0.25% and kept the rates at that low level for nearly a decade before hiking them again. But then, the Covid pandemic that began in 2019 forced Central banks all over the world to slash interest rates again. RBI reduced the policy repo rate by 115 bps between March to May 2020 and subsequently raised the repo by 250 bps between May 2022 to Feb 2023. This is just to give examples of the scale and speed with which interest rates can dance based on evolving economic circumstances. Hence, the difficulty in estimating the interest rates.

While RBI primarily uses the repo rate as its tool, it can also shape interest rates based on liquidity management in the market (by either inducing or absorbing the liquidity). The weighted average call money rate (WACR) is the average of the overnight rates and can sometimes differ vastly from the repo rate based on RBI's intentions. If RBI decides to tighten financial conditions without a formal rate hike, it can use the liquidity lever to achieve its objective.

It is important to appreciate the role of interest rates in determining asset class performance.

Bond Markets: Interest rates determine bond market performance in an inverse way. An increase in interest rates will result in a fall in the bond price (and vice versa). Hence, a falling interest rate regime produces a bull market in bonds and vice versa.

Equity Markets: Interest rates affect equity markets primarily through the valuation angle, where the cost of capital (being the denominator) is again inversely proportional to the value. As interest rates go up, the derived value of a stock falls and vice versa. We can look at the spread between bond yields and earnings yield (the inverse of p/e ratio). This measure is again very volatile and has ranged from zero to, say, 250 bps in the last five years. The long-term average is 120 bps. When stock valuations rise, the earnings yield falls.

Real Estate: In the realm of real estate, the impact of interest rates can be understood via cap rate[12]. Higher interest rates should lead to higher cap rates and vice versa.

---

12 Defined as net operating income divided by the property value.

Currency: Interest rates also affect currency value as higher USD exchange rates will trigger a reverse flow of money from emerging markets like India back to the US, which may well produce currency depreciation.

In conclusion, we can say that interest rates affect corporate profitability and project financing and, hence, capital markets. Economic uncertainty, in the form of higher global inflation, supply chain shocks, and geo-political threats, all shape the yield curve. Inflation and interest rates are connected to each other like the umbilical cord, and hence, forecasting inflation is also ridden with the same uncertainty as forecasting interest rates. If inflation is left unattended at high levels, it can sow the seeds for higher inflation expectations (in what is called anchoring), and when that sets in, it is difficult to control inflation. Hence, Central Banks move decisively the moment they sense trouble in the form of higher inflation by hiking interest rates. Capital market players (be it bond fund managers or equity fund managers) should be adept at forecasting interest rates, though this economic exercise is simply the toughest.

c. Oil

A look at oil price evolution since 1988 clearly shows how volatile the commodity is. After being in a band between $20/bbl to $40/bbl during 1988-2003, it broke out to reach a peak of $140/bbl in 2008 and then entered a highly volatile range, making it impossible to predict for analysts. The Arab-Israeli conflict in 1973 caused the first oil price shock, while the Iranian revolution in 1979 caused the second oil price shock. Subsequently, the world faced many other oil shocks.

Countries like India are highly dependent on this commodity to run their economy. India is the third-largest consumer of energy globally. India's oil imports cost nearly $160 billion every year and therefore are a drag on foreign exchange reserves. India needs to import about 40% of its total energy requirement, primarily that of oil. India's primary energy demand stands at 937 million tonnes of oil equivalent (Mtoe) and is expected to double in the next 15 years. As India matures as an economy, its per capita energy consumption (which is currently 1/10th of the US) would also go up, creating additional pressure. The government will try several alternative sources, including green hydrogen, to reduce its heavy import dependence on oil. Global climate change initiatives will accelerate this process.

Geo-political factors, economic growth, central bank actions, and many other factors shape and guide oil prices. It is interesting to see the tension between producers and consumers of oil. This is an attempt to deduce long-term global trends for energy in general and oil in particular. There are some structural trends that are shaping the course, and they are examined below:

1. **Energy Security:** Before the Russia-Ukraine War, the world was moving with steadfast devotion towards energy transition. The idea was to reduce the share of fossil fuels (now accounting for more than 80% of the pie) and increase renewables and clean energy. New investments, even by traditional oil majors, have always been directed towards renewables to score ESG brownie points and win investor endorsement as well. However, the war changed the narrative completely, as Russia was among the largest producers and exporters of oil and gas to many global destinations, including Europe. When sanctions and

embargoes were imposed on Russia, worries about oil supply mounted, taking the price up as well. Given the fact that the US, Russia, and Saudi Arabia dominate the oil market, disruption in one of the three is bound to stir concerns, especially among major oil importers such as China and India. The good news is that much of Russia's oil, otherwise embargoed in other parts of the world, found its way into China and India, thus making it a zero-sum game. But it did change the narrative from energy transition to energy security. The war kept total oil production almost intact but redirected their flows. However, the worry for the long-term is if current production levels are affected, it can spike oil prices and hence the import bill. Hence, major importers may start focusing on building their strategic petroleum reserves in anticipation of such a trend. While the aspect of energy transition serves the cause of oil importers well in the long-term, I believe it will be pursued less vigorously compared to energy security.

2. **Demand Scenario:** India and China together account for a lion's share of incremental oil demand. Hence, while overall demand for oil is bound to be affected by the economic performance of developed countries, it can very well be balanced out by India and China. Also, the shift in focus from energy transition to energy security may see the demand rise for the short-term. However, in the long-term (next 10 to 15 years), the world will move away from fossil fuels towards renewables as it can meet multiple goals, including climate change pressures on countries. However, that transition need not be as swift as analysts are predicting today. This gives sufficient room for oil demand to taper off in an orderly manner.

3. **Supply Scenario:** The biggest Achilles heel for supply is the decade-long under-investment in oil discoveries and extraction.

Except for national oil companies (NOCs) based in the Gulf, oil majors like BP, Shell, Chevron, and Total have lagged in investment due to investor and board pressures to go clean. The consistent under-investment has been overlooked by many and has laid the foundation for tight oil supply going forward. This has given room for OPEC+ (OPEC+ Russia) to control spare capacity to shape oil prices. Tight supply can also mean that any geo-political disruption to oil fields in the US, Saudi Arabia, or Russia (due to natural or unnatural events) can potentially take some supply off the market.

4. **Peak Oil:** Peak oil is the point in time where oil production peaks and from there it can only decline. Analysts have called peak oil many times in the past, only to be on the wrong side of the call. Since then, the question of peak oil keeps coming back with no definitive answer, of course. This time around, thanks to the Russia-Ukraine War, Europe and to some extent the US will move aggressively towards energy transition via renewables. That could bring peak oil to reality (finally), and major oil exporters (OPEC+) will then focus on maximising revenue opportunities by converting oil below the ground to wealth before it becomes redundant.

5. **Renewables:** Technology advances have reduced the cost of renewables significantly during the last decade, whether it's wind, solar, hydrogen, etc. Hence, the unit economics of generating solar power or hydrogen power are much better today than before and can only improve further. This sets the structural shift towards renewable energy. However, presently, the bulk of electricity generation in the world needs the support of coal, oil, and gas, and in some parts of the world, nuclear power (mostly in Europe). Electricity generation and transport constitute the bulk of energy consumption globally.

The speed with which renewables can replace conventional energy sources for these two crucial consumption items will determine the long-term trend. The aspect of renewables becomes interesting for GCC producers and exporters like Saudi Arabia, Abu Dhabi, and Kuwait. Most of their electricity generation needs are met by oil and gas, resulting in less oil available for export. As these economies are heavily dependent on oil and gas, it makes immense sense for them to accelerate towards renewables and shift their electricity and transport needs away from oil. From an opportunity cost perspective, this can free up more oil for export, which becomes crucial, especially in a peak oil scenario. Another aspect of renewables is the transition towards electric vehicles, touted as the green form of transportation. However, research shows that producing electric vehicles (especially batteries) is a serious call on non-green sources, thereby cancelling out some of the benefits of EVs with their cost. That presents a hurdle that governments will find difficult to overcome.

In summary, energy markets, especially oil, are in for an interesting transition both in the short and long-term. Given their substantial share in energy consumption, the change may be gradual and lengthy. This provides ample opportunity for both importers and exporters to prepare for a world less dependent on fossil fuels. Barring any geopolitical events that could cause significant swings in this assessment, all else being equal, oil could experience a healthy, strong, and gradual decline.

d. Investing during Extraordinary times

What are extraordinary times? It can either be nature-imposed, like tsunamis, earthquakes, floods, and storms, or it can be manmade, like terrorist attacks and wars. While natural calamities tend to be swift with known outcomes, manmade events need not be swift and bear unpredictability regarding the eventual outcome.

The event of 9/11 or the Russia-Ukraine War is a testament to such happenings. History is replete with wars, especially since July 28, 1914, when Austria-Hungary declared war on Serbia, leading to the First World War. Several geo-political events have followed since then, such as the Korean War (1950), the JFK assassination (1963), the Soviet-Afghanistan War (1979-1989), the Iraqi invasion of Kuwait (1990), the WTC attack (2001), the Iraq war (2003), the Russia-Ukraine War (2022), and the Hamas-Israel conflict (2023). This will not be the end, and such events will keep occurring, though we cannot predict their timing. However, whenever such incidents happen, markets exhibit extreme volatility compared to nature-driven calamities. Whether it is manmade or nature-induced, it will be instructive to see how markets react to these extraordinary events.

Generally, the market reaction is in the form of increased volatility leading to dramatic falls (called drawdowns), impacting the currency and commodity markets. This leads to heavy selling of stocks by foreign institutional investors.

In the last three decades, we have had two wars. The first was the Gulf War that broke out in 1991, and 30 years later, the Russian war against Ukraine. Yet, market prices ran contrary to expectations. The Gulf War began one of the sharpest rises in the Indian equity market. And in 2022, after initial hiccups, the markets have taken the war in their stride. Let's look at this a little more closely.

On February 24, 2022, Vladimir Putin launched a "special military operation" against Ukraine in what the world now terms a war. Initially, the military clash was expected to come to a halt in a couple of days, but the war has now been ongoing for years, raising fears that it won't be ending anytime soon. Markets globally have reacted severely to this. The S&P 500 (the bellwether index) fell 5 percent between March 2 and 8, 2022, while India's Sensex tanked approximately 6 percent during the same period.

We saw that just as the Russia-Ukraine War began, Sensex lost 8 percent, while the Indian Rupee fell by 2.5 percent. Oil prices, too, peaked at $139/barrel. All this has seen foreign portfolio investors (FPIs) turn net sellers. Though the Sensex has recovered most of its losses in the subsequent months and so has the currency, FPI selling continued. Thus, it is common for the markets to show extreme volatility during such events, only to regain their footing eventually.

Based on how these events unfold and how long they last, the ruling government of the day tends to implement economic measures that can smooth the impact. If the war is prolonged, leading to severe supply-side bottlenecks resulting in increased commodity prices and inflation, the RBI will increase interest rates as a monetary response. The government may also unleash fiscal stimulus and raise borrowings to meet increased spending, resulting in a high fiscal deficit. These steps will affect different industries differently.

In times like these, can investors spot opportunities? This is a tricky issue. We need to know how long the scenario plays out in advance to act as contrarian buyers. Hence, most investors will initially not enter, fearing the worst. An excellent example to cite would be the beginning of the Coronavirus outbreak in March 2020. Many analysts then predicted a U-shaped recovery for the economy, but it turned out to be V-shaped.

Hence, anticipating a longer play out and waiting to indulge in bottom fishing can be dangerous if the material event ends swiftly.

On the other hand, if one estimates these episodes to end quickly and therefore starts to buy immediately on dips, one may encounter several such opportunities in the downturn if it turns out to be prolonged. Hence, the best response to investing in war is creating scenarios and assigning probabilities. It is advisable to consider three scenarios, i.e., base case, optimistic, and pessimistic.

Optimistic Scenario: We expect the inflation threat to evaporate quickly in this scenario. At the time of writing, inflation was rising in the US and other developed nations. The Federal Reserve (USA's central banking system) initially assessed this as transitory as it felt that this inflation was driven more by supply bottlenecks than demand surges. However, it quickly changed that position and is now using its monetary policy to manage surging inflation by steadily increasing interest rates. The long-run inflation in the US is about 1.5 percent to 2.0 percent, while actual inflation during this period surpassed 7.5 percent.

Also, the Covid pandemic disappeared in certain regions and re-emerged in others (like China and Europe). The optimistic scenario may envision a Covid that can move from being a pandemic to endemic globally. Also, optimistically, we can hope for the supply chain to unclog, leading to lower logistics and commodity prices. All these may keep the Fed on track with its usual rate increase plan. On top of this, we can assume that Russia and Ukraine will come to a long-term understanding, thus swiftly ending the war.

In this scenario, the economy and therefore the markets can recover and produce another bull year.

Base Scenario: In the base case scenario, one can assume that high inflation is here to stay for some more time and can accept that as the new normal. In that case, the Fed may increase interest rates slightly more than anticipated. While supply chain woes would stay, they would not get worse. The Russia-Ukraine conflict would become protracted but contained between them without becoming a global issue. In this scenario, markets may stay flat but may remain highly volatile.

Pessimistic Scenario: In the worst-case scenario, the Russia-Ukraine conflict may spill over to other European countries, and thus NATO would get dragged into the war. This would send commodity prices, including crude oil, soaring, leading to high inflation on the back of severe supply chain disruptions. The economic impact of such a scenario will be market-negative, with earnings and valuations falling steeply.

While we lay out the factors under each scenario, assigning probabilities for those scenarios may be a good idea. However, we should carefully shift those factors from one scenario to another as things unfold and add more elements as we go by. Such changes should also result in reassessing the probability assignment.

Remember, each event is different! Analysing past geo-political events and their market impact is easy in hindsight since all the facts are known. However, studying an ongoing conflict and its effects can be daunting. It is essential to understand that while we can take many cues from history, we should always remember that each event happens in a unique setting; hence, the outcomes can be different.

Building Blocks

(20,000-feet view)

Section 2a: Fund Management

1. Introduction

After viewing the landscape from 30,000 feet through macro research, it is time to move closer to investing by acting on the insights gained. This process can involve formulating an investment strategy and engaging in fund management activities. Fund management is mainly carried out by mutual funds, which have taken up this task as a business.

Mutual funds help investors generate better inflation-adjusted returns without spending much time and energy. Backed by a dedicated research team, investors are provided with the services of an experienced fund manager who makes financial decisions based on market performance and prospects to achieve the mutual fund scheme's objectives.

Mutual funds are an ideal investment option for convenience and time-saving opportunities. With low investment amount, the ability to buy or sell them on any business day, and a wide range of choices based on individual goals and investment needs, investors are free to pursue their life goals while their investments earn returns.

Arguably, the biggest advantage for any investor is the low investment costs mutual funds offer compared to investing directly in capital markets. The benefit of scale in brokerage and fees translates to lower costs for investors.

Following the adage, "Do not put all your eggs in one basket," mutual funds help mitigate risks by diversifying investments across a range of assets. Investors have the advantage of prompt redemption in open-ended schemes based on the net asset value (NAV) at that time.

If invested in close-ended schemes, they can be traded on the stock exchange, as some schemes offer.

Based on medium or long-term investment, mutual funds have the potential to generate a higher return, as one can invest in a diverse range of sectors and industries. Fund managers provide regular information about the current value of the investment, along with their strategy and outlook, to give a clear picture of how our investments are doing. Moreover, since every mutual fund is regulated by SEBI, one can be assured that our investments are managed in a disciplined and regulated manner and are in safe hands. Mutual funds offer a variety of products across asset classes like equity, bonds, money market, real estate, etc.

However, the challenge of managing money through mutual funds is enormous as the primary objective is to beat the index and generate alpha. Over the past 10 years, fewer than 7% of U.S. active equity funds have outperformed the market, according to the Spiva U.S. scorecard[13]. In India, over a 10-year period, more than 60% of actively managed funds, excluding mid – and small-caps, have underperformed their benchmark[14]. If this is the case for trained, qualified fund managers, imagine the plight of retail investors. Remember, fund management is a tough act. Successful investors like Warren Buffet, Peter Lynch, George Soros, Seth Klarman, etc., are rare.

So, where is the disconnect? Let's dive deep to understand the reasons.

When it comes to investing, especially equities, we need to get three things right:

---

13 https://www.barrons.com/articles/active-managers-outperform-passive-index-funds-23723641

14 https://www.thehindubusinessline.com/markets/68-of-actively-managed-funds-fail-to-beat-benchmark-index-last-year/article66724514.ece

- What to Buy?
- When to Buy? And
- How much to buy?

We will have to get nearly right on all three to make it big in our investment adventure.

The first step in investing is to determine what to buy. The investing universe is so huge (more than 5,000 stocks in India) that one can easily get lost in the vast hypermarket. One should be a trained analyst (either by qualification or by experience) and have a robust process of identifying good stocks. It calls for intense research based on vast accumulated knowledge, and this is where experience is a huge plus. There are hundreds of financial and non-financial issues that one needs to consider before making an informed opinion about any company (addressed specifically in section 5).

While historical information in the public domain is a great start, it is only a start. Mostly, it is backward-looking and often comes with a time lag. Any serious research should focus on information lying in fine prints, unexpected places, and regulatory filings. One should develop a filtering mechanism to weed out unnecessary stocks and generate a focus list for further research and analysis. Initial analysis should be followed by detailed fine print research, company visits, and stakeholder interviews. Even then, the picture could be murky as it will still not cover qualitative issues like management quality, ethics, transparency, and operational fairness.

In short, it is a very intense activity and highly time-consuming.

Successful investors like Warren Buffett give it the time needed to form an opinion. Ordinary investors mostly rely on media inputs and sell-side research (research provided by broking firms) and a top-of-the-line research approach. Worse, retail investors mostly follow tips and recommendations from friends, associates, television channels, and YouTube gurus.

The first question of what to buy can help one find good companies. But good companies need not be good stocks as they may not be available at a reasonable price. Usually, companies are available at a good price when there is a broad market sell-off or when a particular company-specific development causes its share price to fall significantly. Such unanticipated broad sell-offs come rarely. The global financial crisis of 2008 and Covid in 2020 are great examples.

To ride against the tide and buy requires enormous guts. Celebrated investors like Warren Buffett precisely do this—wait patiently for a market crash and enter. Retail investors typically do not have the patience. More importantly, individual investors tend to buy at the wrong time when the market is in a bull phase because there is optimism all around, and one can jump in confidently (requiring less guts!). Also, the mood is generally somber and pessimistic when a market sell-off occurs.

Look to wildlife photography for inspiration. The people involved in shooting those engrossing National Geographic documentaries spend days and months in the middle of forests waiting patiently to capture the best moments. In investing, patience is a virtue that pays enormous dividends.

While academic research does not recommend market timing, buying during market crashes can produce outsized returns compared to buying under all market conditions or when the markets are enjoying a bull phase.

To me, the most critical question is how much to buy. There is a difference between buying 50 and 500 shares! After investing considerable time and effort in finding an opportunity and patiently waiting for a favourable market or company event, buying a small part is of no use. The reason is that even if the investment turns out to be a great winner, it will not move the needle unless the original investment is of significant value. The concept of weighted average return on the portfolio is very important.

This is where even institutional investors get caught on the wrong side. Institutional investors are bound by an index and can deviate slightly from the index weights. If a company's weight in the index is two percent, it can at best go up to three percent. Otherwise, they will risk high tracking error. Here, individual investors have a significant advantage as they don't have such constraints. Again, one needs gut in good measure to take a substantial position after convincing yourself that it is a good company available at a reasonable price.

To summarise: Fund management is challenging; one must be right on all three parameters: what to buy, when to buy, and how much to buy. It won't pay off even if we get two out of three right. That's why it is best left to professional managers. If not, be prepared to give it the time, energy, and focus throughout your life.

2. Mutual Funds is a "Desi" game

US asset manager Invesco announced its exit from the mutual fund business in India in April 2024. This is not the first of its kind. We have witnessed several foreign firms like Goldman Sachs, JP Morgan, Fidelity, Morgan Stanley, etc., exit the Indian mutual fund landscape. These are renowned global names in the mutual fund space.

Generally, business exits happen on the back of poor industry performance. But in the case of Indian mutual funds, it is the opposite. From a modest Rs. 10 lakh crores of assets under management (AUM) in 2014, the industry has grown to nearly Rs. 55 lakh crores by the end of 2023. The question then arises: what is forcing these exits in such a rapidly growing industry?

Table : 6 Mutual Fund Market Share

	Fund House	Assets Under Management (Rs. Lakh Cr)	Market Share	Foreign Investor	Parent Type
1	SBI Mutual Fund	9,14,36,530	17%	Amundi (37%)	Domestic Bank
2	ICICI Prudential Mutual Fund	6,83,09,593	13%	Prudential/ Eastspring Investment	Domestic Bank
3	HDFC Mutual Fund	6,12,90,494	11%		Domestic Bank
4	Nippon India Mutual Fund	4,31,30,802	8%	Stand alone Foreign firm	Non-Bank
5	Kotak Mahindra Mutual Fund	3,81,04,582	7%	Stand alone Domestic firm	Domestic Bank
6	Aditya Birla Sun Life Mutual Fund	3,31,70,914	6%	Sun Life	Non-Bank
7	UTI Mutual Fund	2,90,88,085	5%	T Rowe Price Group	Non-Bank
8	Axis Mutual Fund	2,74,26,528	5%	Schrodder Singapore (25%)	Domestic Bank
9	Mirae Asset Mutual Fund	1,61,74,088	3%	Stand alone Foreign firm	Non-Bank
10	DSP Mutual Fund	1,48,06,337	3%	Stand alone Domestic firm	Non-Bank
	Industry Total	**54,13,17,186**			

Source: AMFI, Author Calculations

Before we analyse why this is happening, a look at the top 10 mutual fund houses reveals many things. In an industry populated by nearly 45 players, the top 10 accounts for nearly 80% of the market share. The top 3 accounts for the lion's share of the industry (41%), and all of them have the advantage of tapping their domestic banking channels for sales.

While many foreign firms have exited the Indian space during the past few years, we also notice some stand-alone foreign firms like Nippon & Mirae in the top 10. It is interesting to see them at the top despite not having local bank support.

Some plausible reasons why foreign firms find it too hot to survive the Indian mutual fund landscape can be enumerated here:

1. **High Cost**: Mutual funds are high-volume, low-margin businesses, and hence, controlling the cost becomes very important for survival. Foreign firms, especially the ones based out of the US and Europe, tend to mirror their global cost structures into Indian operations, which can make them unviable in the long-run. Keeping costs low is crucial in an industry that is quickly getting commoditised thanks to the proliferation of index funds and ETFs.

2. **Inability to Scale**: As noted before, the top 3 in the list enjoy the support of the bank branch network to push sales. The top-ranked mutual fund, i.e., SBI mutual fund, can enjoy the backing of nearly 22,000 SBI bank branches, which is not a small advantage by any stretch of the imagination. ICICI Mutual fund and HDFC Mutual fund boost around 5,000-6,000 bank branches, respectively, and hence, they enjoy a head start compared to non-banks. Banks enable mutual funds to establish a strong distributor network that foreign firms may find difficult to replicate. However, the 4th, 6th and 7th in the list are non-banks as well. We also noticed other bank-sponsored mutual funds, especially from the public sector, like Bank of India or Bank of Baroda, which are not at the top of the league at present.

3. **Regulations**: Foreign firms, normally headquartered in the US/ Europe, has to undergo far higher regulatory scrutiny in their

home and foreign markets compared to others. This may have increased their cost and potentially slowed down the speed.

4. **Non-Core**: The AUM of Indian mutual funds at USD650 billion is a fraction of say USD 10 trillion AUM of Blackrock (the top mutual fund in the world). Hence, for most of the global big names, India is still a small market and therefore the struggle may not be worth the effort.

5. **Dynamic M&A landscape:** While the industry is growing rapidly, we have also witnessed several mergers, takeovers, and acquisitions among AMCs in the last few years making the eco system very dynamic. Establishing long-term aspirations in such a robust eco system can be difficult.

For now, the advantage clearly is that domestic bank-backed mutual funds will hold on to their strong market shares while select foreign firms will aggressively compete through innovative product offerings and management styles. Many foreign firms will start with small stakes or Joint ventures and will be willing to test the waters. While most of them see the growth very clearly, operating in India need not be easy. Also, foreign firms are quick to cut their losses when their business plan fails, which can also explain the swift exits of many foreign firms.

3. The Chase for "Alpha"

India's mutual fund landscape is on a rising spree. The last few years have seen explosive growth thanks to aggressive advertisements, product pushing through banking channels, and stock market performance. We often see cricket celebrities endorsing the slogan "mutual funds sahi hai" and a website dedicated to that name to propel investor interest. These endorsements urge investors to look at mutual funds for various needs, varying from children's education to retirement planning. In the equity fund category alone, we have 137 funds[15] spread across seven subcategories. Over the years, the number of fund houses, range of funds, and systematic investment plans have burgeoned to spoil investors with choices. Do funds generate alpha?

Generally, fund managers are paid management fees hoping that they will perform better than the overall market (benchmark). Herein comes Alpha. Alpha is excess return over the stated benchmark. To smoothen alpha calculation, we take five years of rolling annualised return (aka Compounded Annual Growth Rate or CAGR) and deduct five years rolling annualised market return to compute alpha. We have also applied a size filter to remove small funds. We have used the median asset value to eliminate funds below the median. In general, more than 50% of fund managers generated alpha during the period 2019-June 2024. In some categories like multi-cap, it is even higher.

While we have seen managers generate significant alpha, do they do it consistently is the thing to look at. To examine this, we rank-ordered the top 5 performers each year and mapped them to see who stays and who gets out (called the churn). We can compute a Persistence in performance (PIP) ratio that divides incumbents with new entrants to

---

15   As of April 2024

the Top-5 list. In other words, if the PIP ratio is 60 percent, it means three out of five managers in that year were existing incumbents. If that ratio is 100 percent, all the top five managers were the same. A high ratio implies persistence in performance. The following table provides the PIP ratio category-wise.

Table : 7 What's Your Fund's PIP?		
Category	PIP Ratio (%) (Apr 2024)	PIP Ratio (%) (2019)
Large Cap	60%	40%
Flexi Cap	80%	60%
ELSS	80%	80%
Large and Mid Cap	80%	80%
Mid Cap	80%	40%
Small Cap	60%	80%

Note that the persistence factor has been improving over the years for many categories, implying lesser manager churn among the top 5 performers. This has led to higher concentration of fund flows to persistent performers. The market share gainers scored based on their alpha, while losers lost due to negative alpha. Although for most categories, the best-performing fund has witnessed the highest gains in market share, there are also categories where the gainers need not be the market leader but represent those that significantly increased their share. In the large-cap category, the Canara Robeco Blue-chip Equity Fund increased its share considerably from 0.1% in 2018 to 3.5% in June 2024 with a cumulative alpha of 13.1% over the benchmark.

On the other side, Franklin India Smaller Companies lost market share within the small-cap fund universe, declining from 23.1% in 2018 to about 7.1% in June 2024. During this period, the fund's cumulative alpha stood at a negative 4.7%, explaining the loss in market share. It should be noted that the fund's overall AUM did increase during the period 2018-June 2024 at an annualised clip of nearly 14% despite the decline in market share.

Among the losers from a market share perspective, Franklin India funds figure in three categories. Among gainers, the fund managers remain mixed. Increasing market share in an increasing pie size is a significant feat indeed. Losing market share in an expanding pie can still mean period-on-period growth.

A key takeaway from the period 2018-Apr 2024 could be that the market rewards funds/fund houses with consistent past performance with exceptional gains in AuM.

We find that some mutual funds significantly outperform the underlying market, making them a viable investment option. However, we notice a wide variation in performance between leaders and laggards, raising the big question of whether there is persistence in performance. Outperformance is concentrated in a few select fund houses, as the ratio of funds beating the benchmark has reduced to 44% between the 2018-June 2024 period from more than 50% five years ago. Generally, we observe a strong correlation between market share gain and alpha generation, though there are a few exceptions. In short, it is a good investment strategy to bet on market share gainers with a good history of alpha generation.

4. Assessing Fund Managers

Mutual fund investors generally prefer a fund due to its historical performance. In the context of an equity fund, the primary expectation is that the fund manager should outperform his stated benchmark. For e.g., if his benchmark is that of Nifty 50 or Sensex, the fund's performance should be better than the benchmark to justify investor confidence in the fund. The extent to which the manager outperforms the benchmark is the second important element of attraction.

To beat the benchmark, the fund manager is always in pursuit of winners and tactful in avoiding losers while selecting stocks. Where the winners outnumber the losers and where the fund manager's commitment to winners (in terms of allocation) is better than the losers, he or she will generate outperformance or what is technically called alpha (excess performance over the benchmark). In other words, where a fund manager generates superior performance through consistently beating the benchmark, he/she is good at picking winners and avoiding losers. While this assessment sounds simplistic and hence reasonable, often, this 2-dimensional approach to assessing fund manager performance may not be enough.

In my view, the issue of fund management in the context of equity revolves around the concept of bets. There are bets that the fund manager sticks with, and there are bets that he avoids. Hence, we need to view the issue from a 4-D perspective:

Figure : 3 4D Perspective

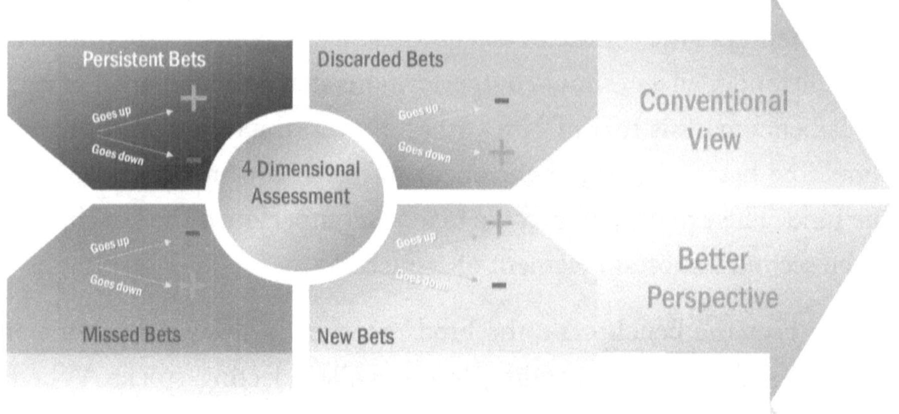

Dimension 1: Persistent Bets: These are bets that the fund manager is sticking with resolutely and believes in them strongly. A simple way to figure this out is to see if a particular stock is present at the beginning as well as the end of an evaluation period. The reason why he persists with these stocks can be borne out of thorough research and fund managers' conviction about its future ability to perform if the stock price of persistent bets moves up, the manager gains and vice versa.

Dimension 2: Discarded Bets: These are bets that the fund manager has lost faith in and therefore sold out. A way to find this out is to see if a particular stock figures in the beginning portfolio but not in the end period portfolio. In this scenario, if the stock price gains after the manager has discarded them, the manager tends to lose out on performance.

Dimension 3: Missed Bets: These are bets that the manager did not take, or we can call it a "failed to buy" scenario. These bets will not figure either in the beginning portfolio or the end portfolio. In such cases, where the stock price moves up, the manager loses out in terms of opportunity gain and vice versa.

Dimension 4: New Bets: These are bets that the manager took recently. A simple way to figure them out is when such stocks are present in the end period portfolio and not in the beginning period portfolio. Like persistent bets, the manager gains when such stocks move up and vice versa.

The idea is to take the literature of fund manager performance one step higher by looking at the opportunity cost of missing something and the opportunity cost of sticking with bad choices, which can take a heavy toll on the portfolio performance. What makes a fund manager stick with a bet, discard a bet, miss a bet, or take a new bet is a combination of several factors, including his ability to pick stocks, ability not to get distracted by peer group pressure, ability to have sound advice and being vigilant. In the end, the aim of any active fund manager is to generate alpha, which is the only reason investors are ready to pay management fees. In the absence of such a proposition, an Exchange traded fund (ETF) can simply do the job. In an ETF scenario, there is only one bet, i.e., index composition!

5. The Stars, Dogs and Darlings

Stock selection has always been difficult, and that's what fund managers are paid for. But how well have they stood up to this challenge?

In the context of the Indian stock market, the game of stock selection can be understood by looking at fund holdings that have managed the best ratings. There were sixteen funds spread across the large-cap, mid-cap, and small-cap universe, and the total number of stocks in the portfolio of these funds, adjusting for overlaps, narrowed down to 335. The Indian stock market boasts listings of almost 5,000 stocks, but surprisingly, the universe of stocks held by leading fund managers is very small (4.9%).

Obviously, some of these stocks enjoy a phenomenal following from the fund managers while others don't. Our classification shows that only 9.3% of the 335 stocks enjoy a tremendous following from fund managers. These 9.3% of the stocks had the approval and investment of 5 to 10 fund managers (out of 16). The bulk of the 335 stocks under analysis were part of only a few funds.

We are still not examining whether fund managers are correct in terms of their stock picking, which we will address shortly. At this stage, we are only looking at whether fund managers pursue a large basket of stocks or a smaller basket of heavyweight stocks.

There is another dimension to this problem. Of these 335 stocks, how many are represented in the index, especially the Nifty index, which has a large following today? The Nifty has three main categories: the Nifty 50 (the bellwether), the Nifty mid-cap 100, and the Nifty Small-cap 100. We found that 13.7% of the stocks fall in the Nifty 50, which predominantly contains large-cap stocks, about 19.7% in the mid-cap index, 12.2% in the small-cap index, and the remaining 54.3% with no index representation, meaning these stocks do not form part of any benchmarks. This is interesting because fund managers take on tracking error risk by investing in such stocks, indicating there are reasons beyond benchmarking that drive them to pursue off-benchmark stocks to enhance performance.

From a performance standpoint, we found that nearly 177 of these 335 stocks, or 45.5%, can be classified as excellent performers (with an annualised return of more than 20%), while nearly 19.3% of these 335 stocks can be classified as poor performers, meaning they showed zero or negative rates of return. Thus, a high percentage of stock selections by fund managers have fared well, with about 20% of the selected stocks disappointing. During this three-year period, the Nifty index returned 14.97% per year, rising from 14,690 points in March 2021 to 22,326 points in March 2024.

Methodology

The data for the mutual funds was sourced from www.valueresearchonline. com, which provides the top-rated funds under different styles and their complete constituent information. The analysis focused on three major styles: Equity Large-Cap, Equity Large-Mid Cap, and Equity Mid-small-cap. The constituent stocks for the top-rated funds in the above-mentioned styles were organised into a single list to facilitate the study of stock selection of different fund managers across the three styles. The index representation of the stocks was another facet of the analysis, which examined how closely the indices are tracked by the different style managers. The indices considered were the Nifty 50, the Nifty mid-cap 100, and the Nifty Small-cap 100.

The presence of individual stocks in these funds was counted, and their annualised returns were calculated over a three-year period from the Reuters database. The returns were then classified as excellent (greater than 20%), Good (between 15% and 20%), Average (between 7.5% and 15%), and poor (less than 7.5%), and the stocks were ordered in terms of returns; from highest to lowest. The top 10 and bottom ten from the list are presented here, as well as their occurrence in the three considered indices.

Another aspect of the analysis is the stocks that are present in most funds, their performance, and if their presence is justified by their performance. Many fund managers have an obligation to closely track the index and to have a minimal tracking error. We examine if this tendency benefits or hurts the investors.

The results are as follows.

Table : 8 Number of Stocks Held by Fund Managers

		>10	5 to 10	2 to 5	1	Total
Performance Classification	Excellent	7	35	102	62	206
	Good	0	3	19	16	38
	Average	5	8	14	29	56
	Poor	0	1	14	23	38
	Total	**12**	**47**	**149**	**130**	**338**

How to read This table? - 12 stocks out of the 338 stocks enjoy the patronage of more than 10 fund managers while 47 stocks enjoy the patronage of 5-10 fund managers

Table : 9 Index Representation

		CNX Large	CNX Mid	CNX Small	Non-Index	Total
Performance Classification	Excellent	28	18	16	144	206
	Good	3	3	6	26	38
	Average	12	4	1	39	56
	Poor	1	4	1	32	38
	Total	44	29	24	241	338

How to read This table? - 44 out of 338 stocks figure in the CNX Nifty index, while 29 stocks figure in the CNX Midcap index. **CNX Large - CNX Nifty 50, CNX Mid - CNX Midcap 50, CNX Small - CNX Small Cap 50 and Non Index - Stocks not included in any of the 3 index**

Table : 10 The Stars

Company	Sector	Count	Index Presence	3 year performance	Annualized Performance	Performance Classification
Rajratan Global Wire Ltd	Manufacturing	1	–	2373%	191%	Excellent
Adani Enterprises Ltd	Industrial	3	–	1895%	171%	Excellent
Tata Elxsi Ltd	Technology	3	–	1273%	139%	Excellent
Cg Power and Industrial Solutions Ltd	Manufacturing	2	–	1128%	131%	Excellent
Greenpanel Industries Ltd	Manufacturing	2	–	1104%	129%	Excellent
Dixon Technologies (India) Ltd	Manufacturing	1	–	769%	106%	Excellent
Deepak Fertilisers and Petrochemicals Corp Ltd	Manufacturing	1	–	749%	104%	Excellent
Apollo Tricoat Tubes Ltd	Manufacturing	1	–	728%	102%	Excellent
Laurus Labs Ltd	Healthcare	4	–	678%	98%	Excellent
Linde India Ltd	Manufacturing	3	–	656%	96%	Excellent

This table represents the best performers in our list of 335 stocks. They need not necessarily be heavily invested by the fund managers as they may lack liquidity. In most cases, they found favour only from one or utmost two fund managers. The stars can be seen mostly in the industrial sector, and they enjoy market leadership, strong distribution channels, brand ownership, new successful product launches, zero-debt status, and high dividends.

Table: 11 The Dogs

Company	Sector	Count	Index Presence	3 year Performance	Annualized Performance	Performance Classification
Suryoday Small Finance Bank	Banking & Investment Services	1	-	-67%	-31%	Poor
Zomato Ltd	Technology	2	-	-63%	-28%	Poor
Dcb Bank Ltd	Banking & Investment Services	1	-	-54%	-23%	Poor
Mrs. Bectors Food	FMCG	1	-	-47%	-19%	Poor
Gulf Oil Lubricants India	Manufacturing	1	-	-45%	-18%	Poor
Nazara Technologies Ltd	Technology	1	-	-37%	-14%	Poor
Jagran Prakashan Ltd	Media	1	-	-35%	-13%	Poor
Engineers India Ltd	Services	1	-	-33%	-13%	Poor
Zee Entertainment	Media	4	CNX Midcap	-32%	-12%	Poor
Gillette India Ltd	FMCG	1	-	-27%	-10%	Poor

This table represents the worst performers in our list of 335 stocks. They need not necessarily be heavily invested by the fund managers as they may lack liquidity. In most cases, they found favour only from few fund managers. The dogs can be seen mostly from financial services, consumer cyclicals and healthcare sectors and suffer from demand decline, order lags, regulatory actions, large debt and capacity constraints.

Table : 12 The Darlings

Company	Sector	Count	Index Presence	Annualized Performance	Performance Classification
Icici Bank Ltd	Banking & Investment Services	19	CNX Large	24%	Excellent
Hdfc Bank Ltd	Banking & Investment Services	18	CNX Large	8%	Average
Bharti Airtel Ltd	Telecommunications	16	CNX Large	27%	Excellent
Reliance Industries Ltd	Energy	15	CNX Large	30%	Excellent
State Bank Of India	Banking & Investment Services	14	CNX Large	17%	Excellent
Infosys Ltd	Technology	13	CNX Large	25%	Excellent
Larsen & Toubro Ltd	Construction	13	–	10%	Average
Gland Pharma Ltd	Healthcare	12	–	8%	Average
Itc Ltd	FMCG	12	CNX Large	4%	Average
Axis Bank Ltd	Banking & Investment Services	12	CNX Large	2%	Average

The above is simply the list of companies embraced by leading fund managers. For example, 9 out of the sixteen fund managers have invested in Infosys, Reliance, ICICI Bank, Maruti and L&T. It is very clear that the simple reason is their presence in the Nifty 50 and hence, fund managers are reluctant to deviate from the benchmark. Also, being index heavyweights, they enjoy good liquidity. On average, the top 10 darling stocks have produced a 13% return on an annual basis during the last 3 years. The sector representation is dominated by financial services, with three banks in the above list of ten companies.

Fund managers are good at avoiding dogs but not necessarily successful in catching stars. Benchmark and liquidity compulsions make them embrace darlings. Fortunately, the propitious market environment has helped them in this process during the last few years. This study simply shows the stock selection from a fund manager's perspective. Whether a stock is a star or a dog, we will know only after the event. However, the list of star performers can be used for further investigation and investment. Similarly, dogs are surely something to be avoided. For liquidity-conscious investors, darlings may be the best bet!

Section 2b: Market Timing

1. Introduction

There is no good or bad time to invest, just like there is no good or bad time to look for a job. Even if there is one, it can be known only in hindsight and becomes useless. Let us flip this question and ask, "How can I time the market correctly?"

This question, in other words, believes that we should be smart enough to buy at the bottom and savvy enough to sell at the top and thus make money. However, the bottom and the top are evident only after they have already occurred. For example, if we look at a historical chart, we can know what the bottom or top is, but if we are asked to draw a graph in the future, constructing the bottom and top is difficult to do with any element of precision.

So, to get the market timing right, we should be right twice (first, in predicting the top and then in guessing the bottom). And more importantly, we should be right both times every time we make an investment call. That's impossible from a probability point of view. Therefore, the best answer is that there is no good or bad time to invest. So long as we have a consistent investment habit over a period, timing will be irrelevant. As experts rightly say, "time in the market" is more important than "timing the market."

Market timing will hurt us if we have sporadic investment habits, as we may be caught in a bad cycle and must wait forever to recover our losses. Alternatively, we may be lucky enough to have a great start and can see through several bad years since the beginning was good.

For example, if we invested in the Indian market at the beginning of 2008, our investment value would be down by 52 per cent at the end of 2008, and we would be smarting our wounds till 2013, which is when we would have broken even. Yet, if we had invested in early 2009, our portfolio would be up by 76 percent by the end of 2009 and another 44 percent in 2010. We would be laughing our way to the bank now. Nevertheless, both outcomes are unpredictable and are purely a function of luck. Hence, the idea of timing the market is a bad one. Instead, one should have a consistent way of investing in the market and invest regularly rather than sporadically.

As per research data from 1992, an investor who invested every year at a 52-week high would have earned an annualised return of 11%, while the same investor would have earned a 15% annualised return if he had invested in the 52-week low year after year. This is just to give an example that market timing is irrelevant as that strategy can only be tested in hindsight since there is no way of knowing in advance what will be a 52-week high or low.

The fallacy of market timing can also be demonstrated by comparing investments by excluding best days. For e.g., if one stays invested all the time (highly recommended), an investment of Rs.10,000 in 2003 would have grown to Rs.21.6 lakhs by 2023. However, if one excludes ten best days, that results in total value dropping down to just Rs.97,036. Even worse, if one excludes the top 60 days from the performance, the investment value would only be Rs 11,017 after 20 years. The danger of exclusion will arise if one tries to time the market.

Another important factor to debate about market timing is the "binary" problem of reasoning. For example, it is quite common to exhibit the performance of the market in a calendar year fashion like it did in the year 2022. This assumes that one invests at the beginning of 2022 and counts the performance at the end of 2022 to appreciate the overall yearly performance of the market in 2022. However, investors have different entry and exit points throughout the year based on market swings and emotional responses to those swings.

Here are two charts that can put this debate in perspective. The first chart depicts the combination of every possible return between the year 1999 and 2022. While investors generally enjoyed gains, it can range from excellent (dark green) to worst (red). While excellent and worst do show up, what shows up mostly is the average performance throughout. Even here, one can notice significant variance in returns based on time of entry and exit. While this chart looks very neat and observable, the second chart depicts the same but for the year 2022 (monthly). Here, it is a completely mixed bag based on one's point of entry and exit.

The final point of this exercise is to show that market timing is futile in prospect but clear in retrospect. Hence, a consistent investing strategy regardless of market levels have produced good outcomes and avoids the risk of timing the market.

While history recommends that we should not time the market, however timing the market is inherent to investment nature for human beings and is difficult to avoid. In such cases where the urge to time the market is irresistible, one should embrace techniques like technical analysis to avoid emotions interfere in market timing decisions.

2. Buy Low, Sell High, But How?

If we ask any investor, the greatest investment challenge is to buy low and sell high. However, many times, we end up buying high and selling low!

While historical returns can look appealing, the exact timing of investment can create a huge divergence between investor returns and historical returns. If timing is wrong, then a buy-and-hold strategy can backfire heavily.

On the other hand, if one is actively trading in the market (what is called high-frequency trading), it will mostly be a negative-sum game that benefits only the brokers to earn their commissions! According to a SEBI study[16], 9 out of ten traders in the equity Futures and Options segment incurred net losses. On average, loss makers registered net trading losses of Rs. 50,000. Over and above the net trading losses incurred, loss makers expended an additional 28% of net trading loss as transaction costs. Those making net trading profits incurred between 15% to 50% of such profits as transaction costs.

Having understood the pitfalls of timing, the question that comes to mind is whether there is any strategy that can time the market without emotions but based on carefully evaluated rules (through an intense study of the past). Can we generate 'above ordinary' returns and live up to our initial expectation of "Buy Low Sell High" ambition? Here, it should always be remembered that no investment strategy beats a buy-and-hold strategy 100% of the time. It always depends on the level of entry and further market movement.

---

16 https://www.sebi.gov.in/reports-and-statistics/research/jan-2023/study-analysis-of-profit-and-loss-of-individual-traders-dealing-in-equity-fando-segment_67525.html

All markets frequently go "underwater" and stay there for longer than what we can anticipate. For e.g., if one invested at 100, and the investment value goes down to say 90, technically the investment is termed "under the water". The problem is that both the depth and the period of investment being under the water cannot be predicted.

The Japanese stock market is a great example. The Nikkei index reached its highest level of 38,915 on 29th December 1989 and breached it on April 5th, 2024 (after 34 years!) Do we have such episodes in the Indian market? For e.g., if we had invested on 14th January 2020 when Nifty TRI was at 17,349, we would have gone under the water immediately and had to wait till 6th November 2020 before we could level our original investment. We had to wait for nearly 10 agonising months, during which our investments dropped by 38% when Nifty TRI reached 10, 710 (23rd March 2020). The probability of something going under the water is high during the peak of bull markets or any unforeseen circumstances, such as the COVID-19 pandemic. Once our investments are "under the water", we take time to accept the fact, during which time it goes even deeper under the water.

When markets go under the water, we often ride it down fully rather than limit our loss by cashing out at some stage. Once our investments are "above the water", our expectation about future profits is unlimited!

Most of our buy/sell points are either determined emotionally or arbitrarily rather than by carefully evaluating our investment environment. Psychology plays a major role in market timing. After we make an investment, and if we move into a profit zone, we attribute that to our "skill" and not "luck." However, when we move into loss, first, we are in "denial" mode (how can I make a bad investment decision?), and then when we are deep in the red, we "resign" to our fate and do nothing. Again psychology!

Can we create a strategy that aims to buy low and sell high? Let us look at this possibility through a series of questions:

The basic idea is to invest only when the market is in a "new low" as determined by a reference to a previous high. For the sake of simplicity, I am assuming that we invest in an ETF-like structure that replicates the broad market.

Table : 13 Investment Indicator

Date	Index Value	Underwater Number	Index High Point	Buy/Sell Indicator
16-11-2022	26,769	100.00	26,769	100.00
17-11-2022	26,673	99.64	26,769	99.64
18-11-2022	26,621	99.45	26,769	99.45
21-11-2022	26,406	98.64	26,769	98.64
22-11-2022	26,528	99.10	26,769	98.64
23-11-2022	26,562	99.23	26,769	98.64
24-11-2022	26,877	100.00	26,877	100.00
Source: Refinitiv, Author Calculation				

Let us look at some historical data to understand this. On 16th November 2022, the Nifty TRI reached 26,769, a new high. One should index this as 100 and keep referencing further moves to this 100. After this, the index offered a "new low" on 17th November 2022 at 26,673. Then offered another "new low" on 18th November 2022 when Nifty TRI reached 26,620 and offered another "new low" on 21st November 2022 when Nifty TRI reached 26,405. As per the strategy, we will invest at all such points of "new lows".

Remember, market can keep going down for a considerable period which means that it will offer us many "new lows". One should then be prepared to invest in every such "new low".

We should start with a defined instalment amount of, say, Rs.10,000 and increase the investment amount as we encounter further "new lows" tracked by the indexing explained above. The following rules can help:

Table : 14 Investment Limits

Underwater Band	Investment Amount (INR)
Less than 50	60,000
51–60	50,000
61–70	40,000
71–80	30,000
81–90	20,000
91 and above	10,000

As we may see, the amount to be invested is based on spotting a new low and the level where it is spotted. Hence, it is variable and cannot be determined upfront. All one can do is to have some amount locked up in a money market fund to be utilised as and when the model screams a "buy". Here, we cannot predict how much to invest since the length of market fall cannot be predicted.

By virtue of the strategy, even the frequency cannot be determined upfront. One may have a situation where one will find the need to invest almost daily, or there may be periods where one will not invest for years.

The strategy sells when the market reaches back a high from where one started (i.e., 100). Continuing our earlier example, while we would have bought on the 17th, 18th, and 21st of November 2022 because it reached "new lows" on these days, we will sell our position on 24th November 2022 when the index reaches 26,877 and surpasses the earlier new high of 26,768 and reached a "new high".

We will sell all the investments that happened during this period at that day's value. The strategy involves buying and selling whenever the model says so. However, we will not know that in advance. Going by the number of buy and sell activities, we can classify the findings as follows:

Table : 15 Strategy Activity			
	3 Years	**5 Years**	**Since 2013**
Total Number of trading days	743	1235	2638
Buy days (a)	110	195	481
Sell days (b)	35	47	113
Total Strategy days (a+b)	145	242	594
% of total	19.5%	19.6%	22.5%
Source: Refinitiv, Author Calculation			

The % number of days on which the strategy will force us to act is 19.5% for the three-year period. In other words, we will have trading action only 19.5% of the time, which is 100% if we are a day trader.

I have tested the concept for several time periods and found that the strategy outperforms the buy-and-hold strategy in the 5 years (30th August 2018 to 29th August 2023) and 10.67 years (January 2013 to August 2023) period significantly, while it slightly underperforms the buy-and-hold in the 3 years category (31st August 2020 to 29th August 2023). Hence, it is worth the time and effort. However, it should be noted that this strategy might underperform a buy-and-hold strategy in an upward-trending bull market.

Table : 16 Strategy Performance			
Performance	The Strategy[1]	The Strategy (w/o transaction charges)[2]	Nifty
3 Years (Aug'20 Aug'23)	16.1%	21.5%	20.8%
5 Years (Aug'18 Aug'23)	26.6%	30.4%	12.0%
Since 2013 (Jan'13 –Aug'23)	20.9%	25.5%	13.2%
1-Based on XIRR & transaction fee of 0.5%		2-Based on XIRR without transaction fee 3-Based on Annualized Return	

The strategy performs best when the market goes one full cycle, i.e., it comes back to a point where it was before. Technically, it is called "Peak-Trough-Peak" (PTP). For e.g., Nifty TRI reached a peak on 3rd March 2015 at 11,856 and thereafter fell continuously till 25th February 2016 to reach 9,282, after which it started climbing back slowly and reached its earlier peak of 11,858 on 2nd September 2016. In other words, if we had invested on 3rd March 2015 and exited on 2nd September 2016 (after almost 1.5 years), we would have just got back our money, implying nil returns. However, this strategy would have indicated buying 33 times all through the fall from March 2015 to Feb 2016. As per the investment band, we would have invested a total of Rs. 5.20 lakhs in this period through 33 buy actions, with the last buy of Rs.30,000 on 25th February 2016 when the Nifty TRI was at 9,282. Remember, as per the band, we start modestly at a Rs.10,000 investment and increase our investment value as the market braces for new lows. Since after 25th February 2016, the Nifty

TRI did not encounter any new low; there was no buy call till 2nd September 2016, when Nifty touched a new high, and the model told us to sell. The sale value would have fetched Rs. 5.97 lakhs, implying an IRR of 14.4% against a 0% return on the buy-and-hold.

Buy-and-Hold	The "Strategy
Invest a fixed sum on a particular date or invest in regular instalments (SIP)	Variable investment that cannot be determined upfront
Passive one-time investment for a fixed period	Active "in" and "out" investment for a variable period that cannot be determined upfront
Responds poorly to a complete market cycle (down and up)	Responds classically to a complete market cycle
Performs well in an upward-trending bull market	Performs well in a full market cycle

As Warren Buffet said (which most of us do not follow), "Be adventurous when others are fearful and be fearful when others are adventurous". When we follow that advice, we can buy low and sell high. The idea of investing a pre-defined amount at a pre-defined time will expose our investment to market timing risk.

On the other hand, the idea of investing when markets are in a free fall and cashing out when markets are in a free rise will make sure that we don't encounter capital loss. The idea espoused above is just that. Given our limited ability to deal with losses psychologically, I feel such a strategy can be of great help. A caveat will be in order. Ready investible cash holding would mean just that and not tied up in a liquid fund or a money market fund, which one can realise only the following day when the market has moved in the other direction. Also, some of the assumptions stated to test the idea may not be rigorous from a conceptual basis. However, the idea is to show an example of rule-based investing, and the rules can be refined further based on rigorous backtests.

3. Investing In Peaks – What Are the Odds?

Should one invest in Indian markets when Sensex is at its all-time high? What are the odds that one will make money from this point forward?

It is common sense to avoid investing in peaks and invest during troughs (when the market hits a bottom). However, this is easier said than done. What if the market is in a secular bull run? Are we not missing an opportunity to make money by not investing just because the market is at an all-time high?

Ironically, markets come to investor attention only when they touch all-time highs. However, an all-time high is also the point at which prospective returns diminish considerably. A look at Sensex from 2005 to 2024 posits that it provided an annual return of 13.5%, and the 10-year period between March 2013 and March 2023 produced an annualised return of 12.8%, sufficient to be attractive even if we factor inflation into the equation. However, this assumes that one invested at the end of March 2013 and never looked back, an assumption that is not easy to make. When markets peak, investor sentiment also peaks, encouraging investment. In addition, peer pressure to perform also increases as we see our friends and colleagues making money (or at least boasting to be making money). Alternatively, when markets are in a trough, fear factor will rule and may force one to cash out earlier instead of investing.

We ran a simple number crunching exercise to differentiate the effect of investing in a peak as opposed to investing in a trough for the Indian market. However, we need to formulate some rules to test the case. Here they are:

As an investor, we expect to make an annualised return of 12.8% (approximately the return Sensex gave during the last 10 years). This is our target return.

1. Our holding period is a minimum of one year since we are not in a trading environment where we buy today and sell either today or tomorrow for a +/-0.2% return in a day. Annualised, this can be equivalent to making or losing 65%.
2. A peak is defined as an all-time high that we have never seen before (quite easy to spot as well).
3. A trough is any point 12.8% lower than the latest peak. (The 12.8% is subjective and is set to align with the long-term performance of the index)

In the period of 2005 to March 2024, Sensex produced 421 peaks (all-time highs), of which the peaks hit the target 285 times. It represents 68% of the time one would have achieved a target return of 12.8% exactly within one year of the holding period, even when one invests at the peak. So, what happened to the balance of the time?

In the same period, we had 1,365 troughs out of which 896 of them were more than 1 year old. In 79% of the trough cases, we achieved our target return of 12.8% within one year holding period. In other words, the odds of not making 12.8% target return when investing in a trough is 21% and this is due to the volatility of the market triggered by several factors. Hence, it is always recommended to invest in troughs rather than peaks.

In other words, when one invests in a peak, there is a 32% chance of waiting for more than a year to make a 12.8% annual return. When one invests in a trough, there is no such risk. The question now is, is the 32% risk of being caught in a peak trap worth taking? It depends on one's risk appetite.

Amazingly, Indian markets have provided far more troughs than peaks! Troughs outnumber peaks by 3.25 to 1. So why not wait for the trough rather than getting lured up in a peak. While the odds of being on the wrong side of a peak investment is just 32%, when we are the odd man/women out in that group, our waiting time to realise our target return can sometimes be endless.

Table : 17 Investing in Peaks

Peak data		Trough data	
Total Number of Peaks	421	Total Number of Troughs	1365
Number of Peaks that have aged over an year	113	Number of Troughs that have aged over an year	896
Number of Peaks that have hit target return within a year	285	Number of Troughs that have hit target return within a year	1076
% of peaks that hit target return	68%	% of troughs that hit target return	79%
Notes: Data for Sensex from 2005-March 2024			

4. The Timing Game: Why Investor Returns Trail Fund Performance

How often have we invested in a fund based on its past performance? In fact, almost all the time. How many times, despite the lofty performance credentials of the fund, the actual return of our investment comes lower than the fund?

The difference lies in the concept of how performance is measured. A fund's performance is usually a time-weighted return (TWR), which is a simple compounding of the fund's net asset value (NAV). This is the return earned by the fund manager on the fund. This measure is presented over various time horizons (YTD, 1-year, 3-years, etc.).

However, this returns metric does not provide a completely accurate view of how much return the investors have made on their investment. To find the correct return, an internal rate of return must be calculated to discern the return on the average capital in the fund. In simple terms, the Capital Weighted Return (CWR) or XIRR considers the cash flows at the beginning and end of the month and is the average rate of return of the investors in the fund.

Why does this difference matter? Because it is vital. The first tells us how well the fund manager did over time, while the second tells us how well their investors did. A fund may gain a TWR of 5% per annum over the last three years, while its CWR may be – 10%. This means that even though the fund manager managed a positive performance, their investors (as a group) suffered a loss. How can this happen? Because investors may be wrong in terms of timing their investments.

Various studies gand reports have been commissioned to analyse and illustrate the difference between CWR and TWR and how using TWR exclusively can be misleading to investors. It has been found that CWRs trailed TWRs in major indices by an average of five percentage points/ year over 25 years[17].

A Wall Street Journal article highlighted the CGM Focus Fund[18] that produced a TWR of 18% over the last 10 years while underlying investors lost 11% per year ending in November 2009! This comes out to a discount of an average of 29 percentage points every year for a decade!

Discounts (CWR being less than TWR) are generally caused by funds rapid asset growth and mistiming of inflows to the fund. In other words, investors' returns may be poor due to wrong timing (subscription and redemption). Conversely, a premium result from a substantial inflow (as a % of AUM) which is also well-timed in market performance.

In short, cash flows into a fund matter more than stand-alone performance. It is no surprise that as per updated standards of GIPS[19], it is now recommended that NAVs be calculated and reported on the date of significant cash flows, reiterating the importance of cash flows.

It is also possible that there may be only a certain number of high probability positive alpha opportunities at any given time that the manager is tracking. When there is excessive capital inflow the manager might run out of "sure bets" and might start to invest in lower conviction ones leading to lower returns.

Fund managers are good at managing funds, and advisers are good at gathering assets, but it does not help investors invested in the fund. Investors consistently make wrong timing decisions (both subscriptions and redemptions), leading to underperformance compared to the fund manager. Fund houses and advisers do not assist

---

17 Enough, John C. Bogle, 2008
18 Named the best-performing US diversified stock mutual fund of the decade by Morningstar.
19 Global Investment Performance Standards

investors in helping them with their timing dilemmas leading to such discounts. For them, investment is recommended at any time of the year/market cycle. Never try to time entry and exit into a mutual fund. A consistent investing approach can mitigate this risk to an extent. Never base our decision to invest solely on the fund's past performance. In the context of MF, rolling period returns enable a better understanding of the past performance of the fund compared to a point-to-point return. Since we cannot successfully time the market, we must spread our investments over a period. This reduces the possibility of a discount in terms of our performance compared to the fund performance. Also, with the proliferation of systematic investment plans (SIPs), which means multiple investments being made at different points in time, CWR or XIRR can be a true measure from an investor's point of view.

Calculations for TWR and CWR

The reasons for the difference between TWR and CWR can be understood from a simple example.

Let us take into consideration three years' time if 1000 investors invest Rs 100 each in year 0. (Y0, AUM= Rs 100,000 & NAV = Rs 100). The fund generates no return in year 1, and hence, the fund situation after year 1 remains the same. (Y1, AUM= Rs 100,000 & NAV = Rs 100). Since the fund generates no return in year 1, 600 investors decide to withdraw their investments at the start of year 2 (i.e., at the end of year 1). However, year 2 turned out to be a good year for the fund manager, who generated a return of 25 %. (Y2, AUM=Rs 50,000 & NAV=Rs125). In anticipation of a greater return, 400 new investors will join the fund at the current NAV at the start of year 3. However, year 3 turned out to be an ordinary year for the fund manager, who gained only 2 % (Y3, AUM=102,000 and NAV = Rs 127.5).

The year-wise data can be summarised as follows:

Table : 18 Cashflow Illustration

Year	Asset Under Management (AUM)(Rs)	NAV(Rs)	Cash flow for investors (Rs)
Year 0	1,00,000	100	-1,00,000
Year 1	1,00,000	100	60,000
Year 2	50,000	125	-50,000
Year 3	1,02,000	127.5	1,02,000

AUM for a particular period has been calculated as follows: [Beginning period AUM (plus/minus) investment made into the fund] × [1 + percent return generated]. Hence, AUM for year 2 has been calculated as [Rs 100,000 minus Rs 60,000] × [1.25] = Rs 50,000.

NAV for a particular period has been calculated as follows: Total AUM at the end of the period ÷ total number of investors in the fund. Hence, NAV for year 2 has been calculated as Rs 50,000 ÷ 400 investors (1000 − 600) = Rs 125.

Since TWR calculates the fund manager's performance, its calculation depends on the NAV. Hence, the 3-year time-weighted annual TWR = (127.5/100) ^1/3, i.e., 8.43%. However, CWR calculates returns generated by the investors, so its calculation depends on the total cash flows for the investors. Using the IRR formula in spreadsheets, the yearly IRR for the following cash flows (Y0 = − 100,000, Y1 = 60,000, Y2 = − 50,000, and Y3 = 102,000) would come out to be 4.96%.

These calculations clearly show that although the fund manager achieved an annualised return of 8.43% over the three-year period, the investors collectively gained only an annualised return of 4.96%

over the same horizon. The reason for this difference is that investors remained invested in the fund during Year 1 and Year 3, which returned only 0% and 2%, respectively. However, investors withdrew from the fund during Year 2, which produced the highest return of 25%. In short, we can say that investors completely mistimed their investment decisions.

Equity Styles and Themes

(10,000 feet view)

01

Introduction

As we ready to land soon, we should now deal with various investment themes and styles as well as concepts that can shape investment decisions.

When we talk about equity markets, we are always reminded of investment stars like Warren Buffet, Charlie Munger, Peter Lynch, Seth Klarman, George Soros, etc. Investment professionals and critics watch carefully how these legendary investors invest and sometimes try to replicate their styles, albeit with only limited success.

While we all know that equity investing is the best bet to beat inflation in the long-term, there are many ways to get there. The multitude of ways is what is generally described as an investment style. They are structured based on their characteristics and have been rigorously tested historically to generate risk-adjusted returns. However, not all of them work very well under all circumstances.

Investment styles are also broadly called factor investing. Celebrated Nobel laureates Eugene Fama, and Kenneth French introduced factor investing to the investment world. In the initial days, life was simple and there was only one factor i.e., the market. The market factor was captured through a simple metric called "beta".

Beta measures the sensitivity of a particular stock to the broad market. A high beta implies more sensitivity and hence high-risk and vice versa. From a one factor model, Fama and French first expanded it to a 3-factor model that included market, size, and style. And then, they expanded it to a 5-factor model with the addition of two more factors, i.e., profitability and investment. Today, investment styles are multifarious and complicated. Some of the styles do well in a recession, while others do well in expansion. Some of them can adapt themselves to the manager in question. For e.g., the momentum style will suit a hedge fund better than a middle-level family business. Mostly, institutional investors and high net-worth clients follow these styles, while retail investors go by the advice given by their investment advisers.

The most prominent, popular, and important style is based on the size as measured by the market capitalisation. We can visualise four such categories, large-cap, mid-cap, small-cap, and micro-cap, by dividing the universe based on their sizes. Usually, quartile techniques are adopted to slice and dice them. As the name implies, large-cap stocks are big companies, mostly market leaders in their respective industries. Many of them can be big family groups, multinationals, and large public sector companies (Navratnas). They enjoy high longevity and set the bar high in terms of governance and transparency. Largely, they are liquid, making it easy for foreign investors to invest.

On the other hand, mid-cap and small-cap companies are smaller, have limited market presence and share, and can represent ordinary entrepreneurs. They normally tend to be newbies with sparse liquidity. Many of them rank low on governance and transparency. Due to this reason, foreign investors are choosy about taking positions in such companies. In other words, they represent higher risk than large-cap companies. It is for this reason that they outperform large-cap stocks in the long-run as they demand more risk premium.

The next popular classification is based on style, i.e., value and growth. Value stocks are stocks with a low price-to-earnings ratio, while growth stocks are stocks with high growth potential. In the case of value stocks, low price is a key determining factor, while in growth stocks, future growth potential is more important than the price. Investors like Seth Klarman are value investors in that they buy good businesses at attractive prices. However, a low price is not always indicative of future value. There is a reason why the market is pricing those stocks in the low range. Hence, it is a lot harder to find good companies in the value space, and research and knowledge play a great role.

We can also blend size and style and create combinations. Investment style based on profitability delineates profitable companies over others (in what is termed quality stocks). In other words, companies with high operating profits generally outperform companies with low operating profits. This is a relatively new investment style that has been proposed by Fama and French and has yet to be rigorously tested.

There is another new style called investment. As per this, companies with high investment and asset growth (asset heavy) will tend to underperform companies with low investment (asset light), though this concept is not yet well tested. The belief is that companies that invest heavily take more risk than companies that invest less especially if their cost of capital is higher than the project IRR. Many times, CEOs embark on huge investment plans just to keep themselves and their teams busy.

The momentum style believes that stocks that go up in price will tend to go up more and vice versa as the market generally is guided more by psychology than reasoning. Hence, it is a good idea to buy stocks whose prices are going up and sell stocks whose prices are going down. Such strategies play very well in a hedge fund context where technology can be employed to spot such companies through what is termed high-frequency trading.

Finally, volatility as a theme is also emerging as an important investment style. Stocks with high volatility tend to underperform stocks with low volatility. However, the problem here is that there is no one method of calculating volatility. While standard deviation is generally regarded as a proven method to measure volatility, there are other measures to capture volatility. Again, this type of style lends itself to more sophisticated investors like hedge funds.

While these represent the broad styles, there are various ways to execute a particular style. At one level, one can have a concentrated portfolio of just 5 to 10 stocks, while at the other extreme, we can have a portfolio with hundreds of stocks (diversified). In addition, portfolio execution can also be active, where the manager includes and excludes stock based on his findings, or passive, where the manager just mimics an index, which does not require any research.

Investment styles and themes also mean appreciating penny stocks and multi-baggers. Many times, investment decisions are influenced by the price we pay. Sometimes, stock prices can be in single digits (called penny stocks), or they can be in five figures (like MRF). The question to ask is whether it matters.

02

Size Based Investing

This may sound like the birth of a baby growing into a full-blown adult, eventually hit by old age and gracefully dying! Yes, the story of a company in the stock market is also very similar to this narrative. Typically, a company debuts on the stock market in the form of an Initial Public Offering (IPO) and most of the time starts the journey as a small-cap or a micro-cap. While many will simply amble along or fall by the wayside over time, some of them will grow to make it to mid-caps and eventually to large caps. A case in point is Eicher Motors, whose evolution is startling over time.

Eicher Evolution

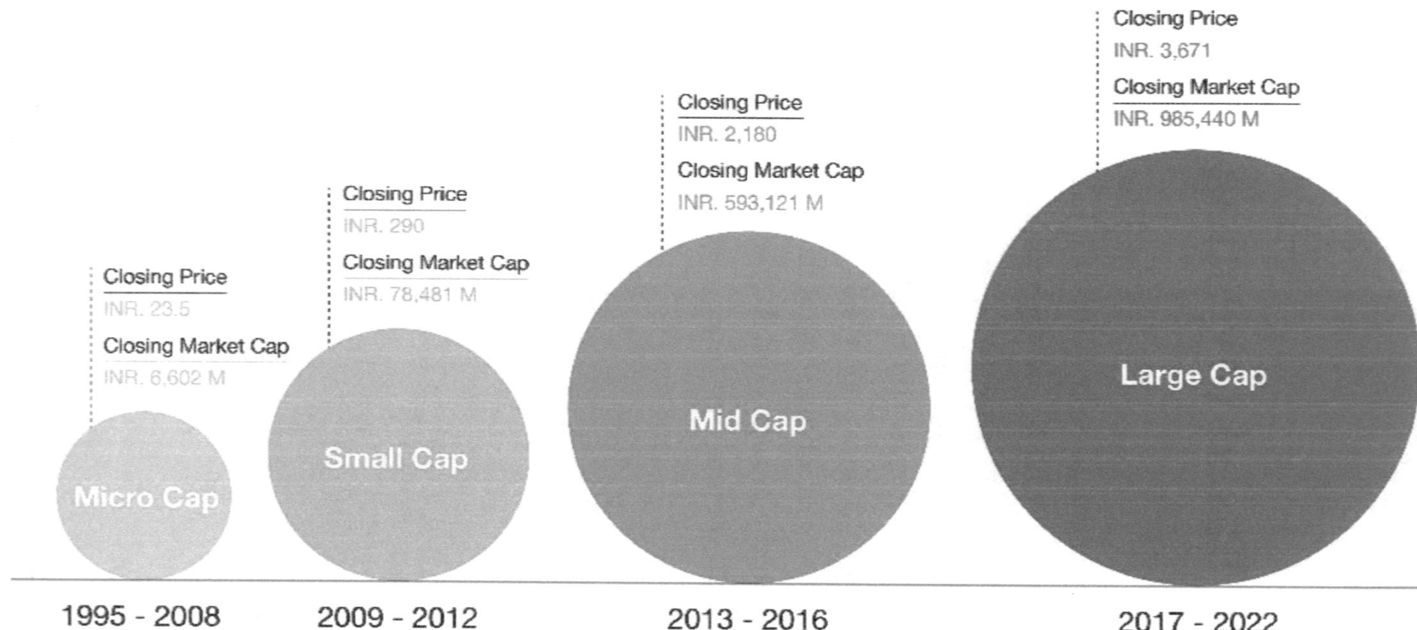

Generally, equity indices are thus divided into three or four categories based on their size, namely large, medium (mid), small, and very small (micro). Index providers have stringent requirements before they qualify a company in the large-cap or mid-cap list. These requirements range from profitability to liquidity as well as free float (% of shares available for trading).

So, if large-cap companies are better in terms of size, profitability, liquidity, etc., then why bother about investing in a mid-cap or a small-cap? The reason is that they have different characteristics and risk profiles as explained below.

Large caps: Typically, these companies adorn the famous indices (S&P 500, Nifty 50, Sensex) and are big in size as measured by market capitalisation, turnover, liquidity, and other parameters. They enjoy excellent research coverage by analysts. For example, large caps constitute 76% of the market cap in the US while the same for India is 53%. Large-cap companies are generally market leaders in their chosen sectors and have strong corporate governance codes and management disciplines. Due to this, they have lower risk profiles. However, most of them may be in a mature phase of growth and hence will offer returns commensurate with the market.

Mid-caps: They are neither big nor small but somewhere in between. Mid-caps account for 14% of the market cap in the US while they account for 7% in India. They may not be market leaders, but they tend to be good-performing companies but sparsely covered by analysts. They normally belong to fast-growing sectors and enjoy reasonable levels of corporate governance. Their management styles will be heterogeneous and are normally majority held by a family or a person. Hence, the performance of these companies hinges on the strength of the person spearheading the story. Naturally, in terms of risk levels, they are subject to higher risks than large caps but with potentially higher returns.

Small-caps: They constitute the bulk of the market in terms of the number of companies but account for a very small share in terms of market capitalisation (7% in the US) with near-zero research coverage by analysts. They normally operate in the support or ancillary sectors of mid-caps and large caps. In other words, they tend to be suppliers of components or services to other companies. Due to their small size, they have cost and margin pressures. They cannot afford strong management teams or risk management resources, resulting in poor corporate governance. Therefore, the failure rates are much higher, resulting in higher risks. However, if identified correctly, they can provide oversized returns that can be unimaginable.

The key differentiating factor among the various size categories now boils down to their risk profiles. There are two ways to measure and understand the risk:

Firstly, the standard deviation (variance of the returns) can be a good measure. The higher the standard deviation, the higher the risk.

Secondly, risk can also be measured using drawdown statistics. A drawdown is defined as the fall of an index from a peak value to a trough value. When the index falls from a high, it is important to see how much it falls and for how long. If the fall is deep and prolonged, it is riskier. Typically, the drawdown for small-caps will be higher and more prolonged than for large-caps. For example, between January 2018 and March 2020, India's small-cap index fell by 65%, and this drop occurred over 26 months. Enduring and withstanding a fall of 65% over 26 months can unnerve even the calmest investor. In contrast, India's large-cap index experienced a drawdown of 38% between January 2010 and March 2020, lasting only 2 months.

Table : 19 Drawdown

Indices	Annualized Risk	Annualized Return	Max Drawdown			
			Peak to Trough	Duration (in days)	Period (From)	Period (To)
US Largecap	20.65%	10.61%	-33.92%	33	43880	43913
US Midcap	23.51%	9.51%	-42.14%	32	43881	43913
US Smallcap	25.75%	10.07%	-45.77%	570	43343	43913
US Microcap	25.91%	6.02%	-47.87%	565	43343	43908
NSE Largecap	20.17%	12.35%	-38.44%	69	43844	43913
NSE Midcap	26.75%	14.86%	-49.06%	805	43108	43913
NSE Smallcap	25.40%	11.00%	-65.14%	799	43115	43914
Source: Refinitiv			Period	Oct 2012 to Oct 2022		

From an investment perspective, size-based investment styles raise an important question: How much to allocate to each style? While for institutional investors, this will be a function of their approved asset allocation structure, for individual/retail investors, this question becomes tricky.

A cursory look at the year-wise performance of various size-based styles from 2013 to 2022 shows the randomness of the performance. For example, a large cap in the US was at the top of the table in 2014, 2015, 2017, 2018, 2019, and 2021 while it was at the bottom of the table in 2013 and 2016. Hence, choosing the style based on future bets is very dangerous given the randomness.

Young investors who are at the beginning of their investment lifecycle (typically aged 25 to 30) can afford to favour small-caps and mid-caps since they have time on hand to compound. The earlier stages of the lifecycle provide an opportunity to target wealth generation, hence this suggested strategy.

However, investors in the middle of their investment lifecycle (typically aged 40 to 50) should maintain a balanced approach between large caps on the one hand and mid-caps to small-caps on the other. Investors nearing the end of their investment lifecycle (typically aged above 50) should favour large-caps and, if possible, avoid mid and small-caps given their high volatility. This is because, at this stage, the focus should be more on wealth preservation than wealth generation.

03

Concentrated Portfolios

"Wide diversification is only required when investors do not understand what they are doing." – Warren Buffet

A classic debate among investors, especially institutional investors, is whether to diversify a portfolio and reduce the risk or concentrate a portfolio and reap rewards. The investment world is still not settled on this issue!

Investment 101 teaches us that portfolios should be well diversified to reduce risk and sleep well at night. While no one can argue the merits of this argument, the issue is what constitutes a well-diversified portfolio.

Benjamin Graham, the father of investing, thinks it is between 10 and 30 stocks; Seth Klarman, the celebrated value investor, thinks it is between 10 and 15 stocks; Warren Buffett, one of the richest persons on earth, thinks it should be 5 to 10 stocks, while John Maynard Keynes, the father of economics, thinks it should be 2 to 3 stocks! In short, there is no consensus on what constitutes a well-diversified portfolio. Peter Lynch, a very successful fund manager for Fidelity, had at one point more than 1,000 stocks in his portfolio!

While experts debate to settle this issue, let us see why a concentrated portfolio is a better idea than a well-diversified portfolio.

1. **Good ideas are scarce:** While an index may have 50, 500, or even 2,000 stocks, only a few stocks perform significantly above the market average. For example, the Nifty 50 index averaged an annualised return of 12% during the 5-year period ending June 2022. However, if we examine the number of stocks that significantly outperformed the market average, there are few. For instance, only two stocks outperformed the market by more than three times, while nine stocks performed between two and three times better than the market. The rest meandered along. A concentrated portfolio would focus on the first two and ignore the last.

2. **Easy to track and research:** If one is managing a portfolio of 10 or 20 stocks, it is humanly possible to keep a close tab on all of them. However, if one is managing a 100 or 200 stock portfolio, attention at best will be paid to 10 or 20 ideas, while the rest will be looked at in a passing manner. In other words, an overly diversified portfolio will mean spreading yourself thin.

3. **Risk reduction still happens:** A common argument for portfolio diversification is risk reduction. However, studies show that significant risk reduction occurs even with as few as ten stocks. Beyond 30 stocks, the extent of risk reduction diminishes to the point where it becomes hardly noticeable.

4. **Moves the needle:** A highly diversified portfolio means that one will have several stocks with very low weights. Even if these low-weight stocks double or triple in value, the impact at the portfolio level will be minimal given their low weights. A better idea would be to spend quality time identifying a few good ideas, invest a substantial sum in them, and reap the rewards for the hard work.

5. **Leverages on skill rather than luck:** Concentrated portfolios will be highly dependent on one's ability to identify a good

investment opportunity. Compensating one for such skill, either in terms of fees or through portfolio performance, is worth it at the end of the day. Alternatively, if one is managing an overly diversified portfolio, portfolio performance will be more of a luck game than a skill game. Why pay for luck?

However, concentration does have risks to contend with:

1. **The "All eggs in…" Syndrome:** Concentration certainly increases the risk, especially when most of the sourced ideas turn sour. Technical ability to identify good ideas is paramount and comes through formal training, business experience, and long periods of observation. Executives in this fast-paced world will be tempted to throw some of these traits out of the window in search of quick success. In the process, they may put all eggs in one basket, and the rest will be history.

2. **Not suitable for retail investors:** Retail investors, especially the non-financial variety, cannot pursue this path, as their risk tolerance can be very low. Hence, they are most often advised to embrace the mutual funds route, where the funds are extremely well diversified.

3. **High tracking error:** Concentration certainly leads to a significant departure from benchmark weights, and this increases the tracking error for managers. Fund managers who manage funds for a living will not want to risk their careers through high tracking errors.

4. **Asset allocation issues:** The focus has shifted to asset allocation funds rather than stock or bond funds. Implementing an agreed asset allocation is best achieved through ETFs or passive funds as they reduce costs and focus one's energy more on asset allocation. Fitting a concentrated portfolio into this asset allocation game can be tricky.

In sum, for professional investors (both individual and institutional) who would like to significantly outperform the market in the long-term, concentrated portfolios are the way to go. However, be conscious of risks and manage them well. Even a concentrated portfolio can and should be diversified, say, across industries.

04

Core & Satellite Approach

The equity investment world is filled with recommendations that are sometimes tricky. Is this a good time to invest in pharma stocks? How about ESG? Can Amazon be a good inclusion in the portfolio now, since it is nearly 26% down from its peak? Should I sell Nifty futures, since I know for sure that markets will tank further, etc. Acting upon them can clutter the investment approach as one cannot assess and provide for the varying risk/return profile of such diverse recommendations. Mostly, these recommendations are analysed from a potential return perspective and not so much in terms of what can go wrong. To provide some method to this madness, sophisticated investors construct something called a "Core/Satellite Portfolio" (CSP).

The simple idea behind the concept is that we keep the unavoidable exposure to the core and avoidable exposure to the satellite part. While the core always remains intact, the satellite options keep changing based on market conditions (also called tactical allocation). The core part would be the equity portfolio with defined exposure to large-cap, mid-cap, and small-cap. The ratio of allocation between these categories is a function of risk appetite.

The core exposure can easily be built in a low-cost manner using Exchange Traded Funds (ETFs), which are like investing in index funds with the additional benefit of ETFs being more cost-effective and liquid, as they are traded in real-time on the stock exchanges. Investing in ETFs can provide market returns, while investing with active mutual funds can generate alpha based on manager effectiveness. If one wishes to avoid manager risk, then the best low-cost option would be ETFs.

At this stage, one should determine how much of the total equity portfolio should be in the core and how much should be in the satellite. Typically, most of the allocation (say up to 80%) should be in the core, and the balance could be in the satellite, again based on risk appetite. Having determined the allocation to satellite, let us now see some options available within the satellite option:

1. **Sector Funds:** While large-cap ETFs that form part of the core are broadly represented by several sectors, satellite options can take some pointed bets on a particular sector based on its attractiveness. Several sector funds are available today, including banking, infrastructure, pharma, technology, etc. One must either be a sector specialist or take advice from an adviser on this type of bet. Sector funds tend to have more volatility than the broad market, but they are very popular.

2. **Factors:** Factor-based investing, also called quantitative investing, can be an interesting part of the satellite portfolio. Typical strands of factor funds involve value, growth, momentum, etc. However, there are not many funds available in the market relative to other opportunities, and hence the choice set is limited.

3. **Thematic:** Thematic funds focus on a particular theme and position investments accordingly. Typical examples of popular themes include ESG, consumption, dividend yield, energy, multinational companies (MNCs), and public sector units (PSUs). There are funds dedicated to such themes, but it would be wise to sift through the stated strategy before committing to such investments. The thematic interpretation can vary from one person to another, hence the problem.

4. **International Stocks:** For an Indian investor, investing in international stocks cannot be a core component, hence it is recommended to be a part of the satellite portfolio. There will not be a dearth of opportunities here, especially if focused on developed markets like the US, Europe, and Japan. Again, one can take the ETF route for this to keep it cost-effective.

5. **Private Equity:** This is an asset class often ignored by retail investors, as the threshold limit to invest in private equity is typically higher. However, one can focus on listed private equity to enter this interesting opportunity space. While for retail investors, this can be a satellite component, for institutional investors and high-net-worth clients, this can be a core component.

6. **Derivatives:** This is the trickiest part, as it can range from options to futures to synthetics. If one has a clear forward-looking market view (like a bear market), one can do well to sell index futures or buy put options as insurance for a core portfolio. However, using derivatives other than portfolio insurance is likely to benefit brokers more than investors.

Having laid out the options, it will be useful to examine the merits of following a core/satellite approach to equity investments.

The main benefit of such an approach is that it is an additional source of return (alpha), which investors are always keen on. Assuming that the core portfolio is invested in ETFs (providing only market returns), it is always good to look for additional sources of return. Also, the inclusion of satellites tends to diversify the portfolio and hence the risk. Also, many satellite options laid above enjoy less or no negative correlation to the core, which adds to the appeal of risk reduction. Since the satellite option is a tactical positioning, one can quickly change their position based on changing market views.

However, the core/satellite approach also suffers from some limitations. The main problem with identifying the satellite options is that it is research intensive and therefore time-consuming. Almost all the satellite options will involve active managers and hence can be expensive. Another troubling issue will be illiquidity with some options like private equity while other options are liquid. Due to these reasons, the core/satellite approach is more suitable for institutional investors and high-net-worth clients.

05

Contrarian Investing

The world's best contrarian investor is none other than Warren Buffett. A contrarian investor will be greedy when others are fearful and vice versa. It simply means going against the grain and prevailing wisdom, doing things contrary to what others are doing.

While, as a concept, it may appear simple, it is difficult to go against the grain in real life. Buying a stock when others are selling requires a different investing approach and involves behavioural biases. Though the concept aligns mostly with value investing, there are subtle differences between the two. Value investing almost always involves buying stocks "cheap", while contrarian investing sometimes can buy stocks even when they are not cheap. A classic global example would be Volkswagen, which sold off 46% in 2015 (from Euro 250 in March 2015 to Euro 109 in October 2015 before recovering to Euro 180 by January 2018) based on news that it was untruthful about emission tests in the US. A contrarian investor would have ignored the negative hype and instead would have bought it, given the brand strength of such a stock. However, that would have involved swimming against all the negative news surrounding the stock.

While traditional portfolio management involves a top-down approach, where one checks the economy and industry before committing to a stock, a contrarian investor is a bottom-up person who ignores the broader macro environment and even the industry setting and instead focuses on the stock to the exclusion of its economic and sector environment.

If one must pursue this investment style, there are some required traits. Most importantly, it includes patience, discipline, conviction, and communication. The opportunities for contrarian investors are rare, and hence, patience is a key virtue here. The efficient market hypothesis says that all the news is always priced into a stock instantly. In that case, finding a stock which has been wrongly evaluated by the market should be a rare event. This investment style requires a much-disciplined approach to identify opportunities, and once an opportunity is identified, one needs enormous conviction to bet against the market. If one is managing money for an institution, then effective communication on why he/she bought those stocks is key to keeping investors glued to the strategy.

The contrarian style is not without its pitfalls. If managing a mutual fund, such a strategy can induce a significant tracking error relative to the benchmark. Tracking error measures the deviation from the benchmark. Most of the bets contrarian managers take may have substantial weightage in the index, thereby contributing to the tracking error. Many institutional investors have tracking error thresholds, beyond which they will have to redeem their investments. Hence, this strategy may not be suitable for all types of investors.

Another problem will be timing the investment. Contrarian investors generally revel in bad news to accumulate their holdings. However, the fall in a stock price can be long and deep, in which case buying them early can induce losses that need to be covered later. When to buy, even when there is bad news, is a tricky question. In most situations, the manager may be hard-pressed to explain the rationale of his investing decisions as it clearly shows that he is doing something out of the ordinary. Many stock price falls invariably have a known or unknown reason. As they say, a stock is "cheap for a reason". If not researched properly to uncover the unknown reason behind a stock fall, a contrarian investor would end up holding a dud stock.

The biggest hurdle of being a contrarian investor is to go against forecasters, both economic and stock. The contrarian investor can ignore economic forecasts as the investment approach is more bottom-up. However, in a recession-driven economic scenario, where stocks are widely expected to perform poorly, holding a contrarian portfolio will raise more questions than answers. However, the main problem would be the equity research forecast that may paint a negative picture, which the contrarian investor overlooks and goes against. In short, a contrarian investor must be "forecast averse" to develop his conviction on the style.

The concept of contrarian investing is normally understood better in the context of buying a deeply undervalued stock (on the back of some verified/unverified information), much against street advice. However, the style works equally well for making sales decisions as well. This is particularly true when the stock has run up beyond expectations and is no longer justifying its fundamental value. In this case, the manager is better off selling. It will also be a good idea to sell when there is over-optimism behind a stock, as the stock will enjoy adequate liquidity and buying interest, and hence realising a good price is quite possible.

While the contrarian style is intuitively appealing, as said before, it should not be an all-encompassing strategy for an investor. While the core part of an investment portfolio should be the time-tested long-only portfolio, styles like contrarian can, at best, be a satellite component to generate additional sources of alpha. There can be other satellite approaches like momentum, disruption as a theme, etc. With such a structure, the risk of a particular strategy pulling away the main source of return is diminished.

A contrarian investment style is suited only for sophisticated investors (institutional and high-net-worth) who can appreciate the inherent risks of the strategy. Embracing a contrarian style involves trusting the manager's judgement in such decisions, which requires a clear understanding of the risks involved. It is certainly not for individual investors with a faint-hearted risk appetite.

06

Value Investing

"It's far better to buy a wonderful company at a fair price than to buy a fair company at a wonderful price" – Warren Buffet.

There is something very nice about the term "value investing". It signifies value and in the investment world if one is not chasing value, what else to chase? When I look back and see the list of value investors in the world, they have some great names like Benjamin Graham, Warren Buffett, Charlie Munger, Seth Klarman, Peter Lynch, Walter Schloss, Mohnish Pabrai, etc. Of course, this list can be extended to include other names. However, they are few and far between. The reason is value investing is easy to understand but hard to practice.

First, let's understand what value investing is. In simple terms, it is buying great companies at a reasonable price. The value chain of value investing involves a series of interesting steps. From the large stock universe (in India, this can mean more than 5,000 stocks), one must sift through to identify "bargains" based on intense research. Once we identify the bargains, we should establish a price point at which we are prepared to buy the stock. This will involve estimating the intrinsic value of a company, the expected price in the future (what is normally referred to as the target price) and waiting for a price that should provide us with a significant margin of safety[20].

---

20 A term introduced by Benjamin Graham, father of investing.

Once such a price point is reached, we jump in and buy. This process has two problems. We need to spot great companies and we should wait for the price of those great companies to be available at a reasonable price. There is a counterintuitive logic here. Why should the market misprice great companies or why should great companies be available at a reasonable price? This is where it gets more interesting.

Analysts love the price-to-earnings ratio (P/E) and one can see its daily use in the financial markets. Value investors focus on the "P" of the P/E ratio more than the "E" of the ratio. Conversely, growth investors focus on the "E" and may be prepared to buy growth companies even at a higher price.

Value investing tends to perform well during strong economic cycles while growth investing performs well during weak economic cycles. According to Fama and French, value stocks outperform growth stocks and hence there is a value premium attached to them. However, value investing is an art which is difficult to master.

There are three reasons why value investing is not a cakewalk:

1. **Intense Research:** To identify great companies among thousands of companies requires very high analytical and research skills. The analyst should develop a strong understanding of the underlying business, company's competitive position, pricing power, balance sheet strength, etc. to identify a needle in a haystack of stocks. The research will also involve estimating future cash flows and therefore expected future prices. Such estimations require a thorough market probe, interaction with company management, sifting through reams of documents (especially the small prints), and making assumptions. As one can understand, the process is intense and requires technical skills. Unless one takes up this activity as a full-time activity, it will not yield results.

2. **Mind Control:** The idea behind value investing is to buy great companies at bargain prices. Generally, great companies are rarely available at bargain prices. Bargain prices are available only during market meltdowns when investor sentiment is negative all around. To have the guts to swim against the tide, identify the bargain, and buy companies requires enormous mind control. The story does not end here. It is highly likely that the price of the stock, post-purchase, can go down further. It is at this stage the role of mind control plays an even more important role. Once the price goes down, it opens several confusing thought trails. Should we buy more, should we panic and sell, should we do nothing, should we revisit our assumptions, etc.?

3. **Patience:** Value investing is more like Sunday fishing and is certainly not Formula One driving. Just as how boring Sunday fishing can be, value investing also requires enormous patience. After identifying a great company, one must wait for it to reach the "desired" price at which it will provide a significant "margin of safety". That price can be obtained in the short-term or medium-term or even long-term. The trick is not to get bored and buy the stock at the current available price. Patience is truly a virtue here.

Great value investors adeptly combine the three factors enumerated above with great zeal. Warren Buffett and Charlie Munger (now deceased), even at this age, spend a lot of time reading (factor 1). When the global financial crisis hit in 2008, they had the mind control to jump in and buy great companies at reasonable prices (factor 2) when the whole world was falling around. Throughout their long career, they have been helped by patiently waiting for an opportunity to throw up (factor 3). A reading of their various annual letters to shareholders will show how they cleverly combined the three factors to become one of the most successful investors of all-time.

07

Momentum Investing

US chip maker Nvidia's share price rose nearly 28,000% during the 10-year period 2014-2024! Other technology stocks like Facebook, Amazon, and Google have provided returns that beat the broader S&P 500 by a wide margin. These stocks have enjoyed tremendous momentum. Hence, momentum investing has gained some attention among professional investors. According to research, on a historical basis, the momentum factor has been one of the strongest generators of excess returns[21]. However, in another research[22], it was stated that "No U.S.-benchmarked mutual fund with 'momentum' in its name has cumulatively outperformed its benchmark since inception, net of fees and expenses", though it must be said that it was based on a relatively small set of samples. Hence, the jury is still not out globally. When I googled "famous momentum investors," I could not get a neat list before me. This shows that the strategy is still not mainstream and clear-cut like say, in terms of value or growth. From a performance point of view, it is still a mixed bag for momentum funds.

What has gone up in the past will go up in the future and vice versa is what momentum is all about. However, a true technical definition found in a research paper authored by Clifford Asness[23] and his colleagues

---

21 https://knowledge.wharton.upenn.edu/wp-content/uploads/2017-11-03-two-centuries-of-value-and-momentum-everywhere-2.pdf

22 https://www.researchaffiliates.com/content/dam/ra/publications/pdf/637-can-momentum-investing-be-saved.pdf

23 https://www.aqr.com/-/media/AQR/Documents/Journal-Articles/JPM-Fact-Fiction-and-Momentum-Investing.pdf?sc_lang=en

defines it as "the phenomenon that securities which have performed well relative to peers (winners) on average continue to outperform, and securities that have performed relatively poorly (losers) tend to continue to underperform."

As we can see, it is the antithesis of the efficient market hypothesis as it is predicated on irrational market behaviour. While it may not conform to standard finance theories, the momentum concept has worked in the past, especially for traders or investors with a short time span. However, we should not confuse it with trend following as taught in the technical analysis course. While trend following looks at absolute price changes, momentum is a relative concept, i.e., it looks at increases or decreases of a particular stock in relation to its peer group. Buying stocks consistently that have gone up relative to their peers and selling stocks that have gone down consistently relative to peers is akin to keeping our winners and shunning our losers. While many investors and fund managers may not refer to their strategy as momentum, they are exactly doing that to reap benefits. A momentum strategy is as much behavioural as it is technical as only that can explain the "herd mentality" of investors.

Of course, momentum does not involve fundamental analysis. Some argue that it can, at best, be a screener and should be reinforced with fundamental research. That would be taking away the concept, though I see no reason why one should not do it. There are several tools available like MACD, RSI, Stochastic Oscillator, Candlesticks, etc. (Did I say it is not technical analysis?). These tools will enable one to calculate the speed of change and act accordingly. Investors can define the timeframe to apply the momentum factor. For example, it can be defined as a day wherein one will buy stocks that have gone up during the day and sell stocks that have gone down, etc. The timeframe can also be past 1 year, in which case the game changes from trading to investing.

However, to buy with conviction stocks that have gone up recently, one should also bet on low volatility. Because high volatility will cause frequent contra trades, thereby increasing trading costs and reducing strategy returns. Essentially, momentum works very well when volatility is either low or when periods of high volatility tend to be clustered together. If one observes VIX, a great volatility indicator, it does go through long periods of low volatility providing immense opportunity for momentum investors. Since the pretext of momentum investing is based on irrationality, market inefficiency also acts as a good context. Most of the emerging markets qualify as inefficient markets, meaning where prices are not fully reflecting all the news and information about the stock. In the Indian context, the markets have exhibited several highs during the last 10 years. However, what is interesting to note is that they tend to cluster around, and this is what provides the needed opening for momentum investors.

The Indian experiment with momentum investing is nascent and still evolving. The National Stock Exchange (NSE) has developed several indices keeping momentum as the focus, post which several fund houses launched momentum funds mostly as index funds or ETFs tracking Nifty momentum indices – Nifty 200 Momentum 30 index, Nifty Midcap150 Momentum 50, Nifty Small-cap 250 Momentum Quality 100, Nifty MidSmallcap400 Momentum Q100. The initial part of the index indicates the universe, and the second part indicates the size of the portfolio (i.e., Nifty 200 Momentum 30 index has Nifty 200 as the universe and selects the top 30 momentum stocks among the 200).

It is instructive to note the methodology framed by NSE for their momentum indices.

- Top 30/50/100 from the universe with the highest Final Momentum Z-score forms the portfolio.
- Final Momentum Z-score of a stock = (50% * 6-month Z-score) + (50% * 12-month Z-score).
- Z-score of a stock = (Momentum Ratio of the stock − Mean Momentum Ratio of All stocks in the universe) / (Std. Dev of Momentum Ratio of Universe).
- Momentum Ratio of the stock = (Price Return of the stock in the past 12 or 6 months) / (Annualised Daily Std. deviation of the stock).

The momentum fund performances that are linked to the NSE[24] indices as ETFs or index funds tasted huge alpha during the one-year period ending June 2024. The alpha was a mouth-watering 45%, though it is a very short timeframe to consider. The UTI Nifty 200 Momentum 30 index fund is the only fund that enjoys a three-year history with an annualised alpha of nearly 12%. However, these are early days and hence no firm conclusion need be derived.

However, there are two fund houses, Quant and Samco, that launched active momentum funds. Both use proprietary algorithms to select stocks, and a cursory reading of the methodology points to the use of advanced statistical concepts as the basis[25]. Some notable academic studies also appeared, of which a very interesting paper by IIM Ahmedabad professors in 2013 combined Fama and French factors with momentum. While active momentum strategies claim certain benefits like better exposure management, rebalancing swiftness, using both relative and absolute momentum factors with no constraints on the number of stocks, the performance of passive momentum strategies seems to be better than active strategies. Again,

---

24   https://www.niftyindices.com/Methodology/Method_NIFTY_Equity_Indices.pdf
25   https://web.iima.ac.in/~iffm/Indian-Fama-French-Momentum/index.php

a word of caution would be worth in terms of the period of analysis which is too short to derive any firm conclusion.

The fabulous performance of momentum-based index funds and ETFs is bound to generate interest among professional investors, and hence it may not harm to commit some money to this strategy. However, what we should observe is the performance of this strategy when markets experience anti-momentum.

08

Active vs. Passive

"Active" is not dead and never will be.

"A ₹10,000 investment in Berkshire would have grown to a mind-boggling ₹10.89 crores over this time, net of all costs. However, if instead of running Berkshire Hathaway as a company in which Buffett co-invests with you, had he set it up as a hedge fund and charged the usual hedge fund fee structure of 2/20 (i.e., 2% management fee + 20% of any gains), then the ₹10,000 investment would've only become ₹89 lakhs — the balance ₹10 crores would've been pocketed by Buffett as fees!"[26]

"By some counts, up to 86 percent of active funds underperform their benchmark, but by definition 100 percent of truly passive funds underperform theirs"– Paul Smith

If there is one thing that has taken the investment world by surprise during the last decade, it is the stupendous growth of passive investing. Passive investing refers to replicating the benchmark either in the form of an index fund or Exchange Traded Funds (ETFs). The only difference between the two is that while the former is a mutual fund where buying or selling should be done with the fund house, ETFs (as the name implies) are traded on the exchange just like a stock and therefore more liquid. However, the key differentiating factor is that

---

26 If Warren Buffet ran a hedge fund..https://medium.com/@vikasbardia/if-warren-buffett-ran-a-hedge-fund-28c99c1f735b

while a passive fund just mimics a benchmark (after fees), an active fund attempts to generate excess returns (alpha) by straying away from the stated benchmark, either by underweighting or overweighting stocks.

In other words, active managers take stock bets to generate excess returns, while passive managers just deliver market returns or benchmark returns (with no excess returns). In anticipation of alpha delivery, active managers charge management fees, while passive managers' fees are modest since they do not promise alpha.

According to Statista, "While passively managed index funds only constituted 21 percent of the total assets managed by investment companies in the United States in 2012, this share had increased to 45 percent by 2022[27]". Slowly and surely, passive funds are strangulating active funds, and at this rate, it is easy to imagine an investment world with 100% passive managers, with active management only finding a discussion in history books!

Not really! When hedge funds became prominent on the back of strong growth in assets, experts had a similar view. However, the growth in the hedge fund industry hit a steady state and later moderated. The debate of active vs. passive can be framed from five angles as below:

Figure : 4 Active Vs. Passive

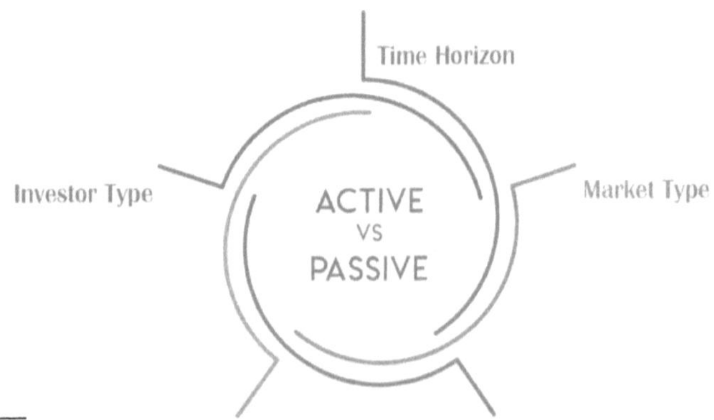

27 https://www.statista.com/statistics/1262209/active-passive-investment-funds-usa/

1. **Market Type:** The meritocratic rise of passive fund management is still a developed market phenomenon, and it is easy to explain why. Developed markets enjoy higher levels of market efficiency, due to which extraction of alpha has become difficult over time. Adjusted for active fees, this means that clients/investors are better off focusing on asset allocation executed primarily through passive funds than investing with active managers. However, if one examines the data for emerging markets, the role of passive funds is still minuscule due to market inefficiency, which gives rise to plenty of alpha-generating opportunities.

2. **Asset Class:** Passive funds are popular among global equities and US equities, which are large and liquid markets. However, their popularity with emerging market equities is still suspect given the alpha opportunities explained above. In addition, the fixed-income market is still not as ETF-friendly as equities. Among alternative asset classes like private equity, real estate, and hedge funds, passive investing is still in the infancy stage given liquidity and cost constraints. Hence, the passive story is for now confined mostly to global, especially US, equities. Due to this, executing a comprehensive asset allocation strategy using only passive funds is proving difficult.

3. **Investor Type:** Adoption of passive funds is mostly prevalent among institutional investors compared to retail investors, though it should be the other way around. If one looks at the data presented by Zinnov and Smallcase, retail investors contribute to only 4% of ETF industry AUM at the end of 2022, while institutional and HNI investors contribute to the remaining 96%.[28] One reason could be that institutions have cost pressures and can be skillful in using passive funds in asset

---

28 Rise of the Indian Retail Investor – Zinnov and Smallcase (internal note: page 15)

allocation, while retail investors may not understand the impact of cost.

4. **Cost:** The rise of passive funds is clearly attributable to cost differentials. For example, in the US, the asset-weighted average expense ratio of index equity mutual funds was 0.05% in 2022, while the same for actively managed equity mutual funds was thirteen times more expensive at 0.66%[29]. In India, the average total expense ratio of ETFs is 0.11%,[30] according to Live Mint. On the other hand, the asset-weighted average expense ratio of equity mutual funds is 0.44%.[31] While retail investors with a short-term outlook may miss the cost factor, long-term investors will certainly have to take this cost differential into account.

5. **Time Horizon:** Lastly, the time horizon can truly change and tilt the balance between active and passive. Let me explain this through an example of HDFC Index Fund S&P BSE Sensex primarily focused on Indian Large cap. As of September 2023, while the fund's rank in the category was 44 out of 143 funds during the last one year, that rank improves dramatically to eight when the time horizon expands to 5 years and impressively to 2nd rank when looked at from a 7-year perspective[32]. In other words, if an investor's time horizon is 5 years plus, they are clearly better

---

29 Source: Trends in the Expenses and Fees of Funds, 2022 – Investment Company Institute – https://www.ici.org/system/files/2023-03/per29-03.pdf (internal note: page 12)

30 https://www.livemint.com/mutual-fund/mf-news/four-surprising-facets-shaping-mf-returns-11687708098880.html

31 Source: Trends in the Expenses and Fees of Funds, 2022 – Investment Company Institute – https://www.ici.org/system/files/2023-03/per29-03.pdf (internal note: page 7)

32 https://www.valueresearchonline.com/funds/31377/hdfc-sp-bse-sensex-etf/#performance

off investing in passive funds than active funds. However, if one is looking at shorter periods, active managers can provide alpha.

In summary, active managers are relevant to emerging markets, where finding excess return is still possible. A 2018 study of 448 mutual funds by IIM Trichy professors (Nilesh Gupta and G Sethu) during the last 21 years found that gross returns by active funds exceed returns from the Nifty total returns index by more than 11%,[33] after accounting for costs on an annualised basis. That is a significant alpha to consider. While passive funds will find increasing prominence in institutional asset allocation in developed markets, active managers will still have a field day in the emerging markets.

---

33 https://www.livemint.com/Opinion/jjLKkYgdOUOZieRc4jg31K/Why-active-funds-beat-the-markets-in-India.html

09

Dividends as a Theme

Have you ever invested in a stock to reap dividends? With an average dividend yield of about 1.5% for Nifty 50 stocks, the answer should be a "no". But the fascination for dividends continues for some unexplained reason.

The dividend is considered a corporate action, and therefore, share prices tend to adjust based on the quantum of dividends declared. At this stage, it is worthwhile to note that all Nifty 50 companies are dividend payers. However, we cannot assume that companies always pay dividends. We have noticed thirteen companies (out of 50) that had some interruptions, mainly during COVID years (2020 & 2021). Given the low dividend yield (calculated as gross dividends/market price), it is not uncommon to see some crazy numbers like 15,750% of the face value (Britannia in FY 2021) to beat the low dividend yield. We have noticed that nineteen companies (out of 50 in Nifty) declared dividends exceeding 1,000%!

As the financial concept goes, dividends are generally paid out of profits and the unpaid part of profits accrues in retained earnings. Also, declaration and payment of dividends involves cash outflow and companies that are in the growth phase may opt to skip dividends and use the profits for expansion. However, most of the Nifty 50 companies are well-settled in terms of their history, profitability and growth and, hence, declaring dividends as an "Image" value. Investors tend to see dividend-paying companies as healthier than others, which may not be true. After the abolition of the dividend distribution tax (DDT), the taxability of dividend income is now in the hands of the investors. Hence, any outsized payment of dividends will invite tax at the hands of the investor.

The pattern of paying dividends is not uniform even for Nifty 50 companies. We can generally classify the pattern as follows:

Consistent and Growing: There were 22 companies that made this cut and have been consistently paying dividends and increasing the quantum of dividends over the years. There is a broad correlation with the price returns of these stocks. Bajaj Finance, Britannia Industries, and Sun Pharma top this list with total returns of 27.1%, 14.3% and 14.5%, respectively. The average dividend yield of 1.2% can be explained by the robust price returns, but that is only a causal factor. Only one stock (Hero MotoCorp) suffers a negative price return (between 2018 and YTD-2023) but makes it up with a high dividend yield, resulting in a positive total return. Interestingly, Bajaj Finance's dividends have grown by 650% between 2018 and 2023. However, that still results only in a dividend yield of 0.3% due to stock price appreciation. Some companies in the list enjoy reasonably high dividend yields (Power Grid, Hero MotoCorp, ITC, and Tech Mahindra). However, most stocks under this category (14 out of 22) have a dividend yield of less than 1%. In other words, investment interest in these stocks stems more from the potential for capital appreciation than dividend yields.

Inconsistent but growing: There were eighteen companies classified under this category that showed a track record of increasing their dividends, but the pattern is not consistent. Because of the inconsistent nature, we can even notice a fall in dividend growth for some companies (Infosys and Bharti Airtel). Except for a few stocks (IndusInd Bank, ONGC, & Maruti Suzuki) that experienced a negative or muted price performance, companies in this category generally enjoy good price and total return. Two public sector stocks (ONGC and NTPC) attract attention in terms of their high dividend yields, though 50% of the companies in this list have dividend yields of less than 1%.

Inconsistent: Three companies from the current Nifty 50 constituents exhibit similar characteristics compared to the previous category in terms of inconsistency, but we have noticed that their dividends have not been growing. The case of Coal India is especially interesting with its mouth-watering dividend yield of 9%!

Erratic: This list mainly comprises seven stocks where there is no discernable pattern in terms of their dividend habits. Some of them enjoyed good dividend growth, while others experienced no growth or negative growth. As a group, they also have low prices and total returns compared to other categories. All calculations are made for the period 2018 – 21st Nov 2023

The idea of segregating stocks in terms of their dividend patterns produces some sort of connectivity to those stocks that exhibit consistency vs companies that do not exhibit consistency. Also, while most of the Nifty 50 stocks delivered good prices and total returns during the five-year period between 2018 and 2023, it is not very apparent that there is a strong correlation between dividends and performance. A good price performance coupled with a good dividend yield is a dream situation but is not practical. High dividend yield will normally be accompanied by poor price returns and vice versa. Based on this analysis, dividends can, at best, account for an additional check box while scrutinising a company and, as said before, have more "Image" value than anything else. All else being equal, a consistent and growing dividend-paying company should be preferred over inconsistent and erratic dividend-paying companies.

10

Penny Stock Investing

Should one invest in penny stocks, also called microcaps? Why not, especially considering they have generated better returns compared to, say, the Nifty 50. The Nifty 250 micro-cap index's five-year annualised return of 13.8% for the period ending July 2023 is higher than the Nifty 50's 10.9% for the same period. After all, many blue chips today started off as penny stocks! This logic likely explains why investors are drawn to these penny stocks. They also have the allure of being cheap (mostly quoted under Rs. 10), leading to the perception that "there is not much to lose but a windfall to gain."

A closer examination, however, reveals a different story.

Table : 20 Index Attributes

Attributes	Nifty 50 Large Cap	Nifty 100 Large Cap	Nifty 150 market Cap	Nifty 250 small-cap	Nifty 250 Micro-cap
Size	✓	✓	—	✗	✗
Liquidity	✓	✓	—	✗	✗
Research Coverage	✓	✓	—	✗	✗
Corporate Governance	✓	✓	—	✗	✗
Historical Performance	✓	✓	✓	✓	✓
Risk (Volatility)	✗	✗	✗	✗	✗
Index Diversification	✗	✗	—	✓	✓
Survivorship Bias	✓	✓	✗	✗	✗
Legends: ✓: Positive Factor	—: Neutral	✗: Negative Factor			

The attractiveness of an asset class should be examined from various factors as outlined in the table. The main stock exchange, i.e., National Stock Exchange (NSE), has seen a robust increase in the number of stocks listed over the period. From approximately 900 stocks back in 2006, the universe of stocks has expanded to more than 2,113 stocks in 2023, offering plenty of scope for stock picking. However, the largest of these are grouped under Nifty 50 (comprising the top 50 stocks) and Nifty 100 (comprising the top 100 stocks), representing large-cap stocks, followed by Nifty 150, labelled as mid-cap stocks. The next tier of 250 stocks is grouped as Nifty 250 small-cap stocks. The Nifty 250 micro-cap index represents stocks even smaller than small-cap stocks, and this is our focus. A review of statistics reveals the sharp contrast that one should observe before deciding to seize this opportunity. Let us examine the attributes for a better appreciation of the issue.

1. **Size:** Penny stocks or microcaps represent the lowest end of the spectrum in terms of size. Size is usually measured in terms of market capitalisation. While the Nifty 50 market cap (free float) is over USD 1 trillion, the micro-cap market capitalisation is just USD 48 billion, hardly 4.7% of the total. The average free float market cap for Nifty 50 is USD 20 billion, while that of microcaps is only USD 192 million (1%). A better measure would be the median market cap, which stands at USD 9.7 billion for Nifty 50, while that of the Nifty micro-cap index is just USD 159 million (1.64%). The universe of microcaps is simply too small, which introduces other problems as well.

2. **Liquidity:** The most significant limitation of the small size of penny stocks is directly reflected in liquidity, as measured by Average Daily Traded Value (ADTV). The ADTV of Nifty 50 is about USD 2.6 billion, while that of microcaps is just USD 386 million. The downside of this extremely low liquidity is the high bid-ask spread, essentially the difference between the bid

price (price to buy) and ask price (price to sell). A higher bid-ask spread increases the cost of acquiring microcaps.

3. **Research Coverage:** Large caps, and to some extent mid-caps, enjoy research coverage by analysts (both buy-side and sell-side). While research opinions (especially sell-side brokerage reports) cannot be completely trusted, at least there is someone providing analysis on the future potential of the businesses involved. The absence of research reports means extensive due diligence is required for micro-cap stocks, which can again be costly.

4. **Corporate Governance:** This is the biggest hurdle and can come in many forms. To start with, high promoter holdings in micro caps can open opportunities for coordinated price manipulation with a motive to "pump and dump" (also called circular trading). Weak corporate governance can also encourage insider trading, where people with inside knowledge can participate in the price manipulation process. Corporate governance is a qualitative parameter that includes the board's strength, ability to communicate proactively and following ethical practices with stakeholders, including tax payments. Micro-cap companies normally score weakly on all these parameters.

5. **Performance:** As noted in the beginning, micro-cap performance was better compared to Nifty 50. In a bull market, almost all stocks (good, bad and ugly) tend to move up in price. However, the real test comes in bear markets where stock prices collapse and may experience serious drawdowns (measured as the extent of fall from peak to trough). The maximum drawdown for Nifty 50 during the last five years is 38%, while that of micro caps is nearly 80%. In other words, investors who can stomach a loss of 80% on their investments can qualify to indulge in these investments.

6. **Risk**: The performance of indices should be looked at from a risk-adjusted perspective. Micro caps' better performance is because they take more risk than other indices. The standard deviation of Micro-cap index is close to 22% compared to 19% for Nifty 50.

7. **Index Diversification**: To be fair, micro caps score better in terms of sector diversification compared to the broader Nifty 50. Micro caps are overweight in sectors like industrial manufacturing, power and consumer goods while they are underweighting in financial services and information technology. Also, the top 10 weight in Nifty 50 is about 42% compared to 25% for Microcaps.

8. **Survivorship Bias**: This is often ignored risk in analysis. This measures how long a company stays in the index. Frequently companies are churned out of the index for various reasons including financial performance and liquidity. Also, mergers and acquisitions can lead to the elimination of a stock from the index. The number of stocks that move out of Nifty 50 is lower compared to Micro caps. When adjusted for this survivorship, the actual performance of the index can be far lower than what is depicted in the analysis.

In summary, investing in penny stocks is like picking nickels in front of a moving steam roller. The risk of getting run down by the steam roller is far higher than the value of nickels one picks up. It is enticing to note that all large caps today started off as micro caps, which is an observation in hindsight or after the fact. Finding the next Infosys or Bajaj Finance is more an exercise in hope laden with huge risks. While institutional investors can afford to take that risk as they can commit resources to due diligence, the same cannot be said about individual investors. If retail investors still want to take the bet on penny stocks, they are advised either to invest a small portion in the micro-cap index (which at least diversifies the risk) through the ETF route or, in cases where they are keen on stock picking, they should devote considerable time and energy in researching the stock before investing.

11

Multi-baggers

With the markets delivering wonderful returns during the last few years, it is now very common to see WhatsApp messages from friends on how they hit the jackpot on some of the small-cap stocks. When our stock investment appreciates not in percentage (like 25%) but in times (like 10x or 200x), that's what we call a multi-bagger. Everyone wants to hit that jackpot, isn't it? However, the odds are extremely low.

Today's blue chips like Infosys, Bajaj Finance, Reliance, etc., all started as micro caps before progressing to become small-caps, mid-caps, and finally large caps. If we were lucky to have identified them early on, we would be sitting on a goldmine today. Hence, the trick lies in catching them early or identifying them early. But then, it is always easier said than done. We have more than 5,000 listed stocks on our exchanges, so we can imagine the enormity of the task at hand and what a nightmarish proposition it could be.

While I said the odds are low, I did not rule them out. So, if we are still on the hunt for the treasure, the key would be to start early and be prepared for a long and arduous journey with these picks. That requires phenomenal mental strength. Furthermore, since the odds are few, it would not be a bad idea to spread our bets far and wide and hope some or a few turn out to be potential winners or multi-baggers. However, to identify them, we need a good investment process. And that is what I will try to explain here.

My suggested investment process has two broad steps with three sub-steps:

Step 1: Do basic checks and identify the stock/s

Step 2: Take a small position (with three sub-steps)

Step 1:

While doing some basic checks, there are some suggested things to look for. One can either take the entire universe and apply some filters (which presumes one has access to enormous data) or apply some checks on recommendations that come our way. Once a name pops up as a great multi-bagger opportunity, one needs to ensure that the said company is financially sound, enjoys healthy margins (implying pricing power), has low/zero-debt, and is not in the news for the wrong reasons (like fraud, regulatory misgivings, etc.). At this stage, it is not essential to look for cheap valuation, high liquidity, or institutional interest in the stock. The reason is that they are almost always thinly traded and hence the price is not a true reflection of value. Only when these stocks successfully migrate from micro to small to mid to large, do they develop good liquidity and therefore, better price discovery. Also, institutional interest in stock investment typically develops only during the mid-cap phase and hence they mostly avoid small-caps.

Step 2:

If a company passes the basic test, it is recommended to take a small position (ignoring market timing). Repeat this process for several companies to spread the risk.

The process gets interesting only after Step 2. Once we have invested in a stock, there are three possible outcomes:

1. The stock price appreciates rapidly:

This may be rare, but it means the lucky stars are well-aligned for us. The suggested strategy would be to set some margin of safety in terms of returns (say 100% or 2x) at which point we may want to double down (buy more) on the stock on dips. The reason being price is a great point of reflection. If the stock price appreciates rapidly, usually there is a good business reason why this happens and hence doubling down may be a good strategy. It also means that we are betting on winners. At this stage, it will be good to cross-check Step 1 again.

2. The stock price stays flat:

This is the trickiest phase to watch as it can test one's patience immensely. The suggested strategy is to remain invested if there is no significant loss or profit (even if this means 10 years!). The reason is that in the history of a company, breakout moments happen but it is impossible to predict them in advance. Selling them out due to boredom will mean missing out on the point when they break out for multi-bagger returns.

3. The stock price falls:

This path is the most painful as the investor is now sitting on a loss. The normal psychology is to think that it is an opportunity for averaging. However, the suggested strategy is to set a "loss threshold" (say 25%) based on one's risk tolerance. The idea is to stick with the stock till the loss threshold is breached, after which selling is recommended. The reasoning again is that price fall embeds some known/unknown bad news. In other words, by selling those out we are eliminating losers. In our quest to find multi-baggers, we generally tend to cash out on winners and stick with losers, with a firm hope that they will bounce-back. This may or may not happen.

Also, when we spread ourselves with several picks, the odds of finding some multi-baggers increase.

When to cash out?

Another key dilemma that an investor may face is dealing with the huge profits of a multi-bagger. If a particular investment has gone up, say, 25x, should we sell at least some part to recover our investment or book profits? The usual temptation is to cash out and enjoy the profits.

However, it is quite possible that this stock is a potential 250x, in which case we will appear silly selling them out early! The best time to sell some stock is not when they are up or down, but when the business thesis has changed (the company is losing margins & market share, debt is increasing, promoters are paying themselves huge salaries, politically compromised groups, etc.). If we are "in the money" on a stock, just stay with them and enjoy the ride. Remember, there is no limit to the upside in a multi-bagger. History is replete with many examples of selling too soon. Softbank sold its 4.9% stake in Nvidia for a profit of $3.3 billion in 2019. If only they had resisted that temptation and held on till 2024, the profit would have reached $160 billion! Similarly, Ronald Wayne, the third co-founder of Apple, sold his 10% stake in 1976 for $800. If he had held on, it would be worth $328 billion in 2024!

12

Primary Market

The primary market is where capital is raised, while the secondary market provides the needed continuity and liquidity. The primary market segment has several terminologies with which one should be conversant.

A key component of the primary market is the Initial Public Offering (IPO), where a company taps the market for the first time through initial listing. However, we may also see subsequent issuances by the same company, which are termed as Follow-up Public Offerings (FPO). When going for an IPO, the amount sought to be raised can either be fresh capital or used for cashing out existing owners, which is termed as Offer For Sale (OFS). We can also see Qualified Institutional Placement (QIP), where the IPO is directed only to qualified institutional buyers. From the data, we notice that QIPs are as frequent, if not more frequent, than IPOs. There is also an active account of OFS among the issuances. The year-on-year trend of primary market activity does not reflect a pattern, as it is highly correlated to the phases of secondary market activity. In other words, during times when the overall market is increasing, we can certainly notice a good number of primary market activities as well.

Table : 21 Primary Market

INR bn	IPOs	FPOs	OFS	QIPs	Total
CY13	13	70	240	81	403
CY14	12	5	50	317	384
CY15	136	-	356	191	682
CY16	265	-	131	47	443
CY17	671	-	181	611	1464
CY18	310	-	107	166	582
CY19	124	-	260	352	736
CY20	266	150	209	808	1433
CY21	1187	-	229	420	1836
CY22	593	43	113	117	866
CY23	494	-	193	543	1231
Source: DAM Capital, CY: Calendar Year					

Whenever we face a new IPO, we wonder how effective it is to invest in one. We've heard many stories of blockbuster returns on IPOs and how investments have turned into multi-baggers thanks to bonuses, rights, dividends, etc. It's worth remembering that all significant rock star companies today (the Nifty 50 biggies) were once IPOs making a modest entry into the investment world.

However, the IPO world is not easy to navigate, as for every rock star, there are many more fallen angels. While it's a challenge to evaluate the issue and decide to invest, it's also a game of "lottery" where probability plays a massive role in achieving results. In attractive issues, the likelihood of allotment reduces significantly, and in not-so-attractive issues, one will be saddled with a loss-making investment proposition. To decide on a good IPO, one needs to look at valuation, recommendations by experts, and the extent of oversubscription.

There are three critical variables to consider while deconstructing the IPO payoff structure.

The first is valuation, the price point at which an issue is offered. While a higher price point is preferred for the issuer, it's vice versa for the investor. Also, a higher valuation implies lower interest in the issue. In general, an issue that is attractively priced garners more investor interest.

The second factor will be an expert recommendation. Since these are new companies on which publicly available information is minimal, investors generally look to expert recommendation/grading while deciding to apply. Expert recommendations influence the decision of retail investors to a great extent.

The third important factor is the extent of over-subscription. The more an issue is attractively priced and receives a favourable recommendation from experts, the higher the degree of over subscription. This may also result in significant Grey Market Premium (GMP). However, a higher over subscription also means a lower probability of getting an allotment.

While the above classification makes an interesting historical analysis, it can also be used for prospecting investing options. As a strategy, one can look at the list of IPOs classified under poor/average and "mine" opportunities by zeroing in on those companies that enjoyed a "subscribe" rating, were highly oversubscribed, and were valued very high at the time of issuance.

Such issues could now be available for a more modest valuation and can thus be investment targets, provided they continue to perform well at a business level. Therefore, the poor/average list is a great place to start and 'mine' opportunities for future investments. On the other hand, the good list may be hard to mine, given the significant jump in their valuation already.

The 502 issues during 2007 to 2022 prove that nearly 50% of IPO's yielded negative returns[34]. However, if one considers listing day gains, nearly 60% of IPO's provided listing day gains[35]. This implies that IPOs generate first day euphoria, eventually when they settle down, it is a 50:50 game.

Unlike the secondary market, where valuation is determined by market price through the interplay of demand and supply, IPO pricing is usually established through a book-building process by investment banks based on the feedback they get during roadshows. At best, it is a guestimate to extract the best value from investors. Of course, the need to walk the fine line of optimally pricing the issue is always there. Huge oversubscriptions often indicate significant listing gains and vice versa. However, this may not always be true.

As indicated before, primary market issuances peak during bull markets as the probability of success improves from an issuer's point of view. However, it also makes it risky from an investor's standpoint. Promoters of weak businesses or promoters with bad intent can collude with investment banks to take advantage of the bull market frenzy. They can mop up money only to disappear a little while later. The Indian IPO landscape is laden with hundreds of such stories. Hence, a careful reading of the Red Herring Prospectus (RHP) will help resolve the puzzle. The RHP provides more comprehensive information about the company, its operations, financials, and risks associated with the investment.

There can be multiple reasons for a promoter to take the company public. The often-cited reason is Capex followed by working-capital

---

34 https://www.chittorgarh.com/report/ipo-performance-summary-ipo-price-vs-current-price/121/mainline/

35 https://www.chittorgarh.com/report/ipo-performance-ipo-price-listing-day-close-price/122/mainline/

needs. However, we also notice debt reduction as another reason to reduce the interest burden and improve net income. However, the exit of current investors/divestment can be problematic.

The biggest hurdle for retail investors, especially those with high-net-worth, is the upper limit of subscriptions at two lakhs per issue that is presently in force. For heavily subscribed issues, the allotment turns out to be a lottery. In other words, if we apply for 200 shares, we may get four shares. The strike rate can be poor. While the profit can be handsome in percentage terms, in absolute terms, it can be so small that one is left wondering whether it is worth going through the hassle!

Even for a listed company, research from analysts builds up only gradually. Until then, the only source of information is annual reports and quarterly updates, which mainly provide information after the fact. In the case of IPOs, information availability is sparse, restricting our ability to make informed decisions. We can only see what is shown, not necessarily what is required.

The arrival of Real Estate Investment Trusts (REITs) and Infrastructure Investment Trusts (InvITs) has changed the landscape of IPOs in India. However, these new asset classes have risk-return profiles different from regular stocks. They are displayed more on the lines of predictable income distribution in the form of dividends and hence cannot be a capital appreciation play. Hence, investing in them during IPO is as good as investing in them, say, a year later.

13

MRF @ Rs1,00,000: What Is in a Price?

As they say, "what's in a name," the same applies to stock price. It is important to dispel the myth that a higher share price is more valuable than a lower share price without considering other factors. I remember this old joke: A man orders a personal-sized pizza. The waiter asks if he'd prefer it cut into four pieces or eight pieces. The man says, "Four, please. I can't eat eight." The price of a stock is like the size of each slice. The value of the company is like the size of the pizza. Without knowing how many pieces the pizza was cut into, we can't conclude that bigger slices came from a bigger pizza.

On 21st June 2023, the tyre behemoth MRF crossed a coveted milestone of Rs. 1 lakh in share price, catapulting the stock to frenzied discussions on Twitter and other platforms, heralding it as a milestone! But is it really a milestone? Very high-priced stocks are a global phenomenon, albeit rare. Warren Buffett's Berkshire Hathaway is a good example, quoting at over $500,000!

This is not to take away from the greatness of MRF, a $3 billion company with a long history. The company was founded in 1946 and went public in 1961, debuting at just Rs. 11. It reached the Rs. 5,000 landmark by 2007, Rs. 10,000 by 2012, Rs. 25,000 by 2014, Rs. 50,000 by 2016, Rs. 75,000 by 2018, and finally the Rs. 1,00,000 landmark in 2023.

It is one of the few home-grown successes that initially collaborated with a foreign tyre company and later crafted its own path to glory. After all, how many companies in India can boast a share price of Rs. 1 lakh? None, in fact. Not even above Rs. 50,000. If we lower the bar to Rs. 10,000, it still yields only nineteen companies. In fact, the numbers swell at Rs. 100 and below. We can count nearly 1,800 companies with share prices of Rs. 100 or more. Hence, the media frenzy over a Rs. 1 lakh share price.

Table : 22 Indian Tyre Companies

Name	CMP Rs.	Mar Cap Rs. Cr.	Sales Rs. Cr.	PAT 12M Rs. Cr.	P/E	CMP / BV	Div Yld %	ROA %	ROE %	ROCE %	Debt / Eq	5Yrs return %	Avg Vol 1Yr	1Yr return %
Balkrishna Inds	2,484	48,016	9,760	999	48.13	6.32	0.64	8.56	13.79	13.79	0.44	16	355442	10
MRF	**1,02,439**	**43,434**	**23,008**	**700**	**62.06**	**2.95**	**0.17**	**2.95**	**4.87**	**7.43**	**0.2**	**5**	**10810**	**26**
Apollo Tyres	421	26,747	24,568	1,080	24.8	2.08	0.95	3.98	8.77	10.21	0.5	8	3313060	100
CEAT	2,460	9,951	11,432	333	29.88	2.89	0.48	2.19	6.14	9.42	0.67	12	325931	106
JK Tyre & Indust	248	6,099	14,645	296	20.64	1.87	0.79	2.42	9.49	11.27	1.44	15	2563628	113
Goodyear India	1,412	3,256	2,928	123	26.57	5.37	1.9	9.36	18.61	25.13	0.02	4	32170	46
TVS Srichakra	3,160	2,421	2,985	82	29.52	2.29	0.52	3.41	8.18	8.95	0.64	1	19190	63
Median: 8 Co's	1,936	8,025	10,596	315	29.7	2.92	0.72	3.7	9.13	10.74	0.52	8	179050.5	54

Source: Screener.com   Data as of 13th July 2023

A stock's attractiveness is always through the lens of shareholder wealth creation, especially when benchmarked with peers or broader index. While MRF's share price is by far the largest not only among its peers but also among all the companies listed in NSE, our focus should be on how much wealth shareholders made over the last few years. In that sense, MRF has been doing very well during the one-year period ending July 2023, clocking a return of 26%, but when we look at the five-year annualised performance, it pales at 4.8%, far lower than the median of all tyre companies at 8% and definitely far lower than say Balkrishna Industries (16%) or JK Tyres (15%).

MRF's market cap is second in the peer group after Balkrishna Industries and is the most expensive when compared to a P/E ratio dividend yield or return on assets. All tyre companies are dividend players and rely less on debt.

As indicated by the risk/return plot, MRF is positioned less favourably compared to the Nifty Auto sector or Nifty 50.

Figure : 5 MRF Risk Return

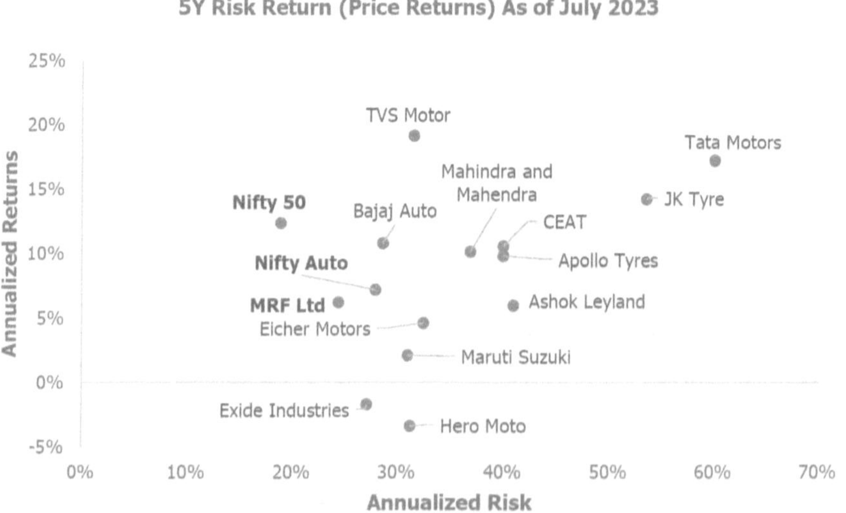

Of course, any long-term movement in share price must be attributed solely to a company's fundamental performance. Since 1995, MRF has delivered an annualised return of 14%, explaining its rise in share price.

However, there are other things also at play, especially corporate actions. Companies announce various corporate actions from time to time that affect their total number of outstanding shares. They mainly include bonuses, rights, and conversions of various types, including preference shares, bonds, and warrants. All these corporate actions tend to increase the outstanding shares and thereby reduce the earnings per share and, therefore, the share price. In addition, other prominent corporate actions include dividends, buybacks, splits and mergers/demergers. Among all of these, the most powerful is the stock split, which is mainly intended to reduce the share price and make it affordable to investors.

A quick comparison of corporate actions among tyre companies can reveal that MRF stayed away from all forms of corporate actions except dividends. This kept its outstanding shares almost at the same level year after year.

Table : 23 Corporate Actions

	Equity								
	Bonus	Profit	Pref share	Warrant	Bond				
			Conversion	Conversion	Conversion	Dividend	Buy Back	Split	Merger
MRF						✓			
Apollo Tyres			✓	✓	✓	✓	✓	✓	
Balkrishna Ind	✓				✓	✓		✓	✓
CEAT		✓		✓		✓			✓
JK Tyre		✓	✓	✓		✓		✓	✓
Goodyear						✓			
TVS Srichakra						✓			✓

Source: Screener.com

The flip side of keeping the outstanding shares constant and letting the share price climb is that it results in abysmally low volume and value traded. The average 1-year volume traded for MRF at 10,810 compares so poorly with, say, Apollo Tyres at 33,13,060! Such low volumes can hamper price discovery and open many other discussions, including the incentive to keep it that way. Promoters that do not want shareholder activity for various reasons, like MRF, will keep it tight-knit. Promoters (28%), Public but inactive (15%), Employees (8.5%) and non-promoter entities (23%) together account for nearly 75% of total outstanding shares, leaving very little for public market trading. By keeping the share price high, only serious investors will be attracted to the stock, which will invest based on the long-term potential as per their assessment. Serious investors will also likely remain invested for a long-time, thereby reducing the volatility of the share price. Lay investors with small capital (less than Rs.100,000) will not show any interest in the stock.

Another incentive to keep the price at the glorious level is to establish "vintage" value and stand out from the crowd. In addition, if one must use share price as a proxy for growth over several decades (like gold), companies like MRF make it easier. However, this story holds well only when we have a one stock portfolio where we tie up all our wealth, which is hardly the case for many investors and goes against the grain of diversification.

If we assume MRF will keep following its strategy of not disturbing its outstanding shares through corporate actions, then it is a plausible assumption that the share price can reach very high levels over the next few years. A range of possibilities has been provided from a conservative Rs.127,628 over the next five years (ending 2028) at 5% annualised growth of its share price to an astonishing Rs.38,33,760 over the next 20 years (ending 2043) at a 20% annual rise in its price. The truth will lie somewhere in the middle. At every step of the way (Rs.5,00,000 or

Rs.10,00,000), the media frenzy is bound to happen, and we can happily partake in the celebrations. However, one's decision to invest in MRF should be purely based on its outlook from a fundamental analysis point of view and not on the level of its share price.

Table : 24 MRF Share Price Scenarios

Annualized Return	MRF Share Price Scenarios			
	5 years	10 Years	15 years	20 years
5%	127628	162889	207893	265330
10%	161051	259374	417725	672750
15%	201136	404556	813706	1636654
20%	248832	619174	1540702	3833760
Source: Author Calculations assuming a starting price of Rs1,00,000				

Sector Ideas

(5,000 feet view)

01

Introduction

The numbers speak for themselves. During the five-year period ending July 2022, if we had invested Rs.1 in the IT sector, it is worth Rs.2.7 by July 2022 as against Rs.1.7 for Nifty and 0.67 paise for the media sector. During this period, IT, energy, Financial Services, and Metal produced far better returns as compared to the Media, PSU Banks, and Auto sectors. Isn't it then time to differentiate among sectors?

Even sophisticated investors do not consider sector bets as seriously as they should. While the broad market comprises many sectors whose performance defines the average performance of the index, investment performance can be significantly enhanced by choosing good sectors and avoiding bad sectors.

The Nifty 50 tracks the performance of 50 of the approximately 1,600 companies listed on the NSE, comprising roughly 65% of float-adjusted market capitalisation. It is a myriad confluence of different sectors, and hence, the performance of Nifty will also be influenced by both well-performing and poorly-performing sectors. Additionally, active fund managers do not make serious deviations in favour of well-performing sectors for fear of tracking errors.

The case of investing in a market index like Nifty will ensure the presence of both good and bad sectors, thereby taking away the benefit of performance in the guise of offering diversification. If academic theory says that it is quite possible to have a fully diversified portfolio with just ten stocks, then identifying those stocks among the well-performing sectors should be the way to go. Hence, investing in a market index fund or ETF may not be as good an idea as investing in well-performing sectors.

Even among well-performing sectors, as per traditional theory, investing should be focused on the index heavyweights whose performance can significantly influence the overall performance of the sector index. For example, in the IT sector, the performance of TCS, Infosys, and HCL should matter as they have a larger share of the index. However, if we look at the leaders and laggards, in most cases, they have names that are not among the heavyweights. Hence, the job is not done by simply investing in sector funds. It is quite possible to improve the portfolio performance significantly by fishing within the sector basket, which calls for stock picking. This argument is even more relevant if we consider the divergence in the performance of leaders and laggards relative to the sector index performance. More than selecting good companies in bad sectors, it may be worthwhile to avoid bad companies in good sectors and improve portfolio performance.

Apart from the annualised performance of the sectors, there can be an inspection of stocks within the sector in terms of outperforming the sector index as well as outperforming the market index (Nifty). Companies that outperform both their sector index as well as the broad market index can obviously be classified as excellent, while at the other end of the spectrum, we may have companies underperforming both their sector index as well as the broad market index (called poor) and all others falling in between.

Hence there is a need to distinguish between good sectors and bad sectors in portfolio investment. However, in the Indian capital market context, the availability and popularity of sector indices/ETFs are still developing making it difficult to implement a sector-based portfolio strategy. As an extension of that research, it may be worthwhile to see the link between sectors and companies. In simple terms, we may have a bad company in a good sector or a good company in a bad sector. How do we reconcile such conflicts?

BSE has nineteen sector indices. If one tracks their annualised performance, we can see that there is a wide variation in their performance. While the annualised performance shows huge variation, even within a sector, we see wide variation in performance among stocks. Hence, it may not be enough to just bet on good sectors as even within good sectors, we notice a wide variation in performance.

Here is the dilemma while choosing companies. We may have good companies in bad sectors or bad companies in good sectors. Hence, it may be worthwhile to regroup the index constituents across these four dimensions and assess their portfolio performance (based on market cap weights):

1. Good companies, good sectors (A)
2. Good companies, bad sectors (B)
3. Bad companies, good sectors (C)
4. Bad companies, bad sectors (D)

The definition of a good company/sector is that it outperforms the Sensex returns, and conversely, a bad company/sector is the one that underperforms the Sensex.

A strong look at the sector to which a company belongs is the key to identifying winners. There may be good companies in bad sectors and vice versa. Hence, a sector bias should not cloud opportunities. In general, good companies come from good sectors. That is a killer combination to have in our portfolio (A) In general. Bad companies come from bad sectors. This should be avoided at all costs. (D)

It is evident that significant enhancement of portfolio returns can simply be achieved by being sector-biased and within sectors stock-biased. Embrace well-performing sectors that are based on solid macroeconomic forces (like demography, consumption, exports, etc.) and avoid sectors that suffer from macroeconomic tailwinds (like high interest rates, capital expenditure, regulatory pressures, etc.). Do not ignore good companies in bad sectors, and at the same time, avoid bad companies in good sectors as they may have company-specific issues (mostly corporate governance) and may not be able to take advantage of a favourable sector atmosphere.

In further sections, we will take a closer look at some sectors/themes to drive the point home.

02

Banks Vs. NBFC's

There are 22 banks and 16 NBFCs in the Nifty 500 index. The financial services segment is a key one for future opportunities. The debate is: where should we bet? Banks or NBFCs. Not an easy question, but an interesting one from an investment perspective.

Table : 25 Banks vs NBFC's

Particulars	Banks	NBFCs
Number	22	16
M.Cap ($ bn) (Mar 2024)	536	145
Median M.Cap ($ mn)	12022	4080
RoE (FY 2019- FY 2023)	11.2%	16.5%
RoA (FY 2019-FY 2023)	1.3%	3.2%
Annualized Share price performance (FY 2020 - FY 2024)	17.0%	21.9%
Source: Refinitiv		

Source: Refinitiv, Banks and NBFCs (Lending) part of the Nifty 500 are considered in the analysis; Aggregate ROE, ROA, share price performance are weighted based on market capitalisation of the respective constituents

As a group, banks are certainly larger than NBFCs whichever way we look at it. However, on performance metrics (Return on Equity and Return on Assets), NBFCs have a clear edge over banks. This is also reflected in the share price performance of banks and NBFCs. Banks, as a group, provided an annualised return of 17% during the last 5 years while NBFCs have provided an annualised return of 21.9%. Looking a bit closer at the share price performance of Indian banks, Public sector banks have underperformed compared to private sector banks for an extended period until 2023.

However, when we extend the time horizon to the past ten years, several mid-sized and small-sized public and private sector banks delivered sub-par/negative returns to shareholders since 2014. This has caused the overall sector performance metrics to be lower. A similar look at NBFCs tells a very different picture. Unlike banks, most NBFCs have managed to create good shareholder value on the back of strong performance metrics. For example, the Return on Assets for NBFCs between FY 2020-24 stood at 3.2%, which is nearly thrice that of banks.

Let us now see what differentiates the business model for banks and NBFCs. Both are in the business of financial intermediation in that they obtain their funding and deploy them with a margin. The segregation of corporates and retail applies on both sides i.e., sources and deployment.

Here is where the key differentiation happens. While banks depend largely on retail sources of funding through deposits, NBFCs depend on wholesale sources. However, when it comes to deployment, banks predominantly lend to corporates, while NBFCs focus on retail. At the heart of this diversity lies the asset-liability mismatch leading to non-performing loans, scams, and scandals. The one with a lower amount of NPAs, scams, and scandals will emerge as the winner.

NPAs have been building up in the banking sector for quite some time thanks to this structure of obtaining funds through retail and lending them to wholesale. In such cases, high-profile defaults (remember Vijay Mallya, Nirav Modi, etc.) will inflict greater pain on the whole sector with a loss of money followed by a loss of confidence.

On the other hand, NBFCs are somewhat in a safer territory since their lending is mainly to retail (consumer loans, mortgage, gold loans, etc.) whose non-performing assets can be controlled. An out of context example in the form of microfinance will be adept here. Microfinance companies mostly lend to rural women with a 95% recovery rate! Retail customers are certainly low-risk compared to corporate bigwigs, especially when they enjoy political clout! The retail focus of NBFCs needs them to build on franchise value more than banks. This is not to say that banks need not have franchise value. It is more at play for NBFCs than banks.

A key factor that can explain the performance differentials of banks vs NBFCs could be the presence and dominance of the public sector in the banking space. More than half of the listed banks in Nifty 500 are from the public sector domain though they constitute only 37% of the market cap. However, the fact is that the presence of the public sector will inhibit nimbleness and can cause governance issues leading to NPAs.

At a broader level, banks as a group performed less compared to NBFCs. Hence, the verdict is clear. However, there are sharp differences in the underlying performance of the constituent companies. Banks like Kotak, HDFC Bank, ICICI, Axis, and IndusInd have produced outsized shareholder wealth over the last decade, compared to other small and medium-sized banks. The same holds true for NBFCs where the performance of Bajaj Finance, Bajaj Finserv and Chola Investment have almost dwarfed most other rivals in the game. In hindsight, it looks like the names captioned above would form good candidates for portfolio inclusion. However, if one can afford a bit closer look and research on the universe of NBFCs, then identify those companies with good governance principles, solid franchises, risk management, and sound business model. When looked at from this prism, NBFCs have a clear edge over banks going forward.

03

Information Technology

Indian IT stocks have a spectacular record of stock market returns on the back of some good long-term moats that are worth explaining at this stage:

1. **Service industry with export focus:** The long growth of the Indian IT sector is purely a home-grown case study that went outside India and captured global attention for its IT attributes. Many of the clients of Indian IT companies are global organisations (banks and non-banks) that depend on Indian IT companies to a very large extent. Some of these multinational companies have set up their back-end units in India and have been seamlessly working with Indian IT companies for many years now. The industry is also viewed positively by the government given the foreign exchange that they bring in good measure, a thing that is highly needed for an emerging market like India with a current account deficit.

2. **Evolving Business Model:** While initially, the Indian IT story started at the lowest end of the value chain (read body shopping and coding), they quickly evolved in the value chain and now aggressively compete in the middle segment of the value chain with immense potential to move up to the higher end. The increasing size, scale, and profitability also enable them to do this. Today, many Indian IT companies are highly focused on the global digital story and provide detailed consulting to global

clients. It can easily be observed that they constantly adapt their business model to maximise opportunities and profits.

3. **Good Governance:** While the biggest risk for emerging market stocks stems from shoddy/suspect governance with family domination, the names in the Indian IT sector have set some good examples for ethics-based governance structure primarily started by Infosys. The big names in the IT sector including TCS, Infosys, HCL, L&T, & Tech Mahindra enjoy good investor backing primarily on the back of good governance. Due to this factor, these names qualify as blue chips in the index.

4. **Long-term returns:** As they say, the proof of the pudding is in eating, Indian IT companies have delivered excellent long-term performance beating the broad Nifty 50 by a significant measure. A look at the risk-return chart for the last five years places the sector in a sweet spot compared to other sectors like Auto, Realty, Metals, private Banks, Financial services, and Pharmaceuticals.

Of course, the sector is not without its risks.

1. **Exchange Rates:** Being predominantly export-oriented in its nature, the industry's fortunes swing widely with the performance of the Indian rupee vis-à-vis global currencies, mainly USD. A strong rupee will hurt while a weak rupee will benefit. Currency hedging will be key to manage this risk. However, the performance of the Indian rupee against the USD has been surprisingly stable given the astute management by RBI.

2. **Macro Risks:** Indian IT companies have global companies as clients, mainly from the USA. Any macro shocks like inflation or recession might slow down global IT spending as it has a discretionary bias. At the same time, companies

also use IT solutions to optimise costs and manage economic downturns. Macro risks are the primary reason for the poor performance of the Indian IT sector during the Covid-led brief recession in the US. Global IT companies have been in the news for massive layoffs as they overstretched themselves during the Covid-19 pandemic. This positions the industry as a volatile sector.

3. **Skill-based Sector:** As a knowledge industry, the IT sector's reliance on people more than machines may result in higher margins but also brings other problems to the fore including intense competition, attrition, and wage growth pressure. The industry must constantly be ahead of the curve to beat these risks and they only get tougher. Availability of superior talent is always a challenge given our patchy education structure that still emphasises on rote learning (memorising). While IT companies are serious recruiters in university campuses, they spend a significant amount to train/reskill the recruits to make them industry-ready.

4. **Moving up the Value Chain:** While Indian IT companies work for the global giants, they are yet to turn themselves into global giants. While the industry has successfully forayed from the low end to the medium part of the value chain, the travel to the higher end will prove very difficult given global pressures especially from the USA/Europe and talent constraints. Companies that successfully navigate this journey will definitely reap great benefits.

In conclusion, we can say that global IT spending at $4.5 trillion is a large pie to provide enough comfort for the Indian IT sector, though domestic IT spending continues to be a modest $109 billion. Globally, companies are embracing some interesting futuristic opportunities around Cybersecurity, Customer experience, Artificial Intelligence,

Automation, and cloud computing. While these are significant trends, many of them are interconnected (like cloud and Cybersecurity). Indian companies are taking interesting steps to get there, including Metaverse. Companies that focus on these emerging digital areas will continue to provide great shareholder returns as opposed to others that are content with being service providers. Given the handful number of blue-chip IT stocks, it may well be worth poring over their annual reports and other filings to see who gets there.

04

Energy

Among the necessities for human survival (food, shelter, and clothing), it may not be out of context to add energy needs. Energy cuts across everything from transportation to electricity. Thanks to a confluence of multiple factors, including geopolitics, oil prices have increased tremendously in the past, inflicting pain on oil importers like India. India's oil dependence is akin to the tale of the boiling frog and imposes a heavy cost on the economy and therefore on companies operating within it. High oil prices impact multiple economic activities, hence most economies around the world heavily subsidise energy to prevent GDP growth from being affected. Before we examine the portfolio context, let's delve into the structural factors shaping oil prices globally.

At a broad level, we have oil producers, oil consumers, and oil exporters/importers. The dynamics shaping this vary based on which lens we use. Major oil producers like the USA are also major consumers, leaving little for exports. In fact, the US produces more oil than Russia. Major producers like Saudi Arabia or Russia enjoy a significant surplus in oil production that they profitably monetise through exports.

However, large economies like China and India continue to be just oil consumers with no significant domestic production. This makes them energy-dependent on oil exporters who control the supply. Hence, studying the factors that influence supply may be crucial here. Presently, OPEC+—which includes major Middle Eastern oil exporters and Russia—tightly controls the market to defend prices. However, the

Russian-Ukraine conflict has created a deep divide between importers (like the EU) and exporters (like Russia). It is highly unlikely that "business as usual" will return anytime soon between Russia on one side and the US/EU on the other. Essentially, oil has introduced a new political cost to buyers, apart from the environmental cost they were paying earlier.

Oil prices experience significant volatility, which affects investments in new fields. Additionally, due to increasing demands for clean energy and appreciation, the conventional oil sector has experienced significant under-investment during the last decade, limiting supply. Most oil-exporting countries need an oil price of $80 and above to sustain their budgets. Anything less would create a deficit. However, oil prices above $100 start to affect consumers. Hence, both consumers and exporters lobby to achieve some sort of equilibrium. Energy demand is highly correlated with global growth, so any recessionary fears can pull down oil prices. Within this interplay between demand and supply come unpredictable geo-political developments (like the Russia-Ukraine War) that can cause temporary spikes in oil prices.

Commodities markets are rarely in equilibrium, and hence, overshoots on both the demand and supply sides can feed high volatility. In short, oil prices less than $80/barrel are good news for consumers and bad news for exporters. Oil prices within a range of $80-$120 can be considered an equilibrium band, while oil prices above $120 are bad news for consumers and good news for oil exporters. The huge under-investment in the sector, coupled with supply outages due to geo-political reasons, makes me believe that oil prices have structurally moved to a band of $80-$120/b in the long-term with significant volatility. Such a trend will also accelerate the move towards alternatives like renewable energy, which can be bearish for oil exporters in the long-run.

Opec+, the powerful oil collective led by Saudi Arabia and Russia, appears to have elected thus far to keep its oil price within a band of $80-$90 per barrel. However, North America's vast shale oil reserves have given the US its own clout. Some experts call the US the global "swing producer" – an honour formerly bestowed on Saudi Arabia. Now, whenever Saudi Arabia-led Opec+ orchestrates production cuts, the US ramps up production and the oil price neutralises. Furthermore, modern shale technology facilitates the opening and closing of oil taps with ease, unlike conventional production methods that can take months to bring oil on stream.

To understand this price war fully, the larger context of energy markets must be considered. The world is still heavily reliant on fossil fuels, despite rapid strides in renewables. While governments contend with intense pressures to transition to clean energy due to climate change, the ambition is at odds with the on-the-ground reality. For example, against the need to add 500GW of additional renewable annual capacity to enable the transition, the current rate of annual capacity addition globally is just 150GW. To put it another way, capital expenditure on renewables is running at a global rate of $300 billion annually. However, a sum closer to $1 trillion per year is needed to close the energy gap sustainably. In contrast, the global oil and gas sector invests about $500 billion annually in maintenance and development. This steady flow of funds to conventional energy players, paired with under-investment in renewables, will only lengthen the time to transition. Some reports estimate that it will take another 50 years for the world to wean itself off fossil fuels.

Saudi Arabia, along with Russia and other Opec+ members, will do its best to keep production under check and not let the price drop below a floor of around $80 per barrel. At the same time, the US will continue to play the role of swing producer to prevent oil prices from spiking above $100 per barrel, which can be understood as the ceiling.

The first immediate touchpoint of high oil prices is through the current account balance. In terms of the impact of high oil prices, it is estimated that a $10 increase in oil price is likely to result in a widening of the current account deficit by 40 basis points from levels of $100/barrel oil price and a similar impact on inflation. Another related touchpoint would be a subset of the Current Account, which is the trade deficit. A trade deficit is essentially the difference between imports and exports. For the 1st quarter of the fiscal year 22-23 (April 2022-June 2022), India's trade deficit was $70 billion, up from $31 billion a year earlier. The cost has almost doubled thanks to the high oil price. Hence, it is a significant pain to contend with.

The second important touchpoint would be in the form of higher inflation. Crude and crude derivatives account for approximately 5% of the weight in CPI and roughly 10% in WPI. Hence, any increase in crude prices will influence the overall inflation significantly. Fuel is the main driver of inflation, having increased 10% in May 2022, while food increased by 8%, taking the overall inflation to 7%. A year ago, there was a fuel increase of 12%, a food increase of 5%, and overall inflation stood at 6.3%. High inflation triggers several policy responses both from RBI and the government, as emerging markets worldwide understand the potential risks of unaddressed inflation over time. Also, high energy prices tend to reduce domestic demand, as people cut down consumption of other products to pay for fuel.

There are many options to manage the dollar deficit induced by the trade deficit. We should either increase exports, reduce imports, or attract capital inflows. For example, higher export growth can happen only when global GDP growth picks up. Reducing imports can occur in the context of a slowing economy triggered by higher interest rates. However, this strategy will take time to produce results and will not yield immediate benefits. The third option of augmenting capital inflows is easier said than done in this volatile geo-political environment. If we cannot reduce imports through increasing interest rates, we can make imports expensive by currency devaluation or depreciation.

The Indian currency has been exceptionally strong in recent years, unlike many other emerging markets. A systematic currency depreciation of, say, 10% annually would also help mitigate the need to use hard-earned foreign exchange reserves to defend the currency. Unlike countries like South Korea or Japan, where high forex reserves are primarily due to trade surpluses (implying a dollar surplus), India's high forex reserves are a function of capital flows rather than a trade surplus. Capital flows can be volatile and can leave abruptly. Hence, it may not be wise to use these reserves to defend the currency.

The economic impact of higher oil prices can also be examined from how the fuel pricing happens in the country. The data depicted in the table shows that there is a heavy tax component to the overall pricing, which can be tweaked based on how it impacts the end consumers. In times of rising oil prices, the government can choose not to pass on the increase by calibrating the taxes and vice versa. Any decrease in taxes will mean a decrease in government revenues, which will increase the fiscal deficit. Hence, using this tool can, at best, be a temporary fix, while in the long-run, higher oil prices will essentially result in high fuel prices at the pumps.

Table : 26 Price build-up of petroleum products

Price build-up of petroleum products	Petrol (RS/L)	In %	Diesel (RS/L)	In %
Price to Dealers (excluding Excise Duty & VAT)	57.35	59%	58.17	65%
Excise Duty	19.9	21%	15.8	18%
Dealer Commission (Average)	3.78	4%	2.57	3%
VAT (including VAT on Dealer Commission)	15.72	16%	13.11	15%
Retail Selling Price at Delhi (Rounded Off)	96.76	100%	89.66	100%
Source: Bharat Petroleum (01/07/2022)				

From a stock market perspective, higher oil prices tend to affect some sectors directly and many other sectors indirectly. However, many of them might experience lags as they need to pass through time. Sometimes, companies may decide to live with lower margins to protect their market share, or market conditions may not be conducive to passing on the cost increase. While others may enjoy significant pricing power (due to market leadership) and hence may have a lower impact. Sectors like Paints, Tyres, Aviation, Chemicals and Logistics will have a direct and immediate impact, while sectors like Cement, FMCG and Discretionary can have lag effects. Nearly 60% of raw material costs are accounted for by oil and oil derivatives for Paints and Tyres. For Aviation, 40% of raw material cost is accounted for by Aviation Turbine Fuel (ATF). Based on a study of quarterly data since 2012, we can see that most of the sensitive sectors felt the heat of lower margins, though we can notice some exceptions as well. For e.g., sectors like Auto, information Technology, pharma and Cement enjoy margin increases during a high oil price regime, while sectors like FMCG, energy, Paints, Tyres and

Chemicals suffer margin erosion during a high oil price scenario. It will be instructive to underweight these sectors in times of high oil prices.

Table : 27 Operating Margins

	(Oil < $ 60)	(Oil b/w $ 60 and $ 90)	(Oil > $ 90)
Auto	6.1%	5.0%	9.3%
FMCG	15.5%	17.6%	14.0%
IT	22.0%	21.9%	24.9%
Metal	5.3%	16.9%	12.8%
Pharma	17.5%	16.0%	20.7%
Real Estate	25.0%	38.9%	28.2%
Energy	10.5%	10.4%	6.6%
Paints	16.0%	15.6%	12.8%
Cement	13.6%	13.3%	14.4%
Tyres	9.6%	9.1%	8.9%
Chemicals	13.8%	15.2%	12.5%
Nifty 50	12.5%	13.5%	13.5%
Source: Refinitiv; Period: 2012-2022			

In conclusion, India's oil trap can have serious long-term implications for economic growth, currency value and stock markets. Understanding this link and the compulsions that define the global oil market can enable portfolio managers to construct portfolios smartly. Any increase in oil prices can also significantly accelerate the adoption of renewables. Macro observations on how this shift plays out are crucial to portfolio positioning for the long-term.

05

Consumer Tech

After telecom companies like Airtel and Reliance Jio, if there is one sector that significantly impacts the lives of ordinary citizens, it is consumer tech. It is the umbrella term generally used to describe the use of technology to reach retail customers. Main categories include food delivery, ticket booking, gaming, education, and healthcare.

The space is inundated with startups. India is home to around 27,000 tech startups growing at an annual rate of 1,300. Nearly 100 of them have claimed the status of unicorns[36]. Presently, it is estimated that about 25 listed consumer tech companies are available for investors.

The interesting aspect of consumer tech is the confluence of technology with several verticals like finance, healthcare, education, and entertainment. Technology knows no borders and can disrupt almost all industries, hence the outsized interest in this emerging opportunity called consumer tech.

There are several macro tailwinds aiding this interest. First and foremost, India is the most populous country in the world followed by China. The per capita income for India has been increasing slowly but steadily from $1,400 in 2014 to $2,300 in 2022. However, what is interesting is the increasing number of households, projected to rise from 190 million (2022) to nearly 300 million by 2030. That is a large enough pie for any business opportunity, let alone consumer tech. In

---

36 Companies with more than $1 billion in valuation.

fact, studies show that India is emerging as a fertile landscape for high-income households as well. The number of high-income households is projected to grow from 15 million (2002) to nearly 30 million by 2030, supporting opportunities in luxury tech. Concurrently, there is growth in disposable income and internet penetration, making the business case very strong.

Companies in the consumer tech business seamlessly integrate three types of technologies: core, adjacent, and transformative. A good example of core technology would be Customer Relationship Management (CRM), while Virtual Reality (VR) exemplifies adjacent technology, and Generative AI represents transformative technology.

While the story of technology companies started very broadly with e-commerce, the hectic growth has now sprouted several sub-layers within the space. Notable among them would be D2C, Quick Commerce, Live Commerce, and social commerce. The D2C refers to direct-to-consumer models where one can eliminate the middleman, leading to higher margins for the service provider. Brand power is an important attraction here. Quick commerce promises faster deliveries (10 minutes in some cases!) and hinges on efficient coordination among technology, operations, personnel, facilities, and promotions. Social commerce enables far-flung consumers to enjoy the benefits of unbranded products based on social media synergies. Live commerce is conceptualised as live interaction to enhance consumer willingness to engage.

The idea is just to explain how the business model of consumer tech is a complicated mix of business and technology and hence not easy to interpret. China can be an interesting example of how consumer tech has evolved, since it happens to be a close comparison from a population point of view. The new e-commerce comprises segments like D2C explained earlier. India has a lot of catching up to do when we look at the comparative numbers with China. This also spells tremendous opportunity going forward.

Consumer Tech companies face several challenges, including funding. Hence, most of them commence their journey as startups and are invariably funded by Venture Capital companies (VCs). In any typical VC funding profiles, the success rate is only about 10%, and hence investment in tech startups is laden with huge risks. While the 100+ unicorns can be good case studies of success, it should be looked at in the context of 27,000 startups, a meagre percentage indeed. In this fiercely competitive environment, companies resort to Growth At All Costs (GAAC) leading to significant price wars and discounts. The idea is to capture a good market share (in what is generally described as Total Addressable Market) which many times results in winners taking it all (like Amazon). Also, most of these startups may show impressive growth due to low base effect but can fail flatly on profitability measures. Therefore, the universe of profitable consumer tech companies is small.

How can one make an investment case here? Since most of them are startups, main funding happens at a VC level. Hence, VC players may have excellent familiarity with the sector. However, many of these VCs eventually look to cash in their investments and hence we can see many IPOs periodically coming up. A look at all the listed consumer tech companies reveals some very interesting aspects. It is a mixed bag with both successes and failures strewn over the place. The list is too small to conclude. However, given the macro backdrop described the potential for growth is huge.

From a portfolio perspective, investing in these companies during IPO can mean that odds are very much against investors. For highly oversubscribed issues, the probability of allotment reduces and hence the final investment value can be very low to make any significant impact on our portfolio. Also, in hindsight it may be possible to see the winners and losers but in prospect, it is almost always impossible to identify them (and this logic applies to all other listed stocks as well). Hence, a prudent portfolio strategy is to invest some consistent amount in consumer tech companies after they are listed (preferably in a systematic way). Post this, one can continue to top up successful companies and eliminate loss-making companies in the portfolio. The success and failures should be measured from a stock market return perspective. As the investible universe expands, investors can look to reap great rewards going forward.

06

Indian Multinationals

We have all been very familiar with multinational companies (MNCs) like Nestle, Unilever, etc., that operate in several countries, including India. Normally, MNCs are bound by the strictures of the parent company in terms of business practices, corporate governance, and other related issues. While they derive most of their revenues from their parent location, the objective is to expand as widely as possible into many markets and capture market share.

Hence, over time, revenues generated outside their home territory may exceed those from the parent country. A notable example is the Las Vegas (U.S.-based) Sands Corporation, which generates the majority of its revenues from Macau, despite being headquartered in the U.S. and listed as an American stock. Another example is Techtronic Industries, based in Hong Kong, which derives most of its revenues from the U.S. through sales of power tools via Home Depot.

From a fund management perspective, investing in MNCs that derive an increasing share of their revenues from emerging markets rather than their home markets can mitigate political and currency risks associated with direct investments. According to one study, the emerging market operations of MNCs have delivered significant revenue and profit growth compared to their home markets. Nearly all major multinational corporations, such as Apple, BMW, Prada, etc., are now focusing more on their exposure to emerging markets than their home markets. Thus, it is common to find these major names present in all emerging markets, including India.

Extending this analogy, it may be interesting to examine how many Indian companies have ventured outside India, the so-called Indian Multinationals (IMNCs)! Typically, these would be companies that generate most of their revenues outside India. We could identify ten companies among the 30 companies represented in the Sensex. The top three names belong to the IT sector, which, by the very nature of their business models, serves clients outside India. This explains the heavy dependence on offshore markets by the IT majors. Together, the top 3 also account for a significant share of the Sensex at 10%. It is also interesting to note names from pharma, energy, Engineering, and Steel. Although it is common sense to assume that IMNCs would be predominantly owned by Indian groups, in cases where foreign ownership is high, it is fully explained by FII ownership, which are entities that generally have their interests of investment at the forefront. All the stocks enjoyed good performance in the stock market.

Among the 30 companies in the Sensex (not necessarily a broad representation, but will suffice for the case), we can notice five companies with significant foreign ownership exceeding 50% that can consequently be technically defined as foreign companies. However, even here, we need to differentiate between FII ownership (which may be subject to quick changes) and promoter holdings (which are always very stable). In that sense, HDFC[37] cannot be classified as an MNC even though its foreign ownership is more than 50% since most of that ownership is due to FII holdings. Hence, the list reduces to Maruti Suzuki (part of Suzuki group), Hindustan Lever (part of Unilever group), Nestle India (part of Nestle group), and IndusInd Bank. In general, they mostly operate within the Indian market space, as signified by the low % of revenue

---

37 Now merged HDFC Bank

generated outside India and tend to represent a sizeable share of the Sensex (measured in terms of market capitalisation).

While MNCs eye the lucrative Indian market apart from other markets, IMNCs eye the huge global markets apart from the Indian market. The trend of Emerging Multinationals (EMNCs) is not a new trend. China's Huawei, Mexico's Cemex, Russia's Gazprom, and Brazil's Embraer are but a few examples. While some of these EMNCs would have internationalised their national experience, MNCs would have nationalised their international experience like that of Hindustan Lever. Of course, there are pure-play IMNCs, like the IT companies (HCL tech, Wipro & Infosys).

In my assessment, IMNCs will prosper immensely as they look at global markets as an opportunity set as opposed to just targeting the Indian landscape. However, operationally it may be challenging to coordinate vast networked operations and generate the requisite profits. Also, they may have to manage political and currency risks in the process. Also, from a governance point of view, the IMNCs may not be able to take with them notable or worthy best practices while they compete in new markets, as India is still learning to draft governance codes and is not widely acclaimed for such metrics. On the other hand, foreign MNCs may have a head start here in terms of corporate governance.

Indian MNCs (IMNCs) and MNCs enjoy good revenue growth relative to the emerging market MNCs. IMNCs also enjoy good net profit margins which probably results in better RoE and RoA.

We can very well conclude that the old concept of MNCs is giving way to a new breed of IMNCs that could add more value to their shareholders by expanding the opportunity set, a move that by itself can diversify and reduce risk. However, they must contend with serious challenges of understanding various geographies, the associated currencies, political, and transaction risks. The sagas and travails of Tata Steel-Corus and Tata Motors – JLR acquisitions are still etched strongly in our memory!

07

International Stocks

RBI now permits Indian investors to invest up to $250,000 per annum in global capital and real estate markets (stocks, bonds, ETFs, and real estate).

The rise of digital banking and fintech means investors may no longer have to visit a bank branch to pay a foreign broker. For instance, institutions like ICICI Bank allow an online process for transfers up to $25,000, i.e., 10 percent of the total limit. This should encourage more investors to consider parking part of their investments in foreign equities.

I will enumerate three reasons why investing in global markets makes sense. It would help one understand the risk-return trade-off well and take an informed decision.

Firstly, the Indian stock market takes pride in having the highest number of listed stocks globally, but from a practical point of view, the opportunity set is restricted to about 500 stocks on the NSE. In fact, realistically, most of the funds are benchmarked to Nifty 50 or Sensex (30 stocks), limiting the universe further. In addition, these benchmarks are dominated by financial stocks and consumer discretionary sectors.

We are all aware of the enormous role Facebook, Amazon, Apple, Netflix, and Google (FAANG) play in our everyday lives in India. In contrast, global markets, including the U.S., are moving in favour of technology, which has experienced multi-decade expansion and is less correlated with cyclical stocks. Hence, exposure to international stocks can allow Indian investors to benefit from the strong momentum in technology sector stocks and their future growth potential. However, these companies are not listed in India.

Secondly, despite the exemplary performance of the Indian stock market in recent times, the long-term performance of its stocks lags its global peers across all periods. In addition to low performance, the Indian market exhibited higher risk (volatility), reflected in a higher standard deviation. In other words, the Indian market provided a lower return for higher risk, while global markets provided higher returns for lower risk. Hence, investing in foreign stocks presents an excellent case for diversification.

In addition, the correlation between the Indian and global markets is not very high, making the portfolio impact much better. Mark it; higher historical returns can also imply lower prospective returns (due to mean reversion) and vice versa. In other words, given the longer than 10-year bull run in S&P 500, foreign stocks (essentially, U.S. equities) may provide lower returns, while Indian equities could outperform. This view again supports the need to diversify, which will help the portfolio be more stable.

Thirdly, technology has now enabled investing to be less costly and speedier. Several platforms are available for Indian investors to directly invest in foreign markets. Examples include Stock, Vested finance, Winvestra, Kuvera, Axis Securities, ICICI Securities, HDFC Securities, Upstox, etc. Thanks to technology, opening and operating an account is relatively seamless.

The reasons above demonstrate the case for investing some part of our wealth in foreign stocks. However, investors should also note the following:

1. There are two ways to invest in foreign stocks. One can take the mutual fund route or the direct investing route. In India, more than 40 mutual funds exclusively invest in foreign stocks, mainly from the U.S. These are primarily structured as funds. Remember, the limit of $250,000 does not apply if investors invest via this route. However, as fund-of-funds, they can be expensive. The other option is to invest directly by opening an account with one of the platforms above. This will enable investors to buy individual stocks directly. However, I would not recommend this option for many reasons.

2. Sharp rallies in GameStop, Dogecoin, Bitcoin, etc., have raised concerns of foul play by vested interests (speculators) where a group of investors formed a cartel-like approach to take penny companies to dizzying heights. The saga of GameStop, a loss-making gaming company whose share price zoomed from $19 to $400 only to drop to $50 within a few weeks, can be an essential lesson for investors. Those following social media influencers' advice and stock tips can easily be lured into this "easy money" syndrome and lose their shirt! Hence, investing only in the index via the ETF route is advisable if one opts for the direct mode.

3. Investors should be aware of two distinct but essential variables when investing abroad. The first is the currency risk. The Indian rupee has been performing very well against the USD, posing little currency risk to foreign investors. However, that may not be the case going forward, as emerging markets always face currency risks, and India cannot be an exception. Hence, investing in dollars (equities) can have dual sources of risk, one of which can be the currency risk, while the other is the market risk. In addition, the tax aspects can be a bit complicated. For example, the short-term capital gain is taxed at a slab rate, while

the long-term capital gain is taxed at 20%. The holding period assumption for the long-term is always higher at two years. In other words, a capital gain qualifies as long-term only if held for more than two years. In addition, dividends are taxed, though this can be offset due to double taxation treaties between the two countries. However, the tax part will need consultation from experts.

4. Direct investing requires an investor to open an account with a technology platform. This will need some due diligence as it involves costs like demat, broking, and currency conversion. In addition, the robustness of functionalities offered by the platform is also essential. All this will require careful due diligence before opening the account.

5. Having established the case for investing in foreign stocks, the key question is how much (portfolio allocation) should it be?

Table : 28 How India Benchmark Compares with Others

	3yr (Sep, 2020 - Aug, 2023)			5yr (Sep, 2018 - Aug, 2023)			10yr (Sep, 2013 - Aug, 2023)			15yr (Sep, 2008 - Aug, 2023)		
	Ann. Return	Ann. Risk	Sharpe Ratio	Ann. Return	Ann. Risk	Sharpe Ratio	Ann. Return	Ann. Risk	Sharpe Ratio	Ann. Return	Ann. Risk	Sharpe Ratio
MSCI Emerging Markets	-1.0%	17.9%	-18.8%	1.4%	19.2%	-4.2%	3.4%	17.1%	6.6%	3.0%	21.1%	2.8%
MSCI India	15.0%	16.5%	76.6%	7.7%	21.8%	25.4%	10.7%	19.4%	43.5%	6.2%	26.0%	14.5%
MSCI World	8.9%	17.6%	37.4%	8.9%	18.3%	36.5%	9.9%	14.6%	52.0%	8.1%	16.7%	34.2%
S&P 500	10.5%	17.8%	46.0%	11.1%	18.8%	47.6%	12.8%	14.9%	71.1%	10.9%	16.2%	53.0%
MSCI Europe	8.1%	20.0%	28.8%	5.5%	19.4%	17.2%	5.6%	16.3%	20.6%	4.3%	19.7%	9.8%
Portfolio												
India/World (80/20)	13.8%	15.6%	73.2%	7.9%	19.9%	28.9%	10.5%	17.5%	47.4%	6.5%	23.3%	17.9%
India/World (60/40)	12.6%	15.3%	66.9%	8.2%	18.6%	32.3%	10.4%	15.9%	51.0%	6.9%	20.8%	21.9%
India/World (30/70)	10.8%	15.8%	53.0%	8.5%	17.7%	35.8%	10.1%	14.5%	54.1%	7.5%	18.0%	28.5%

Note: Based on monthly returns. Risk-free rate for Sharpe ratio calculation is the average US 10Y Treasury yield for the respective period. Data upto August 31, 2023 close has been considered.

A look at the performance of MSCI India with other global indices indicates that India outperforms in the short-term and underperforms in the long-term.

We tested three combinations ranging from a 20 percent global share to a 70 percent worldwide share. We found that in each period (3, 5, 10, and 15 years historically), the higher percentage of global stocks improves portfolio performance significantly. While a 70% share of international stocks in an Indian investor portfolio can be mentally unsettling, this study confirms the importance of having foreign stocks in one's portfolio.

In short, investing in foreign markets, especially the U.S., is welcome for investors. It offers good potential for diversifying one's portfolio and hence reduces risks. It enables Indian investors to participate in the rally in global technology and other stocks not listed in India. However, there may be tax implications. From October 1, 2023, individuals investing in foreign stocks, mutual funds, or cryptocurrencies abroad will have to pay a 20% TCS if they spend over a certain amount in a financial year[38].

My take is that a retail investor should invest only via index funds or ETFs, to begin with, and avoid taking direct exposure to equities. Yet, one must tread with caution before taking exposure to overseas equities.

---

38 https://www.livemint.com/money/personal-finance/have-foreign-shares-in-stock-portfolio-new-tax-rule-applying-from-october-1-2023-20-tcs-rule-11695624740284.html

Analysing Stocks-A Suggested Template

(Ground View)

Analysing a stock is like analysing a person. There are too many moving parts, and it is complex. Hence, the profession of research and analysis when it comes to capital markets is always a sought-after profession!

Of course, our opportunity set will be listed companies in India and even here the focus will always be on the stocks that move the index (mainly large caps and to an extent mid-caps). If we believe in the efficient market hypothesis (EMH), then the current market price of a stock is the best reflection of its value since all information is already and instantly embedded in the price. However, in real life, we know that this is not true. There is a huge information gap between the people that run a company and people that invest in that company. Financial information about a company does come to the market at regular intervals but still with a lag and they are mostly backward looking. Hence, the task of an analyst is to use that information and project the future in terms of profitability and cash flows. Based on this, one can use several valuation models to get a fair value of a stock and conclude if it is attractive based on the gap between fair value and the current market price. Sell-side analysts are also trained to provide target prices based on these fair value estimates. However, this exercise at best is a long shot for the future and analysts love to revise their estimates every quarter based on the new flow of information.

While that time-tested model can still be useful in parts, what I am proposing as a template here is a combination of several metrics both quantitative and qualitative. Also, the idea is not to box a company in terms of a target price but measure them on a scale by giving weightage to both quantitative as well as qualitative factors.

Also, the assessment will differ based on whether a stock is a financial stock or non-financial stock. The reason why this distinction is important is that in the case of financial stocks, money is the raw material and hence high debt should be viewed favourably whereas in the case of non-financial stocks it should be viewed unfavourably. Hence, the framework proposed here will be two i.e., For financial stocks (which includes banking and financial services companies) and non-financial stocks.

The framework has four major tracks:

1. **Financial metrics (40% weight):** This includes key aspects like top line (sales) growth, bottom line (net profit) growth, debt to equity ratio, etc. While analysing the metrics for top line and bottom line, we have considered both the short-term and long-term. The idea is to capture the financial performance of the company.
2. **Non-financial metrics (30% weight):** This includes aspects like foreign ownership, CEO tenure, research analysts' coverage, etc. The idea is to analyse qualitative aspects of a company.
3. **Valuation metrics (20% weight):** This includes the most followed P/E ratio, P/B ratio, enterprise value as a % of sales, etc. The aim is to see if a good stock is also available at a good price.
4. **Others (10% weight):** This includes liquidity and beta.

While the broad framework remains the same for both financial and non-financial stocks, we have considered different metrics to measure financial stocks when it comes to financial evaluation.

Figure : 6 Factors (Non-Banking Stocks)

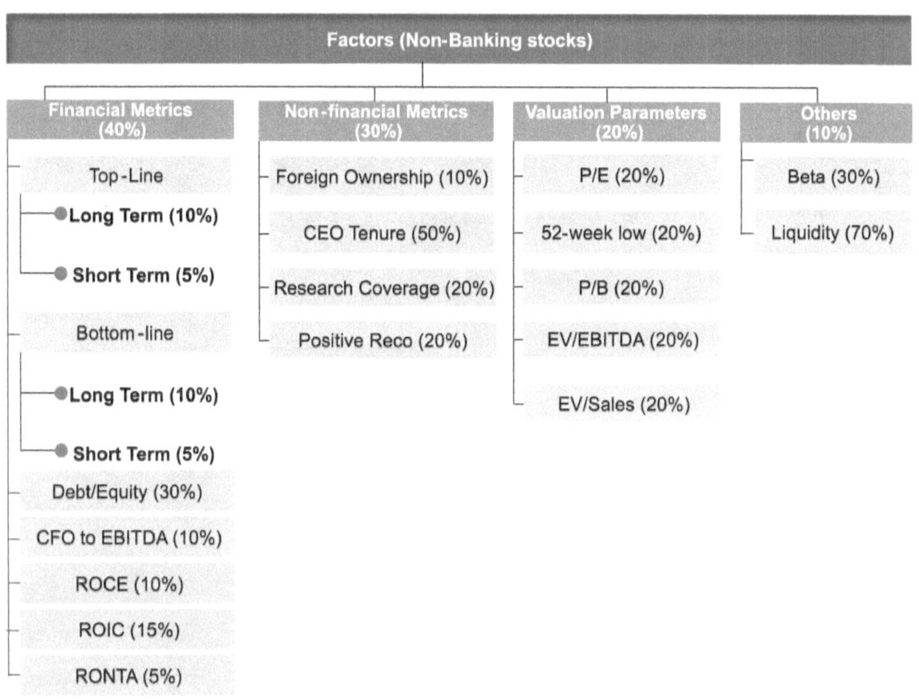

Note: Figures in brackets indicate weights

Figure : 7 Factors (Banking Stocks)

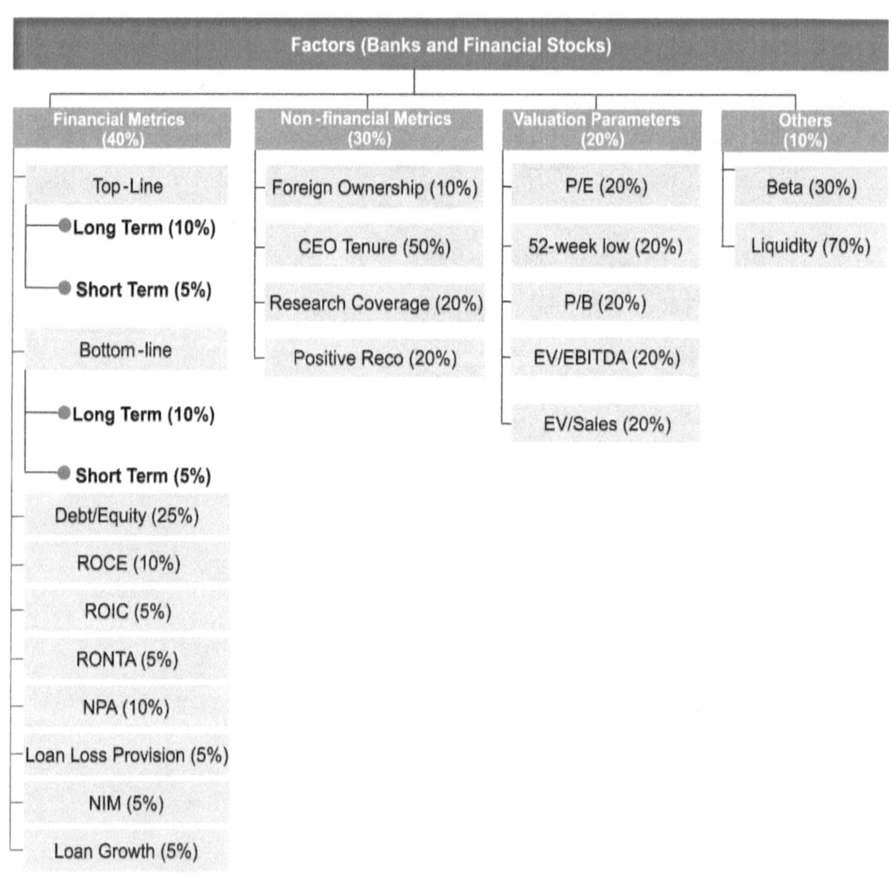

Note: Figures in brackets indicate weights

Methodology:

We define parameters for each metric and score them on a scale of 0-5 based on how they fare.

Category	Financial											
Parameter	Top-Line (5 yr CAGR - Rolling Average)	Top-Line (Past Year)	Bottom-Line (5 yr CAGR - Rolling Average)	Bottom-Line (Past Year)	D/E	ROCE	ROIC	RONTA	NPA Ratio	Loan Loss Provision	Net Interest Margin	Loan Growth
Parameter Weight	10%	5%	10%	5%	25%	10%	5%	5%	10%	5%	5%	5%
Blue=1, Green =5	5%	5%	5%	5%	0.2	5%	5%	1%	1%	1%	1%	5%
Blue=2, Green =4	10%	10%	10%	10%	0.5	7%	7%	2%	2%	2%	2%	10%
Blue=3, Green =3	15%	15%	15%	15%	0.7	10%	10%	3%	3%	3%	3%	15%
Blue=4, Green =2	20%	20%	20%	20%	1.0	12%	12%	4%	4%	4%	4%	17%
Blue=5, Green =1	25%	25%	25%	25%	2.0	15%	15%	5%	5%	5%	5%	20%

For example, if the long-term top line growth is 5% or lower, it scores 1, whereas if the growth exceeds 25%, it will score five. Since this is for financial stocks, the top line would mean revenues. Also, for financial stocks, the higher the debt-equity ratio, the higher the score.

In all, we have considered 23 parameters and provided the formula and rationale for choosing them. The flow chart provides the drill down including the weights that should be applied to get the overall score.

A word about qualitative parameters can be in order here. By nature, qualitative parameters are not easily quantifiable and hence many analysts will ignore them. However, if we can succeed in identifying enough qualitative parameters that can be quantified in some way, it will go a long way in deciphering investment opportunities. A good example can be CEO tenure. Leadership shapes the fortunes of a company, and hence the tenure of a CEO can be a good gauge. The Indian landscape is bound with CEO stories, both success and failures. The longer a CEO stewards a company's ship, the better it is as it provides strategic continuance of the business plan. Deepak Parekh, who steered the HDFC ship for a very long-time, is a classic example.

Table : 29 Metrics

Metric	Financial Stocks	Non-Financial Stocks	Formula	Rationale
Top Line Growth-Long-term	Yes	Yes	5-year rolling average growth CAGR	To assess the long-term growth
Top Line Growth-Short-term	Yes	Yes	1-year rolling average	To assess the short-term growth
Bottom line - Long term	Yes	Yes	5-year rolling average growth CAGR	To assess the long-term growth
Bottom line - Short term	Yes	Yes	1-year rolling average	To assess the short-term growth
Debt to Equity	Yes	Yes	Total Debt/Total Equity	To assess the leverage.
Cash flow to Ebitda	No	Yes	CFO/EBITDA	To assess whether profits translate to cash flows. A good measure to check accounting manupulation
Return on Capital Employed	Yes	Yes	Net Income/(Total Assets-Current Liabilities)	To understand capital productivity
Return on Invested Capital	Yes	Yes	Net Income/(Total Equity+LT Debt)	Invested capital is the amount of capital that is circulating in the business and is a sub-set of total capital
Return on Net Tangible Assets	Yes	Yes	RONTA=Net Income/((Total Assets-Goodwill))	Stripping goodwill to see the real return on assets
Non-Performing Assets	Yes	No	Non-Performing Assets/Total Loans	To assess the impact of bad loans
Loan Loss Provision	Yes	No	Loan Loss % as Provision of Total Loans	To see how much the bank has provided agains loan losses
Net Interest Margin	Yes	No	(Interest Income-Interest Expenses)/Total Assets	To assess the margin a bank makes while lending money
Loan Growth	Yes	No	5-year rolling average growth CAGR	To assess the growth in loans for banks
Foreing Ownership	Yes	Yes	% shares held by foreigners	To assess the extent of foreing holdings
CEO Tenure	Yes	Yes	No of years the incumbant CEO is in the position	To assess leadership continuity
Research Coverage	Yes	Yes	No of analysts covering a particular stock	To assess the extent of research coverage by analysts
Positive Recommendation	Yes	Yes	(Buys+Strong Buys)/Total Recommendation	To assess how many recommendations fall into buys and strong buys
Price to Earnings ratio	Yes	Yes	Price/Earnings (current)	To assess how expensive or cheap a stock is
Distance from 52-week low	Yes	Yes	Current market price/52-week low price	To assess how far is the current market price relative to 52-week low
Price to Book Value	Yes	Yes	Price/Book value (current)	To assess how expensive or cheap a stock is
Enterprise Value to EBITDA	Yes	Yes	Enterprise Value/EBITDA	To evaluate company's value and performance
Enterprise Value to Sales	Yes	Yes	Enterprise Value/Sales	To evaluate company's value and performance
Beta	Yes	Yes	2-year average Beta	To assess how closely the stock price is correlated to overall market
Liquidity	Yes	Yes	Average Daily Traded Value - 52 Weeks	To assess how liquid a stock is

Regarding actioning the scores, investors can do well to form portfolios of stocks with high scores and regularly prune the list as it is quite possible that companies may gyrate within the band and what was considered good sometime back may have deteriorated and hence would warrant exclusion and vice versa.

Score Calculation-Example-Cipla

Table : 30 Score Calculation-Cipla

Stock						
Metric	Result	Score	Group Weight	Final Score	Group Weight	Final Score (Group Weighted)
Top Line Growth-Long-term	8%	1	10%	0.10		
Top Line Growth-Short-term	13%	2	5%	0.10		
Bottom line – Long term	15%	2	10%	0.20		
Bottom line – Short term	47%	5	5%	0.25		
Debt to Equity	2%	5	30%	1.50		
Cash flow to Ebitda	66%	3	10%	0.30		
Return on Capital Employed	19%	2	10%	0.20		
Return on Invested Capital	15%	3	15%	0.45		
Return on Net Tangible Assets	12%	1	5%	0.05		
Total Score			100%	**3.15**	**40%**	1.26
Foreing Ownership	15%	2	10%	0.20		
CEO Tenure	8	4	50%	2.00		
Research Coverage	30	5	20%	1.00		
Positive Recommendation	63%	3	20%	0.60		
Total Score			100%	**3.80**	**30%**	1.14
Price to Earnings ratio	29	4	20%	0.80		
Distance from 52-week low	49%	2	20%	0.40		
Price to Book Value	5	1	20%	0.20		
Enterprise Value to EBITDA	18	2	20%	0.40		
Enterprise Value to Sales	4	1	20%	0.20		
Total Score			100%	**2.00**	**20%**	0.4
Beta	0.3	5	30%	1.50		
Liquidity	50%	3	70%	2.10		
Total Score			100%	**3.60**	**10%**	**0.36**
Note: Calculations as of June 2024						3.16

As we can see from the example of Cipla, a listed pharmaceutical stock, we arrive at a total score of 3.16 on a scale of 0-5. The upside to the score mainly stems from a recent surge in profits, low debt, long CEO tenure, good research coverage by analysts, attractive price-to-earnings ratio, and low beta. However, the stock scores poorly on many parameters including top line growth (both long-term and short-term), bottom-line growth (long-term), return on capital employed, return on assets, foreign ownership, and some valuation parameters.

Table : 31 Final List

S. No.	Score Above 3.8	Score between 3.5 to 3.8	Score between 3.0 to 3.5	Score between 2.5 to 3	Score between 2 to 2.5	Score below 2
1		Berger Paints India Ltd	Triveni Turbine Ltd	Godawari Power and Ispat Ltd	UltraTech Cement Ltd	Thermax Limited
2		Marico Ltd	Safari Industries (India) Ltd	Intellect Design Arena Ltd	HCL Technologies Ltd	Bharat Dynamics Ltd
3			Indiamart Intermesh Ltd	KNR Constructions Ltd	KRBL Ltd	CCL Products (India) Ltd
4			Eicher Motors Ltd	Usha Martin Ltd	Linde India Ltd	India Motor Parts & Accessories Ltd
5			PI Industries Ltd	Emami Ltd	Maharashtra Seamless Ltd	Engineers India Ltd
6			CreditAccess Grameen Ltd	Torrent Pharmaceuticals Ltd	Garden Reach Shipbuilders & Engineers Ltd	Adani Power Ltd
7			Supreme Industries Ltd	Page Industries Ltd	Aryaman Financial Services Ltd	Salzer Electronics Ltd
8			Cera Sanitaryware Ltd	Indian Energy Exchange Ltd	Astrazeneca Pharma India Ltd	Adani Ports and Special Economic Zone Ltd
9			AU Small Finance Bank Ltd	Stylam Industries Ltd	BSE Ltd	Whirlpool of India Ltd
10			Garware Technical Fibres Ltd	Bls International Services Ltd	RHI Magnesita India Ltd	Chennai Petroleum Corporation Ltd

After analysing nearly 600 stocks, we can see how they stack up. Given the diversity of metrics, it is not surprising that only very few made it to high scores of above 3.5 on a scale of 0-5. They are a mix of large cap, mid cap, and small-cap. It is important to note that this list will evolve upon updating, though it is unlikely that a stock will move from good to poor. The descent or ascent in score will be gradual, but it will be useful to monitor. One can access this Excel file here[39].

---

39 https://docs.google.com/spreadsheets/d/1eeMGJnqY8KlmHk-41yqzgrImaT idgO9S/edit?usp=sharing&ouid=112172161087954577165&rtpof=true&sd=true

Index Stories

01

Introduction

"Nifty 50 breached 21,000 in a historic high" goes the headline!

Good or bad, stock market stories always revolve around the index, be it Nifty 50 or Sensex. The role of the index goes beyond creating daily headlines. Producing and maintaining an index has become a huge industry for capital market players, especially fund managers and index providers. In simple terms, an index represents the performance of a group of stocks based on certain criteria. The criteria could be the largest stocks (large cap) or dividend yield or the pharma sector, to name a few.

The stock market exhibits a skew when it comes to underlying stocks, with large companies enjoying a disproportionate share of the total. For example, large cap accounts for nearly 70% of the total market cap while it represents only 2% of total stocks, whereas small-cap accounts for 95% of total stocks but only 15% of total market cap. Even more starkly, from a median perspective, the small-cap median market cap at Rs. 50 crore is just 0.05% of the large cap median market cap. This skew matters greatly in index construction. While it is possible to include all 100 stocks in an index (Nifty 100), small-cap indices often consider only the top 250 stocks out of nearly 5,000 small-cap stocks.

Table : 32 Stock Category

Stock Category	No of Stocks	Total Market Cap (INR Cr)	Median Market Cap (INR Cr)
Large Cap	100	1,86,65,635	1,02,346
Mid Cap	150	45,23,999	27,862
Small Cap	4813	41,41,338	49
Total	5063	2,73,30,972	1,30,257
Source: National Stock Exchange			

Source: National Stock Exchange, Data as of June 30 2023

Another interesting dimension is the user side of the index, primarily mutual funds. Data from the Association of Mutual Funds of India (AMFI) shows that there are 1,350 mutual funds spread across several types, of which equity-oriented funds (42%) and debt-oriented funds (28%) comprise the bulk. A growing but significant category falls under "Other schemes," mainly comprising index funds and Exchange Traded Funds (ETFs).

Table : 33 Indian Mutual Funds

Scheme	No of funds	AUM (INR Cr.)	Share
Growth/Equity Oriented Schemes	418	20,33,407	42%
Income/Debt Oriented Schemes	314	13,57,809	28%
Other Schemes	435	8,22,934	17%
Hybrid Schemes	146	6,23,809	13%
Solution Oriented Schemes	37	40,091	1%
Total	1350	48,78,050	100%
Source: AMFI			

A broad appreciation of the total market size and the number of mutual funds provides the basis for understanding the index world. Indexing essentially involves slicing and dicing within a defined universe. For instance, Nifty indices, launched and maintained by the National Stock Exchange, cover around 750 stocks, with the top 50 designated as Nifty 50 and the top 100 as Nifty 100. Index providers create these segments in the hope that funds will eventually adopt them as benchmarks.

Broad Market Indices

Figure : 8 Nifty Indices

Broad Indices				Stock Group	Cap-based indices				
Nifty 100	Nifty 200	Nifty 500	Nifty Total Market	1-50	Nifty Large Mid Cap 250		Nifty 50		
Nifty 100	Nifty 200	Nifty 500	Nifty Total Market	51 - 100	Nifty Large Mid Cap 250		Nifty Next 50		
	Nifty 200	Nifty 500	Nifty Total Market	101 - 150	Nifty Large Mid Cap 250	Nifty Mid Small Cap 400	Nifty Mid Cap 150	Nifty Mid Cap 100	Nifty Mid Cap 50
	Nifty 200	Nifty 500	Nifty Total Market	151 - 50	Nifty Large Mid Cap 250	Nifty Mid Small Cap 400	Nifty Mid Cap 150	Nifty Mid Cap 100	Nifty Mid Cap 50
		Nifty 500	Nifty Total Market	201 - 250	Nifty Large Mid Cap 250	Nifty Mid Small Cap 400	Nifty Mid Cap 150	Nifty Mid Cap 100	
		Nifty 500	Nifty Total Market	251 - 50		Nifty Mid Small Cap 400	Nifty SmallCap 250	Nifty Small Cap 100	Nifty Small Cap 50
		Nifty 500	Nifty Total Market	301 - 350		Nifty Mid Small Cap 400	Nifty SmallCap 250	Nifty Small Cap 100	
		Nifty 500	Nifty Total Market	351 - 500		Nifty Mid Small Cap 400	Nifty SmallCap 250		
			Nifty Total Market	501 - 750			Nifty Microcap 250		

Large Cap

Mid Cap

Small Cap

Microcap

The two main providers of indices in India happen to be the National Stock Exchange (through NSE Indices Limited) and the Bombay Stock Exchange (through S&P). The NSE has a 75% market share in terms of both the number of indices adopted by fund managers and the consequent share of assets under management. Since indices are used as benchmarks for both active and passive management of funds, they become important from several angles. Some of these are explained here:

1. **Alpha Computation:** The main marketing pitch of active fund managers is alpha generation, which is technically defined as the excess return over the stated benchmark. Hence, the choice of index is critical and should be aligned with the overall objective of the fund. For example, a large-cap fund cannot have a large and mid-cap benchmark, and vice versa. Appropriateness of the benchmark can be vital to attract institutional investors who have a sophisticated understanding of the investment industry.

2. **Price vs. Total Return:** Initially, index launches were mainly based on price returns that ignored dividends. However, this shortcoming has been addressed with the launch of the total return index, which now accounts for dividends. Hence, we can make an apples-to-apples comparison between fund managers and benchmarks.

3. **Providers:** As mentioned earlier, the NSE has a lion's share when it comes to index adoption by fund managers (75%). When choosing between NSE and BSE (S&P) for selecting the benchmark index, one should carefully examine the methodology before deciding.

4. **Regular vs. Direct:** Mutual fund purchasing can be done either directly or through distributors. The latter is termed as regular plans while the former is termed as direct plans. Direct plans

will not have costs associated with distributors, and hence, the performance of direct plans will be superior to regular plans. Given that both will have the same benchmarks, it is no wonder that the alpha generated for direct plans will be higher compared to regular plans.

5. **Tracking Error:** This simply measures the deviation a fund manager takes from the stated benchmark constituents to generate more alpha. While that is the intention, it can cut both ways if the stock selection is poor, which can result in negative alpha. Needless to say, index funds or ETFs will have the lowest tracking error as they are designed to closely match the index. The higher the tracking error for a fund, the higher the risk.

Case Study: Large Cap

The role of the index can best be explained by taking a deeper look at a subset of equity indices. Among the equity categories, the large-cap is the largest in terms of assets under management. Ignoring funds with less than one year of track record, we can count 30 large-cap equity mutual funds managing Rs.286,914 crores. The majority (66%) of the funds are benchmarked to the Nifty 100 Total Return index, while the rest are benchmarked to the S&P BSE 100 Total Return index. It is interesting to note that while both indices take the top 100 companies by market cap, small differences in the list of constituents of these indices produce differences in terms of their performance. The return across time periods (1 year, three years and 5 years) was lower for the S&P BSE 100 TR index compared to the Nifty 100, due to which the alpha generated using the S&P BSE index is lower than the Nifty 100 TR index. Hence, the choice of the appropriate index to benchmark becomes crucial. As a side note, it can also be observed that while active fund managers were successful in generating good alpha in the shorter term (1 year), alpha generated for longer periods came down (for 3 years) and completely vanished for 5 years! The problem is further exacerbated by the regular vs direct investing approach. As explained earlier, regular option performance will invariably be lower than direct due to distributor fees charged.

Table : 34 Large Cap Benchmarks

	No. of Funds	AuM (INR Cr.)	Weighted Alpha - Regular (%)			Weighted Alpha - Direct (%)		
			1 Yr	3 Yrs	5 Yrs	1 Yr	3 Yrs	5 Yrs
NIFTY 100 Total Return Index	19	164,587	3.7	1.6	0.0	4.6	2.6	0.9
S&P BSE 100 Total Return Index	11	122,327	0.2	-1.8	-1.0	1.2	-0.7	0.1
Total	30	286,914						
Note: At least 80% investment in large cap stocks								

In conclusion, we can say that the index world may look unassuming but can be hugely important. Since 1996, NSE has launched over 100 indices spanning four main segments i.e., the broad market indices, sector indices, thematic indices, and strategy indices. A good example would be "Nifty 30 Quality index" comprising 30 best Indian companies evaluated across three important parameters i.e., Return on Equity (RoE), Debt to Equity ratio (D/E), and net income growth.

Given the increasing options facing fund managers, it is important to choose appropriate indices, which can affect alpha generation by fund managers. Managers struggling to generate alpha must have taken higher tracking errors than otherwise. Also, investors should appreciate the subtle but critical difference between price returns and total returns, as well as regular vs. direct options. Benchmarks are central to all such studies and evaluation and hence the focus.

02

Nifty-Fifty Survivors

What's so special about these companies?

Table : 35 Nifty Survivors

Reliance Industries	HDFC Bank	Hindustan Unilever
ITC	SBI	Tata Motors
Tata Steel	Hindalco	L&T

They all survived the index ("Nifty") since the founding of the Nifty index in 1996 until June 5, 2024, the date of data collection. Not a small feat by any means!

Nifty, as an index, is comprised of 50 leading stocks. But the index committee at National Stock Exchange (NSE) does carry out periodic changes (quarterly or more) whereby stocks are excluded and included based on a variety of criteria including liquidity, performance, etc. Since 1996 when the Nifty was constituted and till June 2024, over 130 companies have participated in this ritual of getting in and getting out. (look at the visual description in the appendix).

While nine companies have survived the Nifty since its inception, 52 companies got axed out at some stage during the past 15 years or other due to various reasons, including poor performance, mergers, delisting, liquidity, etc.

Getting included in the index is considered a feather in the cap for a company. Well-governed companies work for such accreditation since inclusion attracts institutional investors (domestic and foreign) and improves the liquidity and profile of the stock. More important than inclusion is the ability to stay put in the index without being axed. Surviving the Nifty becomes important in that context since companies should continuously qualify under various parameters to be part of the index.

The "survivors" averaged an annualised return of 14.3% during these long years of stay in the Nifty compared to Nifty's 11.3% annualised return. HDFC Bank topped the list with a 24.1% annualised return, followed by Reliance Industries (19.1%) and L&T (16.9%). The lowest in the pack was Hindalco at 8.2%. They all enjoyed good daily liquidity and have consistently produced excellent top line and bottom-line growth.

Figure : 9 Nifty Survivors

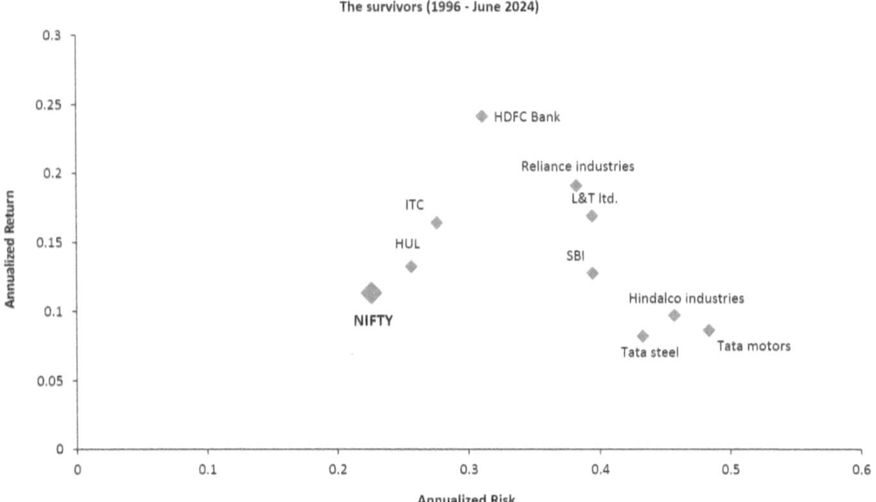

The power of compounding is so astounding that an investment of Rs. 10,000 in HDFC Bank in 1996 would be worth Rs. 44 lakhs as of June 2024, while the same amount invested in the Nifty index would be worth only Rs. 2,05,242. In contrast, an investment in Hindalco would be worth only Rs. 92,346. However, this does not imply that investing solely in one or two companies is advisable, as it diminishes the benefits of diversification.

Table : 36 Nifty Survivors Performance

Company	Annualized return	Market value (INR) of Rs. 10,000 invested in 1996
Reliance industries	19%	13,80,270
HDFC Bank	24%	44,11,490
HUL	13%	3,32,105
ITC	16%	7,26,330
SBI	13%	2,94,312
Tata motors	9%	1,03,150
Tata steel	10%	1,36,524
Hindalco industries	8%	92,346
L&T ltd.	17%	8,18,051
Nifty	11%	205,242
Data: 1996-2024		

The "non-survivors" (52 companies in total) averaged an annualised return of 5.8%.

We can confidently say that investing in the Nifty can be a good idea, as it comprises a diversified basket of companies drawn from various sectors, generally including firms with market leadership and liquidity. However, cherry-picking Nifty "survivors" can be an even better strategy!

The key here is to monitor a company's ability to remain in the Nifty for a substantial period (like 15 years), during which it becomes a strong candidate for inclusion in one's portfolio until it is eventually removed from the Nifty for any reason. All nine stocks that have survived in the Nifty to date qualify for portfolio inclusion. Additionally, eleven other stocks have also survived in the Nifty for over 15 years. A quick evaluation of the performance of these long-term survivors indicates that their performance generally exceeds that of a straightforward investment in the Nifty.

03

Sensex Scenarios

Now that the Sensex has reached its all-time high (74,245 – as of Q1 2024) despite challenging global macros, there are many prophecies on when it would cross 100,000. Of course, the number 100,000 is sensational and represents a milestone for the index and the Indian stock market. Hence, the interest to know more about this. Before we delve into the forecast, let us chronicle the Sensex journey a bit.

Figure : 10 Sensex (1991-2024)

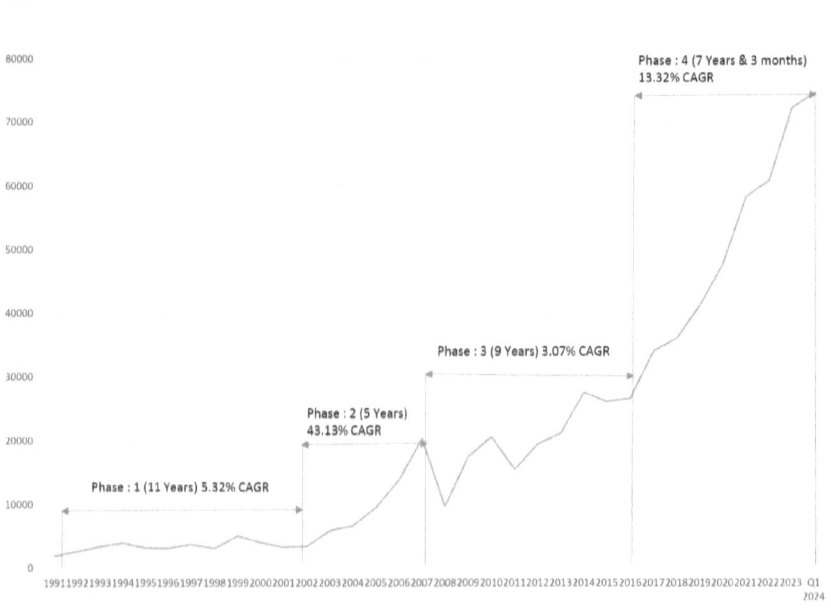

Source: Refinitiv

In its long history since 1991, the Sensex has had four distinct phases.

Phase 1: This was the period from 1991 to 2002 (11 years) when it had only a 5.3% annualised growth for 11 years. During this period, it limped to 3,377 from 1,909.

Phase 2: This was the 5-year period between 2002 and 2007 when it catapulted at an annualised clip of 43.1%, reaching 20,000.

Phase 3: The third phase was from 2007 to 2016 (9 years) when it grew only by 3.1% annualised, limping to 26,000.

Phase 4: The fourth phase is when it touched the current level of 73,651, a period between 2016 and Q1 2024 (7 years), growing at an annualised clip of 13.3%.

Observers can easily notice the difficulty already in terms of charting a future course. Will the next five or ten years resemble the first phase or the fourth phase?

There are many scenarios possible, but I will restrict it to just three. A base scenario where Sensex's annualised growth will be its long-term growth since 1991, i.e., 13.7% from the closing value of December 31, 2023. An optimistic scenario would be an annualised growth of 17%, while a pessimistic scenario would be a growth of 5% annualised. We can now map various milestones like 100,000 or 500,000 or even 1 million through these three scenarios. The table below presents the year by which these milestones would be achieved and the number of years of waiting (from 2023) under the three scenarios.

Table : 37 Sensex Projections

Annualized Returns				Annualized Returns			
Sensex	5.0%	13.7%	17.0%	Sensex	5.0%	13.7%	17.0%
100,000	2030	2026	2026	100,000	7	3	3
500,000	2063	2039	2036	500,000	40	16	13
10,00,000	2077	2044	2040	10,00,000	54	21	17

The 100,000 milestone can be achieved in 2026 under the optimistic case and in 2030 under the pessimistic case.

The 500,000 milestone can be achieved in the year 2036 under the optimistic case and in 2063 under the pessimistic case.

The 1 million mark can be achieved in 2040 under the optimistic case and in 2077 under the pessimistic case.

Now, the billion-dollar question is which path among the three is most likely. Of course, a safe bet would be to anchor on the base case. However, history never repeats but only rhymes. The index performance is a product of two factors: earnings growth and valuation (P/E). Historically, during the last 10 years, the annualised earnings growth averaged 10.4%, and during the last 15 years, it averaged 9.8%. Countries do break out into high growth phases based on reform initiatives, foreign investment interest, and broader economic prospects and growth. If economic growth can be combined with productivity growth (thanks to technology and digitisation with youth adoption), then higher earnings growth of say 13% or 15% is fathomable.

On the valuation side, the 10-year historical P/E (trailing) averaged 24.6, while the 15-year period averaged 23.0. The current P/E for the Sensex (as of December 2023) is around 22.5, a tad below the average. P/E expansion happens when the outlook for the country is positive and vice versa. Here are the combinations of various earnings growth scenarios and the attendant P/E ratios:

If Sensex reaches 150,000 by 2028 where earnings growth is at, say, 9.8%, then the P/E ratio will shoot up to 29.3 from the present 22.5. Alternatively, if the P/E ratio drops to, say, 17.3, then Sensex needs an annualised earnings growth of 22% to touch the magical 150,000. A middle path looks more feasible where earnings growth records an annualised growth of 15.9%, while the P/E ratio softens to 22.4 (close to the 15-year average of 23.0) to hit the 150,000 milestone.

As much as earnings are the prime driver of the market, it is also useful to look at the valuation (P/E) ratio to gauge the excess in the market. To do that, we constructed the historical evolution of the Sensex P/E ratio and applied standard deviation bands where it can be +/ − 1 or +/ − 2 standard deviations from the mean. We also computed the prospective 3-year and 5-year average return for each of these P/E bands historically. Needless to say, prospective return improves when the P/E band is below the average and vice versa.

In the past, Sensex never broke beyond +/ − 2 standard deviations. However, the sharp rise in the index breached that on the plus side, meaning it went above +2 standard deviations. Historical analysis shows that at +2 standard deviations, the prospective return diminishes and vice versa.

Table : 38 Return vs Risk

PE Bands	3yr CAGR, average	5yr CAGR, average	Number of trading days
+2sd to +1sd	8.22%	7.84%	481
+1sd to Avg.	9.42%	9.25%	1,902
Avg. to -1sd	13.11%	11.67%	1,957
-1sd to -2sd	21.82%	11.67%	605

The P/E band analysis shows that the Sensex P/E hovered most of the time within the +/ − 1 standard deviation and very little time in the +1 to +2 standard deviation range. So going forward, this should be the case where P/E would fall back to its preferred zone of +/ − 1 standard deviation. However, if it persists above two standard deviations, then the prospective 5-year annualised return for Sensex can be around 2.8%.

Patience is a virtue in the stock market while volatility can be a huge distraction. At 74,245, Sensex may appear highly priced and expensive, which it is. However, even for someone entering at this level, if they can stay the course for the next 3 years (to experience 100,000 Sensex) or 16 years (to experience 500,000 Sensex) or 21 years (to experience 1 million Sensex), the payoffs are good. For a 29-year-old person, experiencing a Sensex million at age 50 is not a bad deal though!

04

Nifty Top 10 – 2032

Though the Nifty index comprises 50 stocks, the top 10 enjoy a lion's share. In 2012, the top 10 constituted nearly 53% of the index (in terms of market capitalisation), while in 2022, it comprised 45%.

Obviously, the performance of the Nifty itself will be impacted by who is on this coveted top 10 list, and funds flow from institutions (both domestic and foreign) that track this index will also be skewed towards these top 10 companies. Hence, the curiosity to study this in greater detail and to try and figure how this top 10 list will look like, say, in 2032! Also, a look from 1996 to 2022 for Nifty 50 shows that more than 130 companies have been part of Nifty 50 with an average age of 10 years. In other words, if a company has been in the Nifty 50 index for more than 10 years, its probability to continue in the Nifty 50 reduces. In this context, the race to the top 10 gets even more interesting.

Back in 2012, Reliance was the top company in Nifty followed by TCS and ONGC. Fast forward to 2022, the coveted 3rd slot has been taken up by HDFC Bank with ONGC pushed to the 25th spot while Reliance managed to remain in the same 1st spot.

However, the attrition rate of the top 10 between 2012 and 2022 has been 40% in that only six of the top 10 in 2012 made it to 2022. ONGC, Coal India, ITC, and NTPC dropped out of the 2022 top 10 list. Hindustan Unilever, Bharti Airtel, Bajaj Finance, and HDFC Ltd (now merged with HDFC Bank) replaced them in 2022.

Reliance maintaining its top position from 2012 to 2022 is impressive as its market cap compounded at nearly 14% over the same period. While it had a market cap of just $51 billion in 2012, it jumped to $198 billion by 2022, maintaining its reputation as the most valuable company in Nifty 50. The saga of HDFC Bank was even more impressive. Back in 2012, it was in the 7th position with a market cap of $28 billion. It then moved four places up to become the 3rd most valuable company in 2022, with its market cap compounded at a rate of 7.9%. Hindustan Unilever has moved astonishingly from 12th position in 2012 to 4th position in 2022.

While it is useful to know changes that happened in the top 10 coveted list during the last 10 years, it can be challenging to figure out how this list will look in 2032. Current Nifty 50 stocks have grown at a good pace during the past decade. The CAGR among them ranged from 26% (Bajaj Finance) to a negative 9% (Coal India). The positive performers (companies with positive CAGR in market cap) outnumbered negative performers by 44:4. In other words, 44 companies enjoyed growth during the last 10 years, while 4 suffered a negative growth rate. Two companies – HDFC Life Insurance and SBI Life Insurance – were listed in 2017 and were not considered in the calculation.

Going forward, I believe such high growth rates are quite possible for a market like India, which is going to drive global growth along with China. According to BlackRock's long-term capital market expectations, the long-term equity returns for the next 20 years will be nearly the same as witnessed in the last 30 years. While U.S. and European equities clocked 9.6% and 3.6% annualised growth in the last 30 years, they are expected to clock a growth of 8-9% in the next 20 years. On the bonds side, the next 20 years will produce a return ranging from 3-4%.

Hence, it may be prudent to assume that going forward, the CAGR for Nifty 50 companies could be the same as what it enjoyed during the last 10 years (excluding negative growth companies). While this may sound ambitious, in my view, it is more realistic as India is projected to be one of the fastest-growing economies in the next decade. Given this approach, here is the list of the top 10 Nifty 50 companies by 2032.

Table : 39 Nifty Top 10-2022

Rank	Stock Name	Sector	"M.Cap (USD Bn)"	P/E
1	Reliance	Energy	197.6	29.0
2	TCS	IT	135.0	36.1
3	HDFC Bank	BFSI	97.2	21.5
4	HUL	FMCG	77.8	54.2
5	ICICI Bank	BFSI	73.7	20.6
6	Infosys	IT	72.8	36.4
7	SBI Bank	BFSI	58.1	12.5
8	Bharti Airtel	Telecomm	56.5	99.0
9	Bajaj Finance	BFSI	54.4	62.7
10	HDFC Ltd	BFSI	51.0	19.3
	TOTAL		874.0	
	Nifty 50		1,647.5	
	Top 10 Stocks as a % of total		45%	

Table : 40 Nifty Top 10-2032

Rank	Stock Name	Sector	"M.Cap (USD Bn)"	"Implied CAGR (2023 Start - 2033 End)"
1	Reliance	Energy	761.2	14%
2	Bajaj Finance	BFSI	537.8	26%
3	TCS	IT	379.4	11%
4	HDFC Bank	BFSI	335.9	13%
5	Hind Unilever	FMCG	270.8	13%
6	ICICI Bank	BFSI	235.3	12%
7	Asian Paints	Construction	216.7	19%
8	Kotak Mahindra	BFSI	216.3	17%
9	Bajaj Finserv	BFSI	203.3	20%
10	Infosys	IT	193.2	10%
	TOTAL		3,349.9	
	Nifty 50		15,977	
	Top 10 Stocks as a % of total		21%	

Source: Refinitiv

7 out of 2022 top 10 make it to 2032, with Reliance remaining in the 1st position since 2012. Bajaj Finance moves from the 9th position to become the second valuable Nifty 50 stock, improving its market cap from $54 billion to an astonishing $538 billion. TCS would have improved its market cap from $135 billion to $379 billion, implying

a CAGR of 11%. HDFC Bank, HUL, and ICICI would have been downgraded by one position to 4th, 5th, and 6th place. Kotak Bank, Asian Paints, and Bajaj Finserv enter the top 10 league from 12th, 13th and 14th position to 8th, 7th, and 9th position, and Infosys moves to the 10th position from 8th position.

Notable exclusions in 2032 from the top 10 include SBI, Bharti Airtel, and HDFC Ltd (now merged with HDFC Bank). SBI moves to the 15th position from the 7th position, while HDFC Ltd will move out post its merger with HDFC Bank, and Bharti Airtel moves from 8th to 12th position.

Figure : 11 Sector Top 10

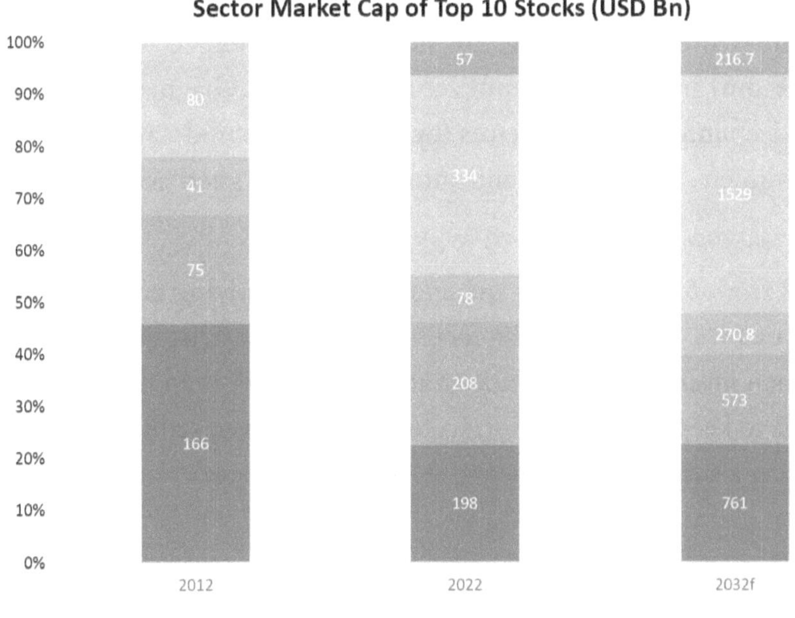

While energy dominated the scene in 2012, it has halved in share by 2032 as ONGC, Coal India, and NTPC exit the top 10 list. BFSI has gained more than double its 2012 proportion (thanks to Bajaj Finance).

IT has its sector weight managed at the same proportion since 2012 whereas the FMCG sector has lost its weight from 11% to 8%. The most important ascent is noticed in Telecommunication as Bharti Airtel had entered the top 10 list. There will be an inclusion of the construction sector in 2032 as Asian Paints enters the top 10 league.

The jostling for space in the top 10 can be important to make investment decisions. Firstly, it will have a huge impact on the index per se. If we are investing in ETFs, we will mostly track the index, which is heavily skewed in favour of the top 10. Index investors will also navigate this process of churning, given the shifts in weights. Index realignment happens over time, and hence, investors in ETFs will underperform active managers, especially in emerging markets like India, where the ability to add alpha is very high.

If one is into stock picking, this study shows sectors to avoid (oil and gas, Telecom) and sectors to embrace (pharma, IT). One may even want to dive deep into attractive sectors (by dwelling into mid-caps) to bet on future winners. Automobiles and auto ancillary are good examples.

The market cap of Nifty 50 is likely to increase to, say, $8.5 trillion in 2032 from $1.6 trillion at the end of 2022, implying an annualised growth of 18%. However, if the focus is on the top 10 list likely to be in 2032, then investment performance should be better than that. What is crucial is to keep an eye on this transformation, as even stable companies can spring a surprise on the negative side at a moment's notice.

Managing Risk & Volatility

01

Introduction

There is not one year that passes by without any crisis. Some are big and tectonic in nature (like the Global financial crisis in 2008 and COVID-19), while others have a limited but powerful impact, like the Asian Financial crisis. When a macro crisis hits the economy, it is natural that companies' risk management systems are tested to the core. However, a company's risk management architecture can also be tested without a macro crisis background. This can be simply due to weak risk management systems and processes in the company. History is replete with several company-specific examples of financial risk management crises, starting from the Bankers Trust derivatives sales scandal in 1994 to the LTCM hedge fund failure in 1998 to the Libor fixing scandal in 2012. Sometimes, the lines can be blurred between a general disaster and a company failure. For e.g., the 2011 Fukushima nuclear accident can be viewed as a market disaster, while it can also be viewed as a risk management failure of Tokyo Electric Power Co.

As finance professionals and CEOs, most of us are trained to focus on performance and results. However, extracting performance and showing results is also concomitant with assuming risk. Return and risk are two sides of the same coin. If we do not have our eyes on risk, we will not be able to distinguish between risks that one can take on a regular basis, risks that one can take occasionally and risks that one should avoid altogether. Without the ability to discriminate in this fashion, focusing purely on performance and results can either be short-term or produce side effects that can sink the whole ship.

From a business enterprise point of view, the higher the risk in a proposition, the higher the return. However, while the return comes from the core business environment, risks can emanate from various sources. A company can face "financial risks" like market risks (interest rates, exchange rates, and stock prices), credit risk and liquidity risk. It does not stop here. The company also faces "non-financial" risks, which can be hard to quantify. Some examples of this would be operations, accounting, taxes, legal, regulations, and finally, model risks. A company stands in the middle between these financial and non-financial risks. Therefore, the main challenge for a financial risk manager is to recognise, measure and manage these risks. Depending on the business in consideration, certain risks may be closer to heart than others. For e.g., a multinational Agribusiness that procures raw materials from different countries and sells the final product in various countries will have currency risk at the heart of its operations. Since the operations are global, it will encounter commodity price risk, foreign exchange risk, equity market risk, and interest rate risk, not to mention credit risk (as its customers tend to purchase on credit) and operational risk where weather-related risk can play havoc. Another challenge is to factor in risks resulting from environmental, social, and governance factors, which are famously termed ESG risks.

Once we capture relevant risks, the next challenge is to quantify or measure them. Fortunately, several readymade tools are available for financial risk managers to use in this sphere. The most practised is the Value at Risk (VaR), which estimates the minimum loss that a party would expect with a given probability over a specified period. Hence, the key issues here are estimating appropriate time periods, confidence intervals, and methodologies. There are advanced tools as well in the form of Monte Carlo Simulation that estimate VaR by generating random scenarios and can handle complex relationships among risks. For the credit risks, the probability of default and recovery rate will be key measures. The Agribusiness example given earlier will have this risk measure for its buyers who buy the product mostly on credit.

The third key challenge after identifying and measuring is to manage the risks. For example, once a firm-wide VaR is computed, and segregated business area-wise, the next question to ask is how much risk the company can take. The answer to this important question will tell us if we are properly covered or exposed. Technically, this is termed "risk budgeting", which enables us to answer questions like "Where do we want to take risk?" and, therefore, which unit can be allocated more bandwidth to assume more risks. In the absence of risk budgeting, all business segments can take equivalent risks disproportionate to their contribution to business goals. In most cases, credit risks are managed by limiting exposure to a party and by marking to market the trading positions. It is also possible to manage this risk through collateral. Some companies have also used Special Purpose Vehicles (SPVs) that have higher credit ratings than the companies that own them.

A related aspect of "risk budgeting" is capital allocation. Risk management has become a key tool for allocating capital across various business units of a risk-taking enterprise. The capital allocation process is a blend of the quantitative mathematical processes using statistical programs embedded with the qualitative decision-making processes.

Managing risks also involves hedging risks through derivatives and other instruments. Corporates normally work closely with the treasury department of banks that provide such customised solutions to clients to hedge risks. However, there are steep costs involved in hedging and will constitute insurance premiums that should be constantly paid. The financial risk manager should eventually take the call to manage the risks through hedging or through other business tools explained above.

In conclusion, it is well known that there is no return without risk, and rewards certainly go where risks are taken. However, there is a difference between taking known risks and taking unknown risks. It is important to know what we do not know (known unknowns). Risk should be discussed openly so that it can be fully understood and, therefore, better managed. While many firms do think about risks, few firms show discipline and consistency in terms of a rigorous approach. A good financial risk management process will ensure consistency and discipline in identifying, measuring, and managing risks. Presently, two professional organisations are dedicated to imparting education and skills in risk management globally. They are the Global Association of Risk Professionals (GARP) and the Professional Risk Managers International Association (PRMIA). Companies should encourage CFOs to acquire these certifications so that best practices can be introduced and followed in the area of risk management.

Last but not the least, financial risk management can easily reduce to a mathematical and statistical process. However, people, not mathematical models, manage risks. Financial risk management, though has rigorous quantitative processes developed over time, has also a good element of common sense embedded. It is better to be approximately right than to be precisely wrong!

02

Dealing with Market Bubble

During February 2024, the Indian capital market regulator SEBI warned investors about froth building up in the small-cap space. They ordered mutual fund houses managing small-cap funds to conduct a stress test after which some funds came out better than others. However, the warning by the regulator led to a fall in the price of small-cap stocks and some panic in the market.

Post Covid, Nifty has been hitting new highs repeatedly. After touching a low of 8,745 on March 20, 2020 (due to COVID-19), Nifty reached 25,010 on August 1ˢᵗ, 2024, implying a return of 286% between the periods. Of course, there were minor corrections along the way, but the ascendancy was very clear. Such a rapid rise in the stock index begs the question – "Are we in a bubble"?

All markets have cycles and so does the stock market. The description of a bubble by Jean-Paul Rodrigue aptly describes the four key phases i.e., stealth phase (when smart money finds its way), awareness phase (when institutional money gets in), Mania phase (when retail public join the frenzy) and finally the blow off phase when all run for cover.

The question now is: Where are we in this chart? While the rapid rise in Nifty during the period 2020-2024 tempts us to flag Nifty in the enthusiasm phase, going by various metrics that I have compiled, it probably indicates that we are in a mania phase.

Table : 41 Nifty Bubble Measure

Parameter	Current	3Y Avg	Peak Value (Since 2019)	Emerging Market Avg.	Peak Value - Period	Reading
Nifty 50 Market Cap / India GDP	106%	99%	120%	63%	Jan 2021 (COVID rebound)	Above Normal
Sector Concentration (Financial)	47%	42%	52%	"Information Technology 25%"	Oct 2020 (post COVID rebound and 5 out of 10 top stocks in N50 were banks)	Above Normal
"Nifty 50 Valuation - P/E - P/B - Div Yield %"	"23x 4x 1%"	"23x 4x 1%"	"42x 5x 1%"	"16x 2x 3%"	"Feb 2021 (COVID rebound) July 2023 (Pre HDFC Merger) Jan 2021 (COVID rebound)"	Above Normal
FPI Yearly Net Inflow (INR Crores)	₹89,808	₹51,446	₹2,37,062	NA	2023	Normal
SIP Avg Monthly Inflow (INR Crores)	₹21,262	₹13,046	₹21,262	NA	Feb 2024 (Current)	Above Normal
Top 10 Companies	57%	54%	63%	26%	Oct 2020 (Surge in Reliance Price)	Above Normal
75th Percentile	26x	43.x	79x	129x	Sep 2020 (Surge in Reliance Price)	Below Normal
Derivatives Traded Volume (Billions)	74	50	74	5	2023	Above Normal
Nifty 50 Avg. Daily Value Traded (INR Crores)	₹37,854	₹25,078	₹78,523	NA	Nov 2020 (COVID rebound)	Normal
"IPOs - No. of Issues - Amount Raised (INR Crores)"	"- 177 (2024 YTD) - ₹39,312"	"- 170 (2021-23) - ₹78,997"	"- 240 - ₹1,19,882"	"- 49 (2024 YTD - Avg) - ₹11,991 Cr ($1,441 mn)- Avg"	"2023 2021 (Zomato, PayTM, PowerGrid)"	Above Normal

For FPI net inflows - YTD 2024 is taken as current value and 3Y average is taken as 2021-23 average; For Div Yield least value is considered as peak

Source: Refinitiv, Author Calculations, Data as of 25th July 2024

*Emerging market countries based on MSCI classification includes Brazil, Chile, China, Colombia, Czech Republic, Egypt, Greece, Hungary, India, Indonesia, Korea, Kuwait, Malaysia, Mexico, Peru, Philippines, Poland, Qatar, Saudi Arabia, South Africa, Taiwan, Thailand, Turkey and United Arab Emirates

We have considered ten important metrics that can measure the bubble. In this, except for three, all other metrics point to normality as of 2024 suggesting that we are sometime away from reaching a bubble.

1. **Market Cap/GDP ratio (Above Normal):** As the formula implies, this measures the relationship between market capitalisation and the broader economy. When the stock market runs itself ahead (a sign of bubble), this surely will be above 100% which is the case now. This ratio is also far higher than the emerging market average.

2. **Sector Concentration among Nifty Top 10 (Above Normal):** Financial services (mainly banks) continue to be the largest sector currently, with a share of 46.5% in the Nifty Top 10, and that has not changed much when benchmarked with the 3-year average but is far higher than the emerging market average.

3. **Valuation (Above Normal):** The three commonly followed valuation measures i.e., p/e, p/b, and dividend yield all plot slightly lower than the 3-year average but is significantly higher than the emerging market average .

4. **Foreign flows (Normal):** Foreign portfolio investors are known to cause bubbles and burst, and hence it is important to watch the flows from foreign investors. During the period under study, this number is above normal but by no measure indicates a bubble.

5. **SIP (Above normal):** While FPIs measure foreign investment, systematic investment plans (SIP) measure the domestic flows into the stock market. Retail investors have been embracing this most recommended investment route for many years now and, hence, keep this tap flowing well above the long-term average. A strong flow of this will imply abundant liquidity in the market that can, in fact, cause a bubble. During the period under study, the numbers were way above the long-term average.

6. **Nifty Top 10 (Above Normal):** This measures the share of Nifty's top 10 companies as a % of total Nifty. Any increase in this number will clearly indicate froth in the market. During the period under study, this metric was well-aligned with the long-term average but significantly higher than the emerging market average.

7. **75th Percentile (Below Normal):** This expresses the value of the largest stock (HDFC Bank) to the 75th percentile stock in the Nifty 500. During the period under study, it was 31 times and was below normal as compared to the long-term average. The wider the gap, the higher the probability of a bubble manifesting. It is interesting to observe the same metric in September 2020, when the largest stock (Reliance) share price was nearly 80 times that of the stock in the 75th percentile. It is also interesting to note that the emerging market average is significantly higher.

8. **Derivatives (Above normal):** India's derivative market growth is incredible thanks to COVID-19, when retail investors found immense time to dabble in markets. Many brokerage firms offer low-cost leverage through derivatives, and this can distort financial markets. The traded volume in derivatives during the study period clearly indicates a bubble, though only 27% of the notional turnover is represented by retail investors. When markets cross sensible limits, regulators take several actions, such as increasing margin level, zero days to expiration, investor education, and increasing minimum contract size, among other things, to warn investors sufficiently in advance. It is good to remember that derivatives trading is a cocktail of risky bets and rare profits.

9. **Market Liquidity (Normal):** During bubble times, market liquidity as measured by value traded normally spikes to unreasonable levels. During the study period this metric indicates parity.

10. **IPO's (Above Normal):** A good indication of bubble is also the unrelenting flows of IPOs in the market. The data clearly indicates that the primary market is running ahead of secondary market both when compared to history as well as emerging market average.

Hence, on a balance of considerations, the Indian stock market is clearly in a bubble zone as of 2024. Therefore, investors should have a plan/strategy to escape the wrath of a market crash. Professional money managers will manage this risk by actively allocating equity and debt and, hence, avoiding steep falls in the market (also called drawdowns). However, retail investors will go through several emotional states like denial, fear, despair, etc., before they can deal with this. Most of the time, retail investors do not see a bubble about to burst due to the high level of market frenzy surrounding them. Even when they see one, they fail to act in time, leading to losses. It takes some experience to look beyond the noise when a market frenzy leads to the metrics discussed above going haywire.

03

Risk Lessons: Global and Desi

The Archegos Lesson

On March 23, 2021, when the world was amid a deadly wave of COVID-19, a hedge fund blowup rattled the US and the global markets thanks to the little-known name Archegos (a Greek word which means "someone who leads the way"). Based in New York, the Archegos family office is a hedge fund owned and managed by Bill Hwang, a US immigrant from South Korea. After working with Tiger Management (of Robertson fame), Bill Hwang went on to find his own hedge fund to manage his wealth in 2013, which had a capital of $200 million. He managed a long-short portfolio (mainly long), which comprised technology stocks focused on Asian geography.

The initial success of Archegos was mainly on star-studded technology names like Amazon, LinkedIn, and Netflix. Emboldened by its success, Bill moved to take bets on lesser-known technology names like ViacomCBS, Farfetch, Iqiyi, Vipstop, etc. Over time, his successful bets enabled him to grow his firm from $200 Mn to $20 bn without the attendant limelight normally associated with such star managers. The fact that Bill remained a low-profile, little-known hedge fund manager speaks volumes about his modus operandi.

Archegos built a portfolio of mainly Asian technology stocks through Total Return Swaps (TRS) with prime brokers. In this arrangement, the prime broker buys the designated stocks (called a portfolio) and swaps the return of the portfolio with Archegos for a fee. Technically, the portfolio risk is assumed by Archegos, while prime brokers make money through the fees but end up holding the stocks in their books. Additionally, the prime broker lends money to Archegos to leverage the portfolio and earn interest on this leverage. Archegos dealt with several reputed prime brokers, including Morgan Stanley, Goldman Sachs, Credit Suisse, Nomura, Wells Fargo, Deutsche Bank and Mitsubishi.

So, what went wrong?

As they say, the party can last as long as the music is playing. In leveraged bets, everyone makes money when the underlying stock price keeps moving up. Technically in that situation, the portfolio value moves up where the investment bank will hand over the profit to Archegos in return for a fixed fee. The increasing value of the portfolio positions Archegos even more favourably now to borrow more and lever up even further.

However, the real fun starts when the opposite happens. When the underlying stock price tanks, the exposed investment bank will now demand more collateral from Archegos. If not provided, then it will resort to a margin call by selling the underlying stocks and reducing its exposure. This triggers a price fall.

In the case of Archegos, the exposure to ViacomCBS turned sour. After experiencing a tripling in the price of the stock, the company decided to tap the market for additional funding in the form of stocks and convertible bonds mainly to shore up liquidity and face intense competition. While the company thought that it was a smart move since it was raising equity at an elevated valuation, the market thought otherwise. The stock price of ViacomCBS tanked 9% on March 23rd, 2021, and 23% on March 24th, 2021. Since Archegos had a concentrated portfolio, it triggered panic among the lenders who rushed to sell the portfolio, which further reduced the value of all the underlying stocks. Few lucky investment banks escaped with little losses, while Credit Suisse and Nomura were left licking $4.7 billion and $2 billion in losses, respectively. Also, Archegos, as a firm, crumbled to the floor and what was a $20 billion liquid empire came to noughts in about 2 days.

There are several interesting risk management lessons from this Archegos saga.

1. **Use of Leverage:** Hedge funds love to make money through leverage, especially in times when rates are near-zero. Leverage is a double-edged sword where it can amplify both profits and losses. Archegos started with normal leverage of 2x, and when it tasted success, it kept increasing the leverage, and before the blowup, the leverage stood at a massive 5x. Well-governed hedge funds and institutions will have internal checks and balances that will limit the leverage in anticipation of troubles. However, Archegos, being a single-man company, did not enjoy that luxury.

2. **Use of Derivative Products:** Archegos did not directly own the underlying stocks but instead owned them indirectly through the prime brokers through the swaps described earlier. This method can escape regulatory scrutiny as regulators cannot determine the positions being built up by Archegos. Archegos also worked with several prime brokers at the same time. While each prime broker can have his exposure worked out, they will not have a composite view of Archegos' total exposure to a particular stock.

3. **Lending is a risky business:** From the prime brokers' point of view, lending is a juicy business as they are covered by the underlying stocks as collateral and can always demand more (margins) when needed. Typically, this works well for small changes in stock prices. However, for large and abrupt changes

in stock price (especially on the downside), lending can be a serious business if proper due diligence is ignored while lending.

4. **Concentrated portfolios can be dangerous:** Archegos ran a highly concentrated portfolio both at a stock level and at the sector level. Ignoring the benefits of portfolio diversification can cause serious problems in sudden market meltdowns. Running a concentrated portfolio that, too, on a levered basis will need very high levels of stock research and the ability to withstand long periods of "against the wind" scenarios. In hedge funds run by a single person like Archegos, both these factors can be missing.

5. **Swimming with Sharks:** Prime brokers, despite their big names, end up dealing with firms like Archegos, where risk management is thrown out of the window. Unless risk management is at the centre of such an investment bank's business model, swimming with sharks will not be pleasant all the time and can end very badly. Most of the big prime brokers cited embraced Archegos as a client despite the SEC slapping fines on Bill when he was with Tiger. It is anybody's guess how this was completely ignored in the risk management due diligence.

6. **Don't wait for the client to decide:** Up to what point one can wait to trigger a margin call is a subjective question, especially when dealing with stocks that have manageable interim volatility. When several prime brokers are involved in lending to the same client for the same stock, a steep fall in the underlying stock price will put them in a situation where, if one pulls the trigger, the whole ship can fall. Before pulling the trigger, prime brokers normally consult the client to see if additional comfort can be obtained in the form of higher collateral or margin money. Mostly, in such situations, the client, instead of putting up with additional collateral, will try to argue about the correctness of his call and punctuate the need to maintain patience. This can

be a recipe for disaster. The biggest risk management lesson here is not to wait for the client's decision.

The investment management business is fiercely competitive and the first casualty of this is risk management. Risk management is a critical function for both the hedge funds and the lending institutions. In many institutions, the unfortunate truth is that risk management is seen more as an irksome middlemen function preventing the business from growing. Some institutions veer around this problem by assigning ex-business heads to lead the risk management function so that they can have a 'friendly' attitude to investing decisions like enrolling risky clients or endorsing risky transactions.

The risk management function should not be a sidekick and should be manned by independent, nonpartisan executives who will not bend, come what may. While this can slow down the growth, at least the institution will survive to analyse. If not, the board meetings will only happen in corporate cemeteries! Corporate failures suck, and financial corporate failures suck big time. Remember the case of the Global Financial Crisis (GFC) and the role financial firms played in creating that crisis. Even after a decade, we still see books published with titles like "*Lessons Learnt from GFC*" or "*What led to GFC.*"

Financial crises leave a grim footmark that is hard to erase. Countries rocked by financial company failures should worry more as they have many connecting dots and impacting points.

IL&FS

IL&FS is a company engaged in infrastructure financing. With more than 250 subsidiaries and not-so-clear ownership structures, its corporate structure is hard to understand. The company was initially started by Central Bank of India, HDFC and UTI. Over time, the ownership changed to LIC, Orix, and the Abu Dhabi Investment Authority (ADIA).

The presence of such globally reputed institutional investors generally gives more comfort and paves the way for better corporate governance.

On the contrary, the executive management of IL&FS used its complicated structure to bestow itself with generous compensations and misplaced incentives, leading to the saga of default that had a humble start in June 2018. At that time, it started off as a delay in repayment of INR 450 crores of inter-corporate deposits from SIDBI. Though credit rating agencies downgraded the rating consequently, the market barely noticed. Unable to conceal the problem, over subsequent months, IL&FS defaulted on several crores of loans, leading SEBI to fire the board and institute a new board. In short, it is a story of poor corporate governance unnoticed by some of the most sophisticated global investors!

DHFL

Dewan Housing Finance Corporation Ltd (DHFL) has a different background but with the same storyline. DHFL was a deposit-taking housing finance company whose business model was predicated on enabling affordable housing to middle-income people. It was spearheaded by Kapil Wadhwan. The trouble started in September 2018 when DSP Mutual Fund sold INR 300 Cr of DHFL papers at 11% in the secondary market, way higher than the traded rates, sparking speculation of a liquidity crunch.

However, the real problem started when Cobrapost alleged in January 2019 that DHFL promoters lent money worth INR 31,500 crores to shell companies that were used to buy assets abroad. As expected, DHFL refuted the claim through a clarification provided to the Bombay Stock Exchange, and rating agencies were quick to reaffirm the high safety rating of DHFL. It was only in May 2019 that care (rating agency) downgraded the Fixed Deposit Programme worth INR 20,000 crores from "A" to "BBB", after which DHFL stopped accepting and renewing fixed deposits and premature withdrawals. DHFL then delayed interest payment on its bonds and bond repayments worth INR 960 crores, and subsequently, in November 2019, RBI dismissed the board and initiated insolvency proceedings. This is another classic example of corporate governance failure, although it is of a different flavour.

These failures, as well as bank episodes (thanks to NPA), have negatively impacted both stock markets and bond markets. The downfall is quite significant to note since such negative performances are observed only in a deep bear market.

However, the impact these had on the bond market is significant. Out of approximately 1,900 funds universe, nearly 105 mutual funds got affected through their exposure to DHFL paper accounting for about 2.5% of total assets.

From an asset value perspective, this is not a number to panic about, but it warrants caution among mutual fund managers. India has been experiencing strong inflows both into equity and debt funds by foreign institutional investors during the past few years. This has increased competition among funds to outperform the benchmark, which warrants them to take a risk to pick up the additional yield. That is when they venture into papers like DHFL and IL&FS, especially corporate bond funds. Bond funds have significant exposure to other low-rated papers by finance companies (in search of yield).

From a portfolio investment perspective, a key question is: Which are riskier banks or non-banks? While banks borrow money from retail and lend to wholesale (businesses), non-banks borrow money from wholesale and lend to retail. So, when banks go bust, the losses will be significant, while non-banks may be slightly better off given their lending exposure to retail.

However, the broader premise is one of corporate governance both in banks and non-banks.

Well-governed banks and non-banks do perform well in the stock market even in these testing times. Hence, research should focus on unravelling this qualitative element rather than labouring on quarterly statements that can easily be doctored. In the case of IL&FS, major lapses on the part of Deloitte (auditors) were also noticed.

With each major crisis, regulators tighten the screws that reduce the intensity of the future crisis. In general, I would say that bank and non-bank regulations are far more advanced today than they were two decades ago. However, regulators must always do a catch-up act rather than pre-empting a crisis. Also, they tend to overreact and over-regulate, which imposes huge costs and kills market growth. Hence, calibration becomes the keyword in terms of structuring regulations to minimise failures and, where it happens, containing the contagion effect.

On a brighter note, the beauty of such financial company failures is that they make available well-governed companies at attractive valuations. Use every such opportunity to build on a quality franchise.

SVB

The collapse of Silicon Valley Bank (SVB) and Signature Bank in March 2023 raised more questions than answers.

The collapse was triggered by the asset-liability mismatch that is typical of many banks and financial institutions that got used to near-zero interest rates. When interest rates went up (that too quickly) to combat inflation, most of them were caught in a balance sheet problem, especially banks that borrow short-term and lend long-term. SVB is a specialised bank that was created mainly to fund startups (as the name Silicon Valley implies). However, SVB experienced a drastic rise in its deposits between 2019 and

2021, which it found difficult to match through its loan growth (mainly to venture capital funds and startups). With an average cost of its deposit at a mouth-watering 25 bps, it sought to pick up some good yields at the long end of the curve (upwards of 150 bps) through Mortgage-backed securities (MBS). Most of its MBS investments were Held to Maturity (HTM) with a 10+ year duration (a space considered risky). The game-changing event occurred when the Fed raised interest rates all too quickly from near-zero to 4.5%, all within one year. This meant that the market value of all bonds (more importantly, long-dated bonds) fell, causing mark-to-market losses. Depositors now sensed better opportunities even in short, dated treasuries, and given this asset-liability mismatch at SVB, they started withdrawing their deposits. SVB's liquidity was tied up in long-dated MBS, which, if forced to liquidate, will be at a steep loss. The drama came to an end when SVB quickly entered receivership. Two days later, another bank called Signature Bank, which was mainly involved in funding cryptocurrencies, also fell. The Federal Reserve was quick to stem the rot by announcing relief for both depositors and banks that were holding these long-duration bonds in their balance sheets. In essence, it gave protection for both the asset and liability sides of banks. The Fed had to do this since the bonds that banks were having as investments were sitting on huge unrealised losses while deposits beyond a small threshold were mostly uninsured.

What is worrying is the magnitude of the failures of these two banks. Back in 2008, when the global financial crisis unfolded, Washington Mutual was considered the biggest bank failure. Now, SVB and Signature Bank will be counted as the second and third-largest bank failures. More worryingly, back in 2008-2010, approximately 25 banks cumulatively accounted for a loss of $375 billion, while in 2023, only two banks (SVB and Signature Bank) accounted for nearly $320 billion in losses. Hence, this episode should count as big enough to warrant comparison with the 2008 GFC.

Fed has a moral hazard issue. While it is primarily mandated to maintain price stability (meaning moderate inflation), it also has the responsibility towards financial system health, where banks happen to be the main channels. The former mandate means the Fed should keep increasing interest rates till inflation cools down, while the latter implies that it needs to either pause or reduce interest rates to prevent further bank failures. The Fed is clearly now in an economic dilemma between containing inflation and protecting banks' health and confidence. Also, any containment of inflation should be demanded by the Fed to have conviction. If it is led by a financial sector-led recession, history suggests that it can be a long and deep recession. The Fed has also come under criticism for ignoring the duration risk that banks were taking without any risk considerations.

Close on the heels of SVB and Signature Bank's failure is the failure of Credit Suisse, a global wealth management institution that was sold to UBS in a deal brokered by the Swiss central bank. Three bank failures in quick succession led to this question about contagion. However, Credit Suisse is a problem unique to the bank and has been in bad news for several years with many leadership changes. The SVB and Signature Bank failures can be a systemic problem across banks as many small and medium banks may have asset-liability mismatch issues and may not be that strongly capitalised to withstand the pressure. With Fed support on both sides of the balance sheet, contagion can be avoided, but that has costs, too.

The SVB incident has a two-fold impact, i.e., funding access to startups and banks' exposure to bonds and its falling values as yields rise.

While we have presented a combination of global and Indian case studies on risk management, the lessons drawn can be overarching. The field of financial forensics is integral to unearthing some of these risks before time and can be a function within the corporate structure. Such evaluations can enable proactive management of potential risks rather than firefighting when they blow in your face.

04

Managing Volatility

Equity markets are not for the faint-hearted as they gyrate a lot due to several reasons. For example, during the first two months of 2022, the Nifty opened at 17,625 and went up by 4% on 17th January, only to fall by 9% to 16,842 on 14th February 2022.

It is important to note, that in 2021 foreign investors poured a net of $38 billion into the market. Due to consistent investing over time, foreign investors now account for nearly 20% of the Indian market capitalisation. Hence, they no longer can be counted as "hot money", as they have good skin in the game.

Stock markets experience volatility for several reasons. Most of the time, it reacts to economic happenings that will have an impact on companies (budget is a good example). Economic discourse normally surrounds broader metrics like GDP growth, fiscal deficit, current account deficit, inflation, and interest rates. For example, increasing oil prices tends to increase inflation, which in turn increases interest rates. These further increase financing costs, and when companies cannot pass on this cost, their margins are squeezed. Hence, markets follow economic events very closely. It is said that a $1 increase in oil price translates into a $1 billion increase in our import bill.

At other times, geo-political reasons could infuse volatility (like the Russia-Ukraine War). These events normally influence investors to react either in a bullish manner (where most of them buy) or in a bearish manner (where they sell). It is important to note that investors are of two types: institutional and retail. Among the institutional category, foreign investors count as the most important as they wield more money power than others. Retail investors normally catch the action after the fact. Always remember that volatility is a permanent thing for capital markets, and hence, markets experience see-saw patterns where some days they are positive while on other days they turn negative.

The key question is how to react to market volatility. To get there, it may be instructive to see what a typical day in a market looks like vis-à-vis a non-typical day.

A look at the data from March 2000 to Feb 2022 (more than two decades) shows that nearly 65% of the time, daily returns for Nifty range between − 1% to +1%. One should consider these days as normal or typical for the stock market. However, there are days when we notice a breakout from this trend, and the market is either extremely bullish or bearish. For e.g., on 12% of the days, the market exhibited a return of +/ − 2%. It is during such extreme movements that investors exhibit extreme tendencies. Smart investors look at them as opportunities to buy or sell, while other investors just watch on the sidelines.

While reacting to market volatility, past lessons are highly instructive. Bear market episodes are captured through a metric called "drawdowns", which measures the fall in the index from a new high to a low and back to a high. This is also called the "peak-trough-peak" study. Each fall from a peak to a trough is termed a drawdown. Here is a list of all Nifty key drawdowns.

Some of the drawdowns are mild and less painful, like the one in 2005. During this time, the Nifty index fell from a peak of 2,169 to a low of 1,903 and then recovered back to the peak with a full cycle of 104 days (roughly three months). The fall from peak to trough is 12.3%, not too steep to worry about.

Table : 42 Nifty Drawdowns

	Peak Value	Obtained on	Subsequent Trough	Obtained on	Drawdown	Peak to Trough-Time duration (days)	Subsequent recovery obtained on	Trough-Peak Time Period (in Days)	Total time (Days) (P-T-P)
1	1756	11-02-2000	854.2	21-09-2001	-51%	588	17-12-2003	817	1405
2	1,982	14-01-2004	1,389	17-05-2004	-30%	124	01-12-2004	198	322
3	2,169	08-03-2005	1,903	29-04-2005	-12%	52	20-06-2005	52	104
4	3,754	10-05-2006	2,633	14-06-2006	-30%	35	31-10-2006	139	174
5	6,288	08-01-2008	2,524	27-10-2008	-60%	293	03-03-2014	1,953	2,246
6	8,996	03-03-2015	6,971	25-02-2016	-23%	359	10-03-2017	379	738
7	11,739	28-08-2018	10,030	26-10-2018	-15%	59	16-04-2019	172	231
8	12,089	03-06-2019	10,705	19-09-2019	-11%	108	27-11-2019	69	177
9	12,362	14-01-2020	7,610	23-03-2020	-38%	69	06-11-2020	228	297
10	18,477	18-10-2021	16,614	20-12-2021	-10%	63			
	Source: Author Calculations								

However, we also have drawdown episodes that are very painful, such as the one in 2008 experienced during the global financial crisis. During this period, the Nifty index fell from a high of 6,288 to a low of 2,524 (implying a fall of nearly 60%!). It took nearly 2,246 days for the market to come full circle (nearly 6 years). In other words, if an investor invested at the peak, he must wait 6 years before he again reaches a no-profit, no-loss situation. The drawdown experienced during the Covid event in 2020 was painful in terms of loss (38%), but it played out swiftly from a time perspective (297 days).

Market drawdowns are a regular phenomenon, and hence, they are very important to understand. Normally, investors panic about a fall and rush to exit their positions. However, this happens after a bit of a wait. Hence, they end up selling at the trough (rather than the peak). The pain point experience is also at its maximum at the trough, and only strong-willed investors can just watch a fall of, say, 50% in their portfolio value and keep smiling or even better buying.

As we have seen from the statistics, all drawdowns eventually claw back, though at differing speeds. If an investor chooses to do nothing (meaning not to panic sell), then he/she would simply have experienced a wild ride but with no financial consequences. However, the problem arises only when investors venture to action during drawdowns.

Every market drawdown gives a feeling that this is the end of the road. However, going by the experience, people who used these drawdowns as buying opportunities have never regretted them.

05

Dealing with Bear Markets

Normally, different countries experience bear markets at different points in their capital market cycle based on home factors. In fact, that is the logic for holding a globally diversified portfolio where when one market declines, others can support it. However, when there is a synchronised bull or bear market, it is normally triggered by macro factors. We are acutely aware of extremely low levels of interest rates since the 2008 Global Financial Crisis (GFC), which triggered a massive bull market both in equities and debt. This almost zero-cost money triggered a liquidity frenzy that created bubbles in asset markets. However, when Central banks around the world finally felt the need to correct this macro imbalance, Covid came and crashed that hope in March 2020, resulting in one of the steepest falls in equity markets. Much against expert assessment, this fall proved short-lived, and the bull party once again resumed with new energy. But it did leave behind the world's worst supply chain dislocations, leading to a consistent increase in many commodity prices. While it was still a reasonably manageable problem, the Russia-Ukraine War ignited a global inflation that could bite deeper. The Federal Reserve of the USA though initially dismissed inflation fears as transitory, then initiated an aggressive increase in interest rates to tame inflation. The stock and bond markets, both in the US and elsewhere, reacted negatively, which triggered a bear market in 2020.

There are many ways to deal with a bear market.

1. **Do nothing**: In this option, one just stares at the losses but essentially does nothing. As markets go through bull and bear market cycles, sustained patience over time will eventually recover all the losses. Measured in the short-term, losses can look outsized. However, over the long-term (10+ years), equity market performance has triumphed. The performance of the Indian equity market, when benchmarked with emerging markets and global markets, has been solid, to say the least. Hence, if one has a sufficiently good time frame of, say, 5 or 10 years, bear markets are just a blip to be ignored.

2. **Average Down**: This is the instant response from many investors, including institutional investors. Being prepared with sufficient cash (dry powder) in anticipation of the bear market can be a great strategy. During these times, exceptional stocks may be available at exceptional prices, and hence, buying those at low levels can produce outsized returns in the future. However, there is a problem with this strategy. It is called the syndrome of catching a falling knife. If one starts averaging at the inception of a bear market, there is no visibility of how far and deep the bear market will last. Hence, if one should average down, one may want to have some rules guiding us[40]. Firstly, have enough dry powder and use it in measured phases. Secondly, if one has a stock already and would want to average on these stocks, do them only when we have sufficient margin of safety already built into those stocks. In other words, the stocks that we intend to average should already be in good profits. This will technically

---

40   Refer the chapter titled "Buy low, sell high but how?"

be averaging up. It is a bad idea to average down on stocks that are already in red. This idea applies to fund portfolios as well (both active and ETFs)

3. **Rebalance:** Instead of viewing a stock portfolio on a stand-alone basis, it is best viewed as asset allocation between equity and debt, where, based on the personal situation, one may want to define a pre-defined split between equity and debt (say 60/40). A disciplined rebalancing (say every quarter or half-year) to restore them back to the stated allocation will mean that we buy equities when the markets fall and vice versa. Intuitively, this is the best thing to do, even though it is also the toughest thing to do.

4. **Diversify into foreign stocks**: With Indian markets opening to investing in foreign stocks, both directly and through funds, one can look at diversification into foreign stocks.

5. **Remember your experience**: The best way to deal with a bear market is to remember and act on past lessons. Market cycles offer valuable lessons, especially in crisis times. The Covid situation has created many first-time traders/investors who have barely seen market cycles. For many, the equity market meant only one thing, i.e., profits and when they are hit by the bear market, there is no experience to guide them safely. The FOMO (fear of missing out) syndrome is what guided many into markets. Investing lessons get better only when we deal with many market cycles (both ups and downs), and unfortunately, that wisdom comes only with age.

In conclusion, investing mistakes are almost always made in a bull market than a bear market. If we ignore the short-term losses and garner sufficient cash to invest, the next bull market will easily wipe out all the losses. However, if we panic and sell out and wait for the return of good times, we cannot enjoy the benefits of investing at low levels.

06

Dealing with Bull Markets

India is entering an exciting growth phase, with its stock markets reaching lifetime highs. Economists and analysts believe this is just the beginning, potentially laying the foundation for multi-decade growth and opportunities. However, the ride won't be smooth, so fasten your seatbelts.

For the uninitiated, the Nifty 50 has clocked a CAGR of 15.6% over the last five years[41], outperforming the MSCI EM index, which achieved just 1.1%. The strong market performance can be attributed to robust domestic flows, thanks to Systematic Investment Plans (SIPs) by retail investors, while foreign flows have also provided support at times. There is a positive feedback loop where good market performance encourages more SIPs, further contributing to good market performance.

However, as with all medicines, this bull market frenzy has side effects, namely a trading frenzy and the gamification of the market. A key reason behind this is the disorderly growth of derivatives trading. The derivatives-to-cash volume ratio in India is now at 422, compared to just 9 in the US. The monthly Average Daily Turnover (ADTO) for derivatives is now Rs 329 trillion, with nearly 36% coming from the retail segment, a fact that should concern regulators.

---

41   As of July 2024

Figure : 12 Equity Market Eco System

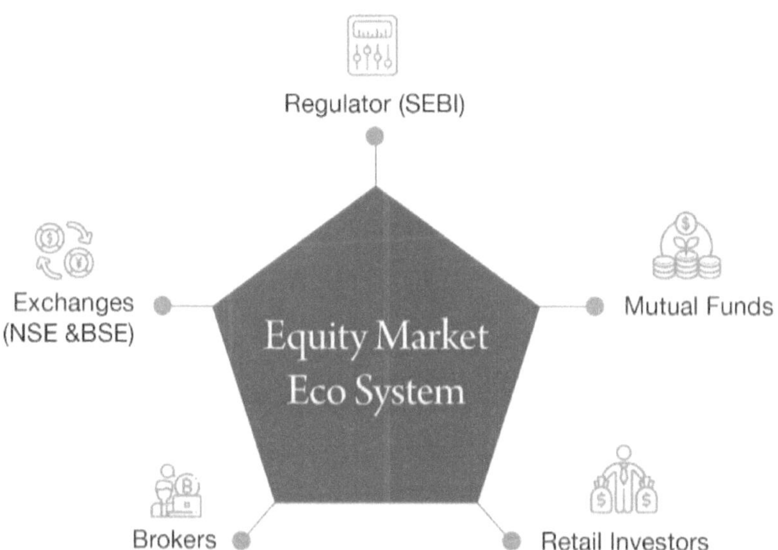

In fact, SEBI published research highlighting that 89% of individual traders in the equity derivatives segment incurred losses, with an average loss of Rs 1.1 lakh in FY22. Experts are struggling to explain this stupendous growth in derivatives trading, though many blame COVID-19. Surprisingly, the same COVID-19 did not induce this investor behaviour in other markets. Such large derivatives trades indicate that speculation, rather than hedging, is at the heart of most trades. Rapid technological development has also enabled exchanges to launch more investor-friendly products like zero days to expiration (0DTE) contracts, which expire on the same day. Combined with 500x leverage and the convenience of online trading, we have a lethal combination fuelling the gamification frenzy.

At some point, this will likely result in a scam-induced crash. Stock market scams are not new to India, with a history of such events including the famous Harshad Mehta (1992), Ketan Parekh, and UTI scams

(2001), the NSE co-location scam (2015), and the Karvy scam (2019). Scams are an integral part of capital market development, triggering tighter regulation to prevent similar future incidents. Currently, SEBI has ordered a probe into front-running at Quant Mutual Fund, which manages funds based on a momentum model. This is similar to the NSE co-location scam, where individuals with advance information about impending trades can front-run and profit.

The risks stemming from hectic stock market growth can be analysed on several fronts:

1. **Controllable vs. Uncontrollable:** Some risks, like front-running, can be detected through regular audits and nipped in the bud, allowing regulators to take action before things get out of hand. However, trading frenzies in derivatives can easily create situations that spiral out of control.

2. **Proactive vs. Reactive:** Regulators are an important part of the equity ecosystem, and their vigilance is key to protecting investors. They should act proactively, as with SEBI's study on derivatives trading, to warn investors of the dangers of speculative trading. Historically, many scams have caught regulators by surprise, leading to reactive measures.

3. **Big vs. Small:** Not all scams are equal. For example, the NSE co-location scam (Rs 75,000 crore) and the KP scam (Rs 40,000 crore) are much larger than the Karvy scam (Rs 2,300 crore) and the UTI scam (Rs 1,800 crore). However, regulations put in place should be evaluated based on opportunity cost more than the direct financial loss.

4. **Systemic vs. Contained:** Some scams can create systemic risks, while others are more contained. This is why the banking industry is stringently regulated by the RBI, as it can pose systemic risks, especially for large banks.

In the complex equity ecosystem, risks can emanate from any player, including stock exchanges, brokers, regulators, mutual funds, and retail investors. Some risks can be anticipated and contained, while others may surprise and quickly escalate into a major crisis.

The biggest source of alpha in equity investing is avoiding drawdowns during market crashes. This requires insuring one's portfolio through asset allocation and diversification and avoiding the gamification of the market through speculative derivatives trading. Investors should focus on long-term investing and avoid speculation, as the odds are against them, much like in a casino. Investing through mutual funds can be a safer approach. Regarding outright frauds like front-running, stringent internal controls and external audits by regulators, along with steep fines, can help prevent such perils. While the current front-running issue is confined to a small segment (Quant), it is conceivable that it could happen with larger institutions if internal controls are weak.

Retail Investing

01

Introduction

Retail investing involves a deep understanding of asset classes, asset allocation and financial planning. It also involves defining the purpose of investment. At a personal level, setting an investment strategy means doing some things right and avoiding others that are clearly wrong.

When it comes to investing, most of us go for the easy option of accumulating our savings in the bank and parking the excess money in fixed deposits. Sometimes, we go by opportunities cited by friends and relatives in the stock market or real estate with occasional gold purchases. In other words, we react to the prospects with no definitive plan backing them.

Instead, we should have a well-laid-out plan to deploy our monthly savings. This plan should consider our family circumstances, our age, our ability to take risks, our willingness to take risks (this is psychological), and our current and future income. While creating a plan, it is also crucial to foresee liabilities like housing, education, healthcare for elders, etc.

Since our earnings are regular (say monthly), our investment should also be regular. There is always this temptation to time the market, be it the stock market or real estate. It is impossible to time the market because we cannot predict when and where the next market-moving event will happen. Hence, systematic investment at regular intervals can smoothen the impact and save us trouble. Technology has made this easier today, where we can instruct our mutual fund to invest even daily or smart SIP. The quantitative merit of SIP is discussed later.

This may be boring, but it is the most important thing to do at least monthly, if not quarterly. Sometimes, procrastination or the tendency to postpone things (let's do it tomorrow) can lead to heavy damage. A timely reckoning can save us a lot of trouble. So, track investment portfolio assets and returns monthly.

Different investment avenues have different risk profiles. For example, equities are very volatile, real estate is illiquid (try selling a home), fixed-income securities are subject to interest rate risk, and gold is linked to the US dollar. Hence, it is important to diversify across asset classes to reduce the risk. However tempting it may be, do not expose yourself to huge bets on one asset class or opportunity.

The importance of a breadwinner of the family can be understood only in times of loss of life for unfortunate reasons like heart attack, accident, etc. We need to take this risk seriously, and besides being careful, one must buy insurance to protect their families after they are gone. Unlike in the past, when we only had one insurance company, we are now offered several products from different companies to suit our requirements. However, we should be careful not to over-insure (as it may be costly) or link insurance to investments.

We have always sought advice from friends and relatives. Still, it would help to seek advice from a professional financial adviser who is trained in this profession of providing advice. The age and experience of the adviser are also crucial factors in building trust towards the advice. However, keep in mind that even professional advisers can go wrong.

02

Asset Class Performance (After Inflation)

When investing, we must always deal with the universal scourge of inflation. Asset class performance can look magnifying before inflation but can look bleak after inflation.

Figure : 13 Asset class performance

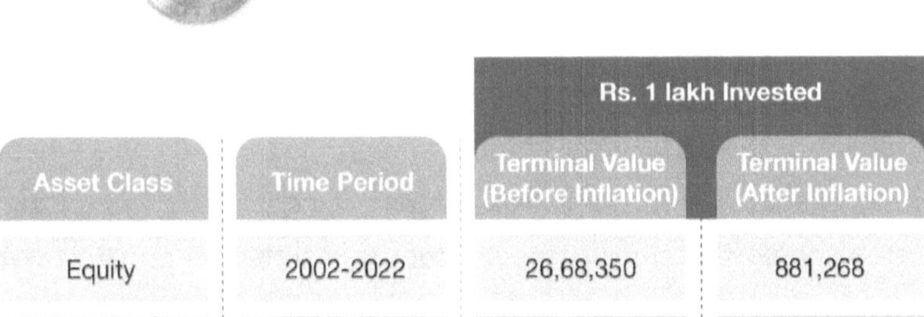

Asset Class	Time Period	Terminal Value (Before Inflation)	Terminal Value (After Inflation)
Equity	2002-2022	26,68,350	881,268
Gold	2002-2022	8,76,157	271,064
FD	2002-2022	5,17,084	154,888

Source: Author Calculation

The three investments and the different time horizons are only meant to drive home the menace of inflation and not to form a judgement on the best mode of investment.

We always make investment decisions based on absolute performance rather than inflation-adjusted performance. This approach can have very costly consequences regarding our wealth creation and overall financial well-being. This is true, although inflation is the same across all investments and may hence not count much when choosing amongst investments.

Without considering the effect of inflation, the investment performance can look dramatic. For e.g., if we have invested Rs 1 lakh in a fixed deposit in 1997, it will be worth Rs 10 lakh by October 2022. But when adjusted for inflation, it is worth only Rs 1.75 lakhs! Also, inflation is a steady and silent killer – it creates more havoc in the long-run than in the short run.

Most of us deal with bank fixed deposits without realising the meagre return (after inflation) that they offer. While banks have benefitted from the fixed deposits as they make nice spreads (the difference between lending rates and deposit rates), investors have yet to make any significant returns since inflation eats much away, leaving significantly less on the table.

Generally, the RBI pushes banks to increase interest rates whenever inflation increases. In other words, interest rates also rise when inflation increases, thereby technically protecting the real rate of return. However, as data shows, inflation has had the upper hand, resulting in a dismal performance by the fixed deposits. In the long-run, a 2 percent real return rate can seriously hurt.

Unlike fixed deposits, gold has always produced an excellent rate of return in the long-run (15, 20, and 25 years). It had a good time during the 5-year period between October 2017 and October 2022, which was mainly attributed to global uncertainty and the Covid crisis. Gold has generated 10 percent nominal returns annualised (before inflation) and

5 percent real return (after inflation) in that period. It has also enjoyed a nice run in a twenty-year context, with inflation-adjusted annualised returns at nearly 5 percent compared to the 2 percent returns on fixed deposits.

Indian Equities, by far, has the best story to narrate. In the (5 years ending October 2022), the equity performance is a 10 percent real rate of return. It produced a real return of 11.5 percent annualised during the previous 20 years (ending October 2022) compared to 5.1 percent for gold and 2.2 percent for fixed deposits. If we muster some patience, it is the best hedge against inflation.

Though there is no statistic to back the claim, the real estate does an excellent job of protecting value against inflation. In the absence of treasury inflation-protected securities (TIPS) as it exists in the US, the only place to hide from inflation is equities. If we have a time frame of 10 years, we can expect equities to protect us from inflation.

03

Asset Allocation

It is frequently suggested that as investors, we should invest across various asset classes, i.e., fixed deposits, equities, bonds, real estate, gold, etc. Investors with a non-investment background may not appreciate the nuances or differences between various asset classes.

Before getting to various asset allocation theories, let's find out the answer to the question: 'What should be the purpose of investing?'

In simple words, managing investments should

- be age agnostic.
- be treated as a flow rather than a stock
- let you sleep well at night
- never result in capital erosion and
- take care in old age

We are often advised to be aggressive in our investment during our young age and conservative during our middle and old age. In other words, we should be risk-seeking when young and risk-averse when elderly. While this has its merits, it usually does not happen that way. When we are young, we may not have sufficient knowledge and experience to understand the risk inherent in an investment. With age and experience, we are more capable of appreciating genuine risk. Also, we usually tend to invest our surplus. Now, the surplus tends to be less at a young age. Moreover, surplus generation happens all through our life span, so investment decisions must be made even when we age, and we must seek reasonable risk at all points in time.

A 'flow' is a recurring item. Since surplus flows every month, investments should be viewed as a flow. In other words, occasional decisions on where to invest should not be the case since the surplus keeps accruing. However, traditional asset allocation assumes that our wealth is a stock rather than a flow. More simply, a 'stock' is a one-time event consolidated in nature.

A risk-focused diversified portfolio will experience lower volatility compared to concentrated portfolios of stocks. The idea of bringing disparate asset classes into a portfolio is to minimise volatility. While it is human nature to check the value of our portfolios (sometimes even daily), if we adopt a diversified approach to portfolio construction, the risks will balance out and will not produce any significant deviations. This will let one sleep well at night.

The most significant risk of the all-equity portfolio is the erosion of capital. If our investment value of 100, say, drops to 70, it will be psychologically unnerving. A well diversified portfolio of various asset classes can reduce the probability of capital erosion. That is why it is said that time in the market is more important than timing the market.

Retirement planning should be one of the key pillars of wealth management. Thanks to strides in life expectancy, people are now expected to live much longer than before. The average global life expectancy is inching towards 80 years. Assuming one retires at 60, it means providing oneself with retirement funding for twenty long years. Portfolios that are constructed keeping this in mind will make sure that one lives comfortably during their retirement phase from a financial point of view.

With this basic understanding, let's understand how to allocate the surplus by following a few unconventional theories.

While investing, we have three scenarios viz.

- We are familiar with the investment, and we fully understand what it is (say, fixed deposit)
- We are partly familiar with the investment, and we have difficulty understanding what it is (say, mid-caps stocks in equities)
- We are totally unfamiliar with the investment and have no clue what it is (say, Bitcoins)

Let us call the first category "Familiar", the second "Not so Familiar," and the third "Unfamiliar". The irony is that we do not end up constantly investing only in familiar investments. We often invest in the other two categories based on the advice tendered by friends, relatives, and associates, only to rue such decisions later in life. The investments should be familiar and reduce our anxiety about investments. A Brazilian stock may be familiar to Brazilians but not to an Indian! Risk is a perception based on familiarity.

Here is a list of investment opportunities classified as per this understanding:

Table : 43 Asset class familiarity

Familiar	Not so Familiar	Unfamiliar
Gold	Midcap Equities	Exotic Currencies
Real Estate	Soverign Bonds	Art
Fixed Deposits	IPO's	Small and micro cap
Sovereign Bonds		High Yield Bonds
Large Cap Equities		Hedge Funds
Mutual Funds		Derivatives
		Structured Products
		Crypto Currencies
		Commodities
		Private Equity

How do we make this classification? We should put them in the following framework whenever we see an opportunity.

i. **Probability of loss:** This is the true definition of risk. Familiar investments are when the likelihood of loss is minimal or well known.

ii. **Liquidity:** Investments should be reasonably liquid. If not, they only have paper value and not realisable value. Familiar investments are highly liquid.

iii. **Transparency:** The opportunity should be easy and straightforward to understand, even for a layman. Avoid structured products as even professionals do not understand them sometimes!

Table : 44 Asset class familiarity

	Familiar	Not so Familiar	Unfamiliar
Probability of Loss	Low	High	Very high
Liquidity	High	Medium	Low
Transparency	High	Low	Very Low

Predominantly, we should invest approximately 60% of our investible surplus in familiar investments. However, to enjoy higher returns, we should allocate 30% of our surplus towards the not so familiar category and 10% towards unfamiliar investments. However, as we tread into the not so familiar category and unfamiliar categories, it is best to get professional help while deciding on the investment.

Investment opportunities can also be categorised based on their risk, i.e., high, medium, and low-risk. High-risk means the probability of losing all our investments is very high. Medium-risk acquisitions may result in a loss, but not entirely, and low-risk investments will not result in a capital loss. The increased risk may also result in high returns, while low-risk will result in nominal returns and, in most cases, does not beat inflation. Opinions may marginally differ on the classification, but not so much that a high-risk investment can be considered low-risk. We would not risk losing our assets in the low-risk segment, while in the high-risk investments, the risk of losing our investments would be very high.

How much of my money should I commit to each of the three risk categories?

The answer depends on our age and liquidity requirements. When we are young, we have more time, so we can afford to take more risks. The reasoning is that even if we lose a significant amount, we have time to ride it out and hope for recovery. As we move towards a later period (50-plus), our ability to take risks is reduced, and the need for liquidity increases. At this stage, we don't have the luxury of time. Hence, as we age, we should initially focus on our high-risk investments and gradually reduce them in favour of low-risk. The following chart illustrates this transition:

Table : 45 Age and risk

Age (years)					
Risk	20-30	30-40	40-50	50-60	60-70
Low	10%	20%	30%	40%	60%
Medium	30%	30%	30%	30%	30%
High	60%	50%	40%	30%	10%
Low-Risk: Gold, FD, Government Bonds, Post Office Medium-Risk: Real estate, Balanced Funds, Corporate Bonds High-Risk: Stocks, Equity Funds, Commodities					

Low-Risk: Gold, FD, Government Bonds, Post Office
Medium-Risk: Real estate, Balanced Funds, Corporate Bonds
High-Risk: Stocks, Equity Funds, Commodities

Let's understand this in more detail. When we are between 20 and 30 years old, our income may be low, but our liquidity needs are also low. When we move to the next age bracket, i.e., 30-40, we need to reduce our allocation towards high-risk in favour of low-risk.

The amount we can save monthly (Remember the golden formula: Expenses = Income − Savings) must be channelled towards high-risk investments like equities. This can happen either by selling our high-risk investments (hopefully after making good profits!) and investing them in low-risk or by committing our new money more towards low-risk than high-risk. As we can see from the chart, when we move into the 60-70 zone, most of our investments are low-risk, income-yielding investments since that is when we need income to support our retirement. A key opportunity in the medium-risk is real estate. Real estate makes up a large part of their total wealth for most people.

Also, one may argue that real estate has no risk since it does not generally depreciate. This may be true, but most buy real estate through mortgage loans for several years. During this time, the interest rate may fluctuate and cause hardships. Also, sometimes, if we decide to buy real estate at the peak of the bubble, then the price may start stagnating and sometimes fall. Hence, it is prudent to consider this as a medium-risk investment rather than a low-risk investment. The increased allocation towards low-risk as we enter our 40s and 50s is to ensure that we have enough liquidity to fund our children's higher education expenses or marriage expenses.

Prudent financial planning and inspection of our investments is the master key to economic prosperity. Investing money in an intelligent and organised style by realising its risk is as important as earning money through hard work.

04

Financial Planning

Professional independent financial advisers can help one flip the equation in favour of disciplined investing and balanced emotions. They will caution us when we start becoming greedy and will encourage us to take a risk when we are afraid. The financial adviser's fees will only turn out to be a worthy investment in the medium to long-term. A professional adviser should be qualified in their chosen field through recognised accreditation. Some informal feedback from their current and past clients can also be of great help.

Most importantly, they must be independent. In other words, they should only be taking the fees from the client, and not from any product providers typically the financial institutions. If some advisers claim that they can help for free, remember that there is no such thing as a free lunch.

It is also important to note that a periodic performance evaluation of the adviser is necessary (just like our job appraisals!). However, in real life, we have a serious reluctance to engage a financial planner to manage our money. There are some reasons for that.

1. **Overconfidence:** We generally overestimate our driving skills. We tend to do the same when managing our money. For some reason, we believe we can do it ourselves. This belief cuts across professions: engineer, doctor, lawyer, or CA. Everyone believes they can better manage their wealth until something goes terribly wrong.

2. **Not sure where to go:** Even if we decide to opt for financial planning, we may not know the right place to approach and the right person to ask.

3. **I am too small:** Many of us think we are too small to have an adviser assist us and that the game is only for the rich!

4. **Things are okay:** If things are normal and reasonable, we think that an adviser is unnecessary. Why have an adviser when we can do it ourselves? It's like the feeling of going to a doctor to get the periodic tests done and then hearing, "Oh, the reports are all normal!"

5. **Reluctance to pay:** Independent financial planning means payment of fees to the financial adviser. We are often not too keen on that.

How we manage our wealth is as important as how we work our health, albeit with one difference. Regarding health management, we do not think twice about taking expert help. However, when it comes to managing our wealth, we invariably feel that we can do a better job than an adviser.

Many of us take investment calls casually and without serious research. And when they do go sour, we refuse to accept the fact and persist with the wrong investment till the losses mount to levels from where reversing course becomes tricky. The occasional wins are invariably attributed to our innate skill rather than pure luck! This is true for all types of investing, be it equities or real estate. The only investment we all make consistently with the least risk is fixed deposits.

The need for an independent adviser to guide us mainly arises at the mid-career level, typically when we are between 40-50 years old. This is when we would have accumulated reasonable savings, developed many failed experiences, and significant expense planning like children's education, marriage, or apartment purchase requires serious planning. This is also a phase where we might be receiving some inheritance or ESOPs that require expert management.

While getting professional help to manage our savings is easy, it is difficult to identify the right adviser.

The current crop of advisers mainly stems from banks with which we have our account. Other advisers can be aligned with major brokerage houses. Banks or brokerage houses are incentivised to sell third-party funds/products for commissions and fees.

Also, given their aggressive targets, these institutions experience high resource turnover, making continuity a significant problem. An NRI that visits India every year or two may be meeting a new face during their visits to their banks. In the western world, they have a concept called independent financial advisers who charge their clients for the service rendered and are not incentivised to push products. It is important to verify advisers' independence and question them on the source of their revenues and how transparent they are in this respect.

Independent financial advisers can provide better continuity and build trust and relationships. Remember, wealth management is more about service rendered than about performance. Professional advisers offer regular updates, assuage clients' fears when markets experience corrections, counsel clients from being aggressive when markets go through euphoria, explain new trends, encourage clients to embrace technology to keep a tab, etc.

In India, SEBI regulates the registration of investment advisers (IAs) under the SEBI (investment advisers) Regulations, 2013. The regulations define an investment adviser as someone who advises about investing in securities or provides research analysis. Any individual or entity that falls under the definition of an investment adviser must register with SEBI. This includes individuals, partnership firms, LLPs, companies, and any other entity that provides investment advisory services for a fee. Employees and representatives of investment advisory firms who interact with clients and provide advice should also be registered with SEBI. However, anyone engaged in incidental advice, such as a banker, chartered accountant, or insurance agent, is not required to register as an investment adviser. But, if such a person wishes to provide investment advice as a primary service, they can register with SEBI as an IA[42].

Another problematic angle for a High-Net-worth Individual (HNI) is the diverse nature of investments. They may range from equities to real estate to individual businesses or private equity. If the asset size is significant, having a dedicated family office to manage the affairs may be worthwhile. The family office should be headed by a qualified professional who will make decisions in the client's interest. However, if the wealth level is not very high, then the unit economics may not warrant setting up a family office. In such a case, either one can enrol into a multi-family office or source independent advisers for each asset class.

While advisers may be inclined to advise across asset classes, it may not be in the client's interest to mix up equity advice with real estate advice or insurance advice. They are so different in expertise that they all need careful attention from their respective specialists, just like the medical profession where ENT specialists cannot attend to broken joints! Ironically, clients, often, tend to view wealth management as a holistic function!

Many NRI and other HNI clients share an ephemeral relationship with their auditors and tax advisers. It is also natural for them to look up to their auditors for financial advice. While some auditors have developed the expertise over time and, therefore, are able to discharge that duty, they are often not trained for a different function. Hence, it may be a good idea not to mix the two.

---

42 https://www.5paisa.com/stock-market-guide/stock-share-market/sebi-registered-investment-advisor#:~:text=In%20India%2C%20SEBI%20regulates%20the,securities%20or%20provides%20research%20analysis.

Let us also understand financial planning from the lens of income and expenses.

We generally depend on our careers to provide us with income. In some cases, there may be other sources of income (like inherited properties and wealth). However, our job, business, or profession is the primary source of income for most of us. Keeping this income in mind, we have certain expenses. What remains after this is 'Savings' which we 'Invest'.

So, the equation is:

- Income – Expenses = Savings = Investment

Thus, in the traditional form, whatever is left after expenses is considered our savings, which we invest in whenever possible. But if we tweak the equation a bit, we can get into smart financial planning.

The new equation becomes:

- Income – Expenses – Investments= Savings

In short, instead of investing what is left after savings, we will be spending what is left after investing. This form can lead to long-term outcomes that can lead to excellent financial well-being. The merit of financial planning will become clearer once we understand the sequence involving income, expenses, savings and investments and the complexities surrounding each.

While income from a job can be the only source during our initial days, in the medium to long-term, income from accumulated wealth can be a larger source of income. Warren Buffet's net worth is estimated at $120 billion. However, 99% of his wealth generation happened after he turned 50 years of age. This is a good example of the power of compounding and appreciating the importance of income from wealth, which turns out to be a more significant source of our wealth than salary and other income after a certain threshold.

In case of income, the popular narrative is that our career is the primary source of income. However, financial planning can become another great source of income, thanks to the power of compounding! A good financial planner would explain the benefits of starting early and disciplined investing which can produce outsized returns in medium to long-term. Thanks to credit cards (the easiest but costliest source of money) and UPI, it is now possible to indulge in a shopping binge.

Sometimes, we erroneously associate buying an expensive watch or a fancy car with an asset. It is vital to note that a sound investment produces income and grows in value. Fancy assets are either non-income creating (like gold) or income-and-value-depleting (like a car involving maintenance and depreciation). Such expensive lifestyle habits through easy spending sources can cause "lifestyle inflation," eroding our savings. Since access to money is now easy (though not cheap), it may quickly result in debt.

Equated Monthly instalments (EMIs) are a troublesome part of our financial life. Even if one does not go on a buying spree, aspects like uncovered medical expenses for our family and ourselves can drain money at record speed. In other words, expense planning and management are critical aspects of financial well-being. We will certainly not consult our financial planner about buying a Rado watch, but he/she can explain the outsized influence of growing EMIs on our finances.

Assuming we earn and manage our expenses well (double pat), the main question is: Are we investing our savings wisely?

Traditionally, savings are either invested in fixed deposits (even though some pay an interest rate lower than inflation!), real estate (how can one go wrong on this!) or gold (best hedge in times of crisis!). We may also have a skewed understanding of these options based on our risk perception. This is where the role of a financial planner is precious.

In the absence of professional financial advice, it is common to make investment mistakes.

- Did we not buy XYZ stock based on a tip?
- Did we not purchase that property because a friend did?
- Did we not invest in an insurance product mistakenly, thinking that we would get a return in the future?

Our mistakes in investment can lead to an undiversified portfolio of assets. Also, the emotional aspect of investment alternates between greed and fear. We all want to double our money in six months (Greed). But if we lose money once, say, because of a wrong stock choice (thanks to a tip), then we fear reinvesting in the stock market (Fear). Our emotions alternate between greed and fear throughout our lives.

Also, three trends are worth noting from a lifestyle point of view:

- We will live longer than we think. More importantly, women will live longer than men (based on life expectancy).
- Our investment will produce lower returns after adjusting for inflation, yielding lower income. And,
- Our cost of living will increase more than our current/original estimate.

The power of inflation comes directly in the last trend, i.e., cost of living, and to an extent in the second trend, where the net returns will be lower after inflation. The outcome of these three critical trends is that we will experience a lower standard of living in retirement.

So, what should we do to stay ahead of it?

- Focus on health – be more than content with maintenance. Spend money on building a healthier body.

- Develop an investment strategy that is inflation-proof.
- Work longer by moving your retirement age higher than 60.
- As investors, before framing money decisions, we often ask ourselves, "Can this investment fetch me good returns?"
- As a group, we are widely varied in terms of age, qualification, salary, and geographical lineage, and this is often reflected in our investment habits as well. However, regardless of this diversity, we decide on investment options through the frame of returns. In many cases, we build our decisions based on information collected from friends in social meetings. We invest when we have money (liquidity) based on available options.

Throughout this entire process of managing savings, a cardinal mistake that many of us make is not involving our spouses. Many men believe that it is a "man thing." They think that since they earn the money, they have the right to decide where to invest it. Nothing can be farther from the truth. Many women, including in rural India, are quite investment/money-savvy and have self-sustaining independent careers. Ultimately, wealth creation must take the family's well-being into account; hence, it is a bad idea to exclude the spouse from the conversations with financial advisers. In fact, one should actively encourage their spouse and children to take part in these conversations.

We must remember that financial planning is like medical consultation. We can rush to a doctor when we have a mild heart attack or have regular health check-ups, which will help avoid the heart attack.

05

Systematic Investment Plans (SIPs)

As stock market investors, these statements look familiar:

1. One cannot and should not time the market.
2. One should consider investing regularly (say daily/weekly/ monthly) to take advantage of market volatility &
3. Regular investments or systematic investment plans (SIPs) are easy and flexible and can inculcate savings habits.

To add to the emphasis, imagine one invested a lump sum in an index fund during October 2021 when Sensex was at 61,700. At the end of May 2022 (55,566), the portfolio would be down by 10%. Hence, the case for SIP.

Based on data from May 2012 to May 2022, over different time horizons (1-year to 10-year periods), SIPs outperformed lumpsum strategy in eight of the ten considered time periods. The SIP performance is calculated using the internal rate of return (IRR) method since it involves regular cash flows. For e.g., if we had invested Rs.10,000 every month for the last 3 years, the IRR of our investment at May 2022 value (assuming we cash out) would be an annualised return of 20.2%, while a lump sum strategy would have yielded an annualised return of 11.8%, a difference of around 8.4% annualised. Except for the periods 2 years and 10 years before May 2022, lumpsum returns have lagged SIP returns.

In a consistently rising market, SIPs can produce an average purchase cost lower than the peak value thereby benefiting the investors. Markets by nature gyrate between optimism and pessimism and hence produce volatility.

The best news for SIPs lies with the fund houses, which aim for consistent and measured growth in their assets under management (AUM) by enabling one to commit a fixed amount of investment every month. It is good news for them since they earn their fees on the AUM.

Also, once we sign up for an SIP, rarely ever do we take the pain of monitoring its performance vis-à-vis a lumpsum strategy. Hence, SIPs, once started, invariably run their course, which again is music to the ears of fund houses.

Basis the above data, the argument in favour of SIP is that it has performed better than lumpsum return and it is easy on liquidity, especially if investors have a monthly income matching monthly investments. No wonder, there are now more than 90 million SIP accounts in India with annual gross inflow touching Rs.2 lakh crores during FY2024[43]!

---

43   https://timesofindia.indiatimes.com/city/mumbai/mutual-fund-share-in-indian-stocks-at-record-high-fpis-at-12-yr-low/articleshow/110343902.cms

Table : 46 SIP Outperformance

	Lumpsum Return	SIP Return	Diff
1 Year	24.9%	22.9%	2.0%
2 Years	12.1%	17.7%	-5.6%
3 Years	14.2%	14.5%	-0.4%
4 Years	25.7%	17.4%	8.4%
5 Years	13.8%	16.3%	-2.6%
6 Years	14.3%	15.4%	-1.1%
7 Years	13.9%	14.8%	-0.9%
8 Years	14.3%	14.6%	-0.3%
9 Years	11.4%	14.1%	-2.7%
10 Years	12.6%	13.4%	-0.8%
Data: April 2014–March 2024			

Source: Refinitiv

Soft Aspects

01

Introduction

The task of investing is almost as much of mind as math. The advent of quantitative investing or passive investing is predated on lessening the mind over math, as even professional investors suffer from severe biases which can cloud their investment decision-making. While investing in the market, an investor's state of mind will oscillate between greed and fear based on the investment outcome. Investment success will lead to greed, which may then result in unwarranted bets, losses, and fear. The journey can also be reversed, where one starts with losses and is therefore gripped by fear, which then leads to extremely careful investment decisions that lead to outsized returns that will eventually lead to the path of greed. The market always works to extremes, and at any point, we have analysts who provide a future view that can be either very good or very bad. But the truth lies somewhere in between always and psychologically, one should train to operate in the middle, which can keep them levelheaded.

Quantitative finance eliminates the influence of the mind and works mostly on a pre-determined formula which is agnostic to feelings. This probably explains the stupendous growth of passive investing and the decline of active managers. Behind the oscillating feeling between fear and greed lies the ability to analyse success and failures. Many times, we will mistake our investing success for our skill and attribute our investing failures to bad luck, while smart investors just do the opposite. Analysing one's investing failures threadbare enables one to learn the necessary lessons which can avoid repeating them in the future. Also, smart investors do not take investing success too seriously and fear that some portion of that could have come through sheer luck or market timing. Downplaying success and analysing failures takes a large chunk of the effort and is not easy to achieve, given the way our mind plays most of the time. Even at cocktail parties, we love to broadcast our multi-baggers because humans want to look good in front of others. Discretion more than public validation is key, or else we are playing the wrong game. If one is forced to say, a smart conversation should look something like this: *"I completely misjudged this stock and lost 70% even though the broad market did well. Where do you think I went wrong?"*

An important bias is overconfidence, which is often mistaken for conviction. Analysts are frequently called to provide "high conviction" ideas, and conviction develops over long years and after intense research. Warren Buffet studied Microsoft for many years, yet he kept admitting in his annual report that he could not understand how the information technology industry works. In the meantime, the stock was moving up, and he was missing out on fun. But he waited for the conviction to develop before he finally invested. At a psychological level, investors mostly play to win, while the smart thing to do is to play, not to lose. While playing to win will make one aggressive and overconfident, playing not to lose (an element of tentativeness) can signal conviction and risk management. Playing not to lose embeds a statement, *"In spite of my careful research, I can still be wrong."* Conviction in one's investment process is different from conviction in the investment itself. The former takes care of risk management, while the latter just enables one to discover the business context.

Many star fund managers of the likes of George Soros or Stan Druckenmiller would first invest and then investigate. They place more value on their "gut" feeling than analysis, and that gut feeling is generally shaped by decades of observations. This is quite the opposite of what they teach at business schools, where one is trained to analyse before deciding. In investing, speed is of the essence, and hence, gut feeling driven by psychology plays a larger role than analysis based on historical facts. This is not to say that these fund managers totally shun analysis. In fact, once they make an investing decision based on gut, they commission their analysts to investigate and if the recommendation is negative, they will quickly close the position and move on. The need to first act and then investigate is not to lose time in the process.

Many investors also like to play the investing game on their own instead of getting help. In the investing world, taking help is akin to declaring to the world that I don't know how to do this thing. But even in the medical world, the most celebrated surgeon should still get this surgery done by another surgeon! Even while we are perfectly right in believing that we can control our own investing destiny, it still pays to get outside help, get an investment doctor's advice, and manage one's portfolio. Apart from getting a second view of things, this can also help one to be more disciplined than if he/she manages investing affairs all by themselves. More importantly, if one does not have the time or inclination to learn, it is best to outsource the process to outside advisers.

One must also master the art of saying "no". In investing parlance, it can also mean going short. Our investing minds are more trained to say "yes" when we see an opportunity after careful research. It is easier to go long on the market or stock than go short because going short means we must train ourselves to say "no", which is not easy. Even in life, we struggle to say no more than yes, which can be the chief cause of many problems. The ability to say "no" becomes more important if we have a sizeable investing amount at stake, which is normally the case for high-net-worth individuals or fund managers.

The ability to hold on to an investment or dispose of it is a function of the state of the stock more than the state of our investments. If we have a multi-bagger where one is sitting on, say, 200x type of profit, there is no justification to sell unless it is driven by liquidity considerations. Also, if one is down on a stock, it is not a reason to sell unless the business situation surrounding that stock has changed for the worse. Having said this, our mind still "anchors" our investment returns to decision-making. Remember, the market does not know how much profit or loss we make on an investment. That is the key to understanding.

Therefore, psychology plays a huge role in our investing decision-making and if we must do it ourselves, we better control our mind and make it free of biases. That is easier said than done.

02

Learning From Mistakes

Human psychology is a powerful force and, at times, can be a spoiler, especially in the world of investing. We tend to glorify our successes and ignore our mistakes by giving them a passing reference on coffee tables. Stock market investing is treacherous and requires strategy and monitoring. Even if our strategy is sub-par, a good monitoring system can save the day. On the other hand, a great strategy with sub-par monitoring can be disastrous.

If we earn money, we are savers and investors. Hence, it may be worthwhile to recount some of the mistakes I have made while handling my savings, especially in stock markets.

1. Not Having Endurance

Markets, by nature, are volatile and hence make our emotions swing. It is normal to get upbeat in a bull market (and laud our expertise) and disheartened in a bear market (and curse bad times and luck). However, what is critical is our endurance during the down market, where our emotions are tested to the hilt. I remember buying some of what is called today as blue chips way back in the 1990s when I stepped into a career. If only I had the endurance to have held them today, I could have retired a while ago! Instead, I gave into the market psychology of selling when everyone was selling.

Sometimes, our investments go nowhere even though they do not produce any losses. They can test our patience since we will have the urge to compare them with broader markets or with other stocks. Stock price appreciation can never be a straight line. Many stocks have a long period of flat performance and then a take-off (what I call an inflexion point). But the point is we cannot predict when that take-off will happen. Since we cannot predict this, we sometimes lose interest and exit the investment. That can prove costly as well. Here is an example of Eicher Motors, which had a long stretch of flat stock prices (2001 to 2009) hovering between Rs. 24 and Rs. 400, and then a sudden burst of performance taking the stock price all the way up to Rs. 21,000 within a short span of time. If we had been holding this stock since 2001, it would have really tested our patience!

2. Going by the Herd Mentality

Identifying investment opportunities is time-consuming and lonely work. It requires validation from several fronts including financial analysis, qualitative analysis, and connecting all the dots that are strewn all over the place. Even then, one cannot be sure about the prospects as of the date of investing.

However, there is an easy way of doing all this. Just go by what our friends/colleagues/relatives are doing or what our brokers recommend. If they are buying ITC, buy it. If the markets are going up, keep buying when the trend is positive, regardless of whether valuations are reasonable. This is a sure-shot recipe for underperformance. I used to compile the top holdings of all the leading fund managers to see where they were investing and mimic their investments, only to realise that such a strategy was very similar to herd mentality.

3. Mistaking Name/Brand for Profits

The key indices (like Sensex and Nifty) are always dominated by large caps. Most of them would be market leaders in their respective industries (Bajaj Auto, Infosys, Reliance, ITC, to name a few). Market leaders are big brand owners. But being big and owning great brands does not equate to good performance all the time. Sometimes, it is the small, seemingly boring businesses without any recognisable brand power that can create enormous shareholder wealth. Also, once a company becomes a large-cap and a brand leader, it may unnecessarily spend money to keep that status, which can be a big negative for the shareholders. No wonder many of the large caps in the index have a poor performance track record in terms of creating shareholder wealth.

4. Not Acting When I Should Have

It is said that the easiest thing in the stock market is to buy, and the toughest is to sell. We will be forced to take a sell decision under three scenarios, i.e., when we made good money and wonder if we want to take some profits, when we have lost significantly and wonder if we should cut further losses or when we have a liquidity need where we are forced to sell regardless of the situation. The first is a good problem to have, and the third is a bad problem to have. However, the trickiest part is the second. This is where psychology comes in and acts as a spoiler. When our investment is down, our psyche refuses to accept it as we feel we have grossly erred in our judgement. And there is this innate feeling that this is temporary, and the value will come back. This feeling need not be backed by any logic. It can just be a feeling. Also, we have a reference point, i.e., our purchase price, and our psychology is swayed by this reference point. Unfortunately, the market does not know or does not care what our reference point is. Hence, once the investment goes down in value, it need not come back (as we innately feel). Rather, it can go down even further. I remember being caught in one such investment cycle where I invested in a Gulf stock. Relative to my investment value, my realised loss on that investment was 98%! A classic example of not acting when I should have.

5. **Averaging on the Downside**

This probably counts as a very common reaction when our investment value is down. When the stock price tumbles, instead of fearing further downside our instincts let us think that "if it was attractive at the earlier level when I bought, it should be even more attractive now, so let me buy more".

Again, the spoiler in this situation is the reference point, which is our initial purchase price. Our reference point has no reference value for the market, and hence, averaging down on the downside can only result in "throwing good money after bad". Since markets are volatile, bounce-backs are common and can make us feel that we have a great opportunity to average our purchase price when the bounce-back happens. However, if the price bounces back, it will also make our investment look good, and hence, we should be less worried. But if our averaging down does not pay off, the net loss on that investment will be manifold. Hence, the need to wait for the right price to buy stocks so that we are not caught in this dilemma of "double down."

6. **Not Being Affected by Loss in Profits**

Not all losses are the same. A loss of capital can produce more pain relative to, say, the loss in profits. Hence, complacency to deal with losses in the second case. We panic the moment we have a loss of capital. But we do not show the same panic when our profits are reduced, though, in theory, a loss is a loss. At least, that is how I dealt with my losses – worrying the most in cases where the capital is negative and not worrying about those where there is a loss in profit situation. The best way to deal with this problem is to equate our year-end market value to 100 and look at the appreciation/depreciation from that perspective. Appended is a table with some hypothetical numbers to explain the concept.

Table : 47 Loss in Profit

Year	Value	CAGR	If equated to 100 every year
0	100	-	-
1	120	20%	20%
2	150	22%	25%
3	130	9%	-13%
4	120	5%	-8%
5	100	0%	-17%

If our investment starts at 100 and in a 5-year horizon touches a peak of 150 and reverts to 100, our compounded annual growth rate (CAGR) will be 0, with no negative performance highlighted in the interim 5 years. Since we don't see any negative performance, we may turn complacent to a loss in profits. However, if we equated the year-end value to 100 every year, years 3, 4, and five would have highlighted negative performance. Such a performance highlight could either have enabled us to take the profits or do something else other than stare at the stagnant performance.

7. Not Insuring the Portfolio

Insurance need not be restricted to just life, cars, and bikes. Even our stock portfolio requires insurance lest we run the risk of swinging along with the market. Like life insurance or other insurance products, portfolio insurance also will cost money. But that cost is bearable given the downside protection it offers during sharp market downturns. A simple portfolio insurance example is to buy put options. Fortunately, Indian markets now offer such portfolio insurance products. Even where we have investments only in mutual funds or ETFs (for some reason, many think they are safe investments!), we still need to insure our investment, as our fund manager will not do it for us.

8. Mistaking Performance for Stability

When a stock performs well on the back of good company performance, we can mistake it for stability and hence may fail to check the story at regular intervals. Turning points, even in a good scenario, can be sudden and can wipe out gains in no time. An example could be Motherson Sumi, an auto ancillary company. Like Eicher, the company had a long streak of ordinary performance and then had a nice take-off. From Rs.88 in Sept 2013, the stock went up to Rs.348 in August 2015. Not many paid attention to its over-dependence on Volkswagen (40%), and when bad news came in the form of a scandal involving VW, the stock price of Motherson Sumi plummeted 42% in just two months!

9. Mistaking Performance for Skill

The biggest mistake we can make as investors is to attribute success to our skill and failure to luck! (or bad luck!). The performance of a company and, therefore, its stock price is dependent on scores of quantitative and qualitative factors. While through skill we may be able to crack the quantitative part, it is a time-consuming and innate exercise to look through a company qualitatively.

Qualitative factors include a deep understanding of the Board and the executive management, their track record in terms of corporate governance, ethical conduct of the company and its owners, employee remuneration, tweaking books to show a certain performance number, political connections, front-running the stock, insider trading, etc. Either we devote considerable time to unlocking these essential elements to develop the needed conviction or go with a gut feeling on the subject. Given our inability to find time, we normally resort to the second tactic. When our decision turns positive, we feel we are in control of this process. Always double-check the story during a good performance period just to be sure we can keep the profits.

Honestly, I have been through all these mistakes in one form or the other. This list of mistakes may not be exhaustive, and I may unravel many more as I reflect.

03

Managing Conflict of Interest

In our day-to-day work, we come across several situations where we face a severe conflict of interest. If we are in a situation faced with a conflict of interest, ethics demand that we disclose and move away from the situation that creates the conflict.

However, if we are faced with a situation where there is a potential conflict of interest that we note but cannot do anything about, that would probably not be as simple to deal with because the ability to remove the conflict of interest is not within our hands. Here is a simple list of certain conflicts of interest that I have observed mostly within the finance/commerce space over time, and it would be interesting to see how they play out in terms of business decisions.

Credit Rating

This is the mother of all conflicts of interest that I have ever observed. The credit rater is paid by the credit rating. This conflict probably was at the heart of the global financial crisis. However, the model continues to operate the same way. Even now, credit rating companies are paid by credit-rated companies and not by any independent agency. Well, to an extent, credit rating agencies can appear to be unaffected by this conflict of interest, but I am sure that down the line, there would be an impact of this direct conflict of interest between the rating agency and the rated company. The best way to resolve this is to create an independent credit rating agency fully funded by the government. The government can impose some sort of tax on corporations on an overall basis and try to do this as an independent exercise completely devoid of any conflict of interest. A credit rating borne out of such a process can be more unbiased and objective.

Sell-side Research

The brokerage industry thrives on brokerage commissions. Brokerage commissions are derived from the extent of trading by clients (investment companies or asset management companies). To elicit interest in trade, brokerage companies come out with a series of research notes on companies in what is now popularly known as sell-side research. The idea is to trigger either buying interest or selling interest about the client firms so that the commission earned can be increased.

Obviously, this sort of research is not going to be independent or objective because the purpose of this research is basically to trigger trade actions and not to enable unbiased, objective investment decisions. There is still no way out of this sell-side research dilemma. Investment communities continue to depend highly on sell-side research even though they see this conflict of interest very clearly. Of course, certain regulators mandate publishing details like investment banking business done in the past year, the number of sell call/buy calls, and the history of calls along with actual performance. Often, these disclosures come in small print!

Media

Media is probably one of the best examples of a conflict of interest. The most popular newspapers and magazines almost completely thrive on advertising revenues. Nearly 90% of their total income accrues from advertising revenues rather than subscription revenues. So obviously, this poses a limit on how far we can go to be independent of client companies, lest our main source of revenue be hit. This is true for print media, television channels, and digital media too. We all know that views that are being aired about these companies and their clients can never be independent or objective since their existence depends on the continuation of their advertising contracts. And curiously enough, the client list can also include political parties!

Audit and Consulting

Auditors normally are mandated to be extremely independent, and they must provide an independent view of the financial status of the company. Like credit rating agencies, auditors are being compensated by the company that is being audited, which itself is a potential conflict of interest, but by virtue of their access to almost all records and status of the company, they are also able to see what type of consulting mandates can be obtained and executed by the audit firms. Technically, they may not do it under the same name, but there are ways to get around this.

Board of Directors

The board of directors can either be independent businessmen, in which case they would try to push their business opportunities, or they could simply also be a client or vendor for the company. It may not be done directly, but there is always a conflict of interest between being on the board and trying to influence the company to use the services of the businesses with which they are directly or indirectly connected.

Hospitals

Major hospitals and, to an extent, even clinics of a decent size have their own testing laboratories. These laboratories house expensive, often imported, medical equipment whose capital costs need to be recovered as soon as possible. Hence, doctors have an implicit incentive to refer patients to sometimes necessary but, most of the time, unnecessary tests to recover capital investments. I believe that many hospital doctors have targets when it comes to recommending tests!

In summary, conflict of interest abounds and surrounds us in our everyday lives. It may be a source of intense frustration when it impacts our personal lives (like the hospital example given above). In corporate situations, it may affect our performance as investment or portfolio managers, as we rely on credit ratings or equity research to make investment decisions. In most cases, the cost of conflict of interest is not straightforward or apparent, although we know it exists. It may pay well to be conscious of this while making decisions, though in many cases, it cannot be avoided. By no means is this list exhaustive.

04

Power of Networking

It's not just for marketing people to be well-networked. It applies to every profession and every community. Networking implies enabling active interaction among people that we can connect to receive and provide knowledge. It is important because it can make a huge difference to our career, enable us to meet people that we can appreciate, build very crucial bridges in our lives, and make a world of difference when things challenge us on many fronts. However, there are many roadblocks to effective networking. The question is how to overcome them and effectively network.

The first rule is 'Overcome hesitation' – Many times, we are very hesitant to really make an acquaintance with a stranger, saying Hello!! Or writing a small memo introducing ourselves. There is the hesitancy in us to really make that first phone call or write that first email. But if we overcome that hesitancy, we can feel that we are much more comfortable in terms of how we start building our network. This is the first and most important step that one should take to overcome hesitation.

The second important thing is 'Don't hesitate to ask for advice or opinion'. People really respect being asked for opinion. We always have a very high level of tendency to talk more and listen less. Just reverse the process, make your contacts talk more and provide yourself the opportunity to listen.

The third aspect to networking is 'Perseverance'. Don't be afraid of dead ends. They happen all the time. Not every step that we make towards building our contacts and networking can result in a success. It doesn't mean that we should give up our networking efforts. We should just put behind those things that doesn't work and keep moving with the single objective of building effective networking.

The fourth important aspect is when we network, try to follow basic etiquettes. Thanking a network that just got connected with is a basic requirement. If we have approached a particular person for a particular aspect, keep him posted about subsequent steps that we take. This will really help them appreciating us in the long-run. People do remember small things.

The fifth important aspect is, 'Don't restrict networking group to professional job colleagues'. It's a huge temptation to really reach out and build our network only among job colleagues. It is important to expand network to ex-colleagues, friends, educational acquaintances and to a host of other people that can really widen our perspective.

Finally, social media can be used to build networks. Among the most popular social media platforms today, LinkedIn is one of the most important tools for building a professional network. One can be very effective by being an active LinkedIn member. We can browse people of repute and request them to connect with us and keep actively engaged on LinkedIn by contributing to occasional articles, sharing updates and appreciating people when they move on to something very important. This is the most effective method of networking, and it is freely available, and people should make full use of this powerful engine.

Research Tips

Research, in general, is hard, and equity research is even more so. Research is about looking at history and guessing the future direction. The first part may be easy and doable, but the hardest part is the second aspect of guessing the future. Most of us are trained to handle equity research as a quantitative process that includes setting the context, establishing a framework, collecting data, analysing data, and writing the report. Most probably, this is how the equity research process is drilled into us in business schools and other learning places.

While this process is obviously a good place to start, it cannot stop there. There are many qualitative aspects to equity research and taking cognizance of that can greatly improve the way we analyse and present things.

Here are some research tips drawn from my experience over the years.

1. **Using Adjectives:** It is very tempting to use adjectives while making a point just to give it more emphasis. Analysts also give emphasis by showing a word or group of words in bold or italics or underlined. However, the use of adjectives can be superfluous and can take attention away from the meat of the argument. Adjectives like extremely, wonderful, worst, etc., tend to be used more often, and the same sentence will look much better without adjectives. Avoiding adjectives can bring seriousness better than otherwise, though it appears counterintuitive.

2. **Using Colloquial Words:** After the advent of social media, the use of short phrases and colloquial words has increased (for e.g., pretty much). Speaking form is different from writing form. It is best avoided in writing form. In other words, do not write like you speak.

3. **Do not Plagiarise:** One may get inspired from someone but should never copy which is technically what is called plagiarism.

There are software programs to check and hence it is not easy to plagiarise anymore. Still, due to time pressure, many resort to convoluted plagiarism, which may still be detected. It is best that one reads, understands, and then develops an argument using one's own thinking.

4. **Be mindful of Sources:** The research process is highly based on tapping several sources. In this age, these sources can be formal (like academic papers or equity research reports) or informal like chats that happen in WhatsApp groups etc. Newspapers are a resorted source when it comes to research. However, it is best to avoid newspaper citations as newspaper reporters or analysts aim for sensation more than correctness, and pressure to file reports leaves them with little time to fact-check. In addition, the style of newspaper reporting tends to rely more on personal quotes (Oil minister said so and so or Mr. X said so and so). Hence, the flavour is different and, therefore, the purpose. It is better to go to the source, delineate and then present rather than blindly relying on the first point of the source.

5. **Visualising a pre-existing context in a new context:** A pre-existing context (like national champions in country X) can provide fodder for reimaging them in a different context (national champions in India). In my long years of research experience, this served me very well. While I normally enjoy a well-presented context, I try to imagine them in a new context, and this has produced some good findings. (I could have said "fantastic" findings, but I am mindful of my first suggestion to avoid using adjectives!).

6. **Observe unusual patterns:** Research analysts are normally bogged down so much in numbers sometimes it can really create a numbness in the brain. This will not enable one to observe unusual patterns due to data errors. For e.g., the INR/

USD number can be stated as 825 instead of 82.5 and can go unnoticed if we fail to question the pattern. Of course, a feeling for unusual patterns comes out of experience (knowing well that Rupee cannot be 825), but it is worth examining unusual patterns one more time just to avoid embarrassing findings.

7. **Share Knowledge:** The more we give, the more we get. Analyst day job is spent mostly reading several articles and research papers. However, only some will get used where many will be either dropped or filed for future use. However, if one develops the habit of sharing some interesting articles (may or may not be useful in the current context) generously with others, over time we will also start receiving many in our inbox.

8. **Seek Research mentorship:** Mentoring is normally understood in a career sense more than anything else. However, every activity that one pursues can be actively supported by way of mentors who are good in that field and whose expertise can be helpful. Research is no exception. As equity research analysts, one can seek and get research mentorship from other experienced analysts (inside or outside the system) and constantly bounce ideas and get valuable perspectives.

9. **Read Books:** As analysts, we read many articles, but reading books is slowly becoming out of fashion, mainly due to a lack of time. However, the experience of devouring a book is quite different from that of an article or a research paper. Books are more intense and, therefore, require more time. However, the deep understanding one gains by reading a book is no comparison to other avenues. Successful fund managers and corporate CEOs have this one habit running across.

10. **Promote your Research:** It is important that we promote our own research though many social media handles that are available today. Promoting one's work is as important if not

more important than the work itself. It can help receive counter viewpoints as well as accolades. Shyness can prevent one from promoting their research, but it is a bad idea.

11. **Establish your Style:** Each person has a unique writing style. Some have a straight way of explaining things, while some other can have a great sense of humour while presenting something. (For e.g., economists successfully predicted the last 7 of 5 recessions!). It is important to identify and hone your own style to create a long-term impact.

12. **Some Writing tips:** Do not write long sentences. If they get long, break them. Also, try to be grammatically correct. Again, there are software programs that one can get help with. Presenting ideas in correct and cogent language can improve the appreciation value.

Reprinted from

The COMMERCIAL *and* FINANCIAL CHRONICLE

Thursday, December 6, 1951

The Security I Like Best

WARREN E. BUFFETT

Buffett-Falk & Co., Omaha, Nebr.

Government Employees Insurance Co.

Full employment, boomtime profits and record dividend payments do not set the stage for depressed security prices. Most industries have been riding this wave of prosperity during the past five years with few ripples to disturb the tide.

The auto insurance business has not shared in the boom. After the staggering losses of the immediate postwar period, the situation began to right itself in 1949. In 1950, stock casualty companies again took it on the chin with underwriting experience the second worst in 15 years. The recent earnings reports of casualty companies, particularly those with the bulk of writings in auto lines, have diverted bull market enthusiasm from their stocks. On the basis of normal earning power and asset factors, many of these stocks appear undervalued.

The nature of the industry is such as to ease cyclical bumps. Auto insurance is regarded as a necessity by the majority of purchasers. Contracts must be renewed yearly at rates based upon experience. The lag of rates behind costs, although detrimental in a period of rising prices as has characterized the 1945-1951 period, should prove beneficial if deflationary forces should be set in action.

Other industry advantages include lack of inventory, collection, labor and raw material problems. The hazard of product obsolescence and related equipment obsolescence is also absent.

Government Employees Insurance Corporation was organized in the mid-30's to provide complete auto insurance on a nation-wide basis to an eligible class including: (1) Federal, State and municipal government employees; (2) active and reserve commissioned officers and the first three pay grades of non-commissioned officers of the Armed Forces; (3) veterans who were eligible when on active duty; (4) former policyholders; (5) faculty members of universities, colleges and schools; (6) government contractor employees engaged in defense work exclusively, and (7) stockholders.

The company has no agents or branch offices. As a result, policyholders receive standard auto insurance policies at premium discounts running as high as 30% off manual rates. Claims are handled promptly through approximately 500 representatives throughout the country.

The term "growth company" has been applied with abandon during the past few years to companies whose sales increases represented little more than inflation of prices and general easing of business competition. GEICO qualifies as a legitimate growth company based upon the following record:

Year—	Premiums Written	Policyholders
1936	$103,696.31	3,754
1940	768,057.86	25,514
1945	1,638,562.09	51,697
1950	8,016,975.79	143,944

Of course the investor of today does not profit from yesterday's growth. In GEICO's case, there is reason to believe the major portion of growth lies ahead. Prior to 1950, the company was only licensed in 15 of 50 jurisdictions including D. C. and Hawaii. At the beginning of the year there were less than 3,000 policyholders in New York State. Yet 25% saved on an insurance bill of $125 in New York should look bigger to the prospect than the 25% saved on the $50 rate in more sparsely settled regions.

As cost competition increases in importance during times of recession, GEICO's rate attraction should become even more effective in diverting business from the brother-in-law. With insurance rates moving higher due to inflation, the 25% spread in rates becomes wider in terms of dollars and cents.

There is no pressure from agents to accept questionable applicants or renew poor risks. In States where the rate structure is inadequate, new promotion may be halted.

Probably the biggest attraction of GEICO is the profit margin advantage it enjoys. The ratio of underwriting profit to premiums earned in 1949 was 27.5% for GEICO as compared to 6.7% for the 135 stock casualty and surety companies summarized by Best's. As experience turned for the worse in 1950, Best's aggregate's profit margin dropped to 3.0% and GEICO's dropped to 18.0%. GEICO does not write all casualty lines; however, bodily injury and property damage, both important lines for GEICO, were among the least profitable lines. GEICO also does a large amount of collision writing, which was a profitable line in 1950.

During the first half of 1951, practically all insurers operated in the red on casualty lines with bodily injury and property damage among the most unprofitable. Whereas GEICO's profit margin was cut to slightly above 9%, Massachusett's Bonding & Insurance showed a 16% loss, New Amsterdam Casualty an 8% loss, Standard Accident Insurance a 9% loss, etc.

Because of the rapid growth of GEICO, cash dividends have had to remain low. Stock dividends and a 25-for-1 split increased the outstanding shares from 3,000 on June 1, 1948, to 250,000 on Nov. 10, 1951. Valuable rights to subscribe to stock of affiliated companies have also been issued.

Benjamin Graham has been Chairman of the Board since his investment trust acquired and distributed a large block of the stock in 1948. Leo Goodwin, who has guided GEICO's growth since inception, is the able President. At the end of 1950, the 10 members of the Board of Directors owned approximately one-third of the outstanding stock.

Earnings in 1950 amounted to $3.92 as contrasted to $4.71 on the smaller amount of business in 1949. These figures include no allowance for the increase in the unearned premium reserve which was substantial in both years. Earnings in 1951 will be lower than 1950, but the wave of rate increases during the past summer should evidence themselves in 1952 earnings. Investment income quadrupled between 1947 and 1950, reflecting the growth of the company's assets.

At the present price of about eight times the earnings of 1950, a poor year for the industry, it appears that no price is being paid for the tremendous growth potential of the company.

24

Note: This is a research note by Warren Buffet back in 1961. Picture Perfect and a great case study to show case the research tips.

Key Takeaways

You have now reached the end of the book.

Investing is always a tricky art and needs constant attention and specialisation. Active fund management has been facing the heat from passive funds for a long-time now. The promise of generating alpha can fall flat, considering historical data. Investors would want to ride a wave but avoid shocks (or drawdowns).

Considering these, what are the key takeaways from the book? Let me summarise them here:

1. **Observe the Macro:** I am not an economist by qualification, but I benefitted a lot by focusing my interest on the subject. Macro observations can be less noisy but more difficult due to the complex economic web. It may be a good idea to learn economics even if we are not a student of economics as macro binds everything and shows us the path. A sharp understanding of how different economic parameters interact with each other can keep one slightly ahead of the curve and avoid major crashes.

2. **Retail Investing is different:** While this book is about researching Indian equities, it provides some insights on how to focus on managing one's own personal money. It is important to be a successful investor of our personal money before we can claim that position for managing institutional money. A good analogy is for a doctor to remain healthy to infuse confidence in his/her patients. The book has focused on the aspects of retail investing, which is mainly for this reason. If we are a professional investor, we can do this ourselves. If we are not, we will be well advised to take the help of an independent financial adviser. Be clear about the purpose of investing. Stick to easy bets if we are starved of time and venture into wild bets (like Crypto or hedge funds) if we have time in hand to do thorough research and see all the dimensions clearly.

3. **Handle the "Market Timing" question:** Timing the market is difficult and should be avoided at all costs. Most probably, an investor in a fund experiences lower returns compared to the fund due to the wrong timing of his/her entry and exit into the fund. The reason why investors experience a lower return compared to underlying funds in which they are invested explains the hardship of market timing. A systematic investment at regular intervals will avoid the dangers of getting caught on the wrong side of the timing cycle. Having said that, one should also seize extraordinary times (like war, floods, crisis, etc.) and be willing to move against the tide. It is essential that one has some dry powder (meaning some cash at all times) to seize such extraordinary times. A good example is COVID-19, during which the markets crashed very quickly and regained all the losses in no time.

4. **Understand Mutual Fund Ecosystem:** Whether we are individual investors investing in a mutual fund or a professional managing a mutual fund, it is imperative to have a solid understanding of the mutual fund landscape to differentiate funds. For e.g., in the race between Exchange Traded Funds (ETFs) and index funds, ETFs apparently will win hands down in terms of costs. However, if one factors other costs like market impact, brokerage, and volume, the conclusion can be different.

5. **Choose your Investment Style:** The book discusses several investment styles that one can practice as a professional. It ranges from portfolio construction (active vs passive, concentrated portfolios) to various styles (like value, contrarian, and momentum). It is important to identify the style that best suits one as a professional investor and keep excelling at it.

6. **Be a Sector Specialist:** Sector specialisation is becoming very rare as fund managers want to be generalists and have a sense of

all the sectors that go into the portfolio. However, understanding banking is not the same as understanding energy. It pays to be a sector specialist with a realisation that it may take years, if not decades, to get even a sense of what moves within the sector. However, in the end, sector specialisation would give one an edge that others will find hard to match.

7. **Discriminate Stocks:** Stock selection is the game funds managers play in pursuit of alpha and is at the centre of what happens in the mutual fund world. If we are a direct stock investor, it is important to discriminate between long-term value creators and short-term fads. Many quantitative and qualitative variables are used to select stocks. Create your own template and use it to derive the benefits.

8. **Understand index Ecosystem:** Indices are normally used as benchmarks to measure the performance of funds. However, they come in many shapes and sizes (price vs total return for e.g.). Given the explosion of the mutual fund industry, the slices and dice of the index have also exploded. Indices suffer from survivorship bias in that one sees only the current constituents of the index. However, companies do come in and exit the index for various reasons. It is important to understand companies that survived this process. Also, be it Sensex or Nifty, it is at the heart of analysis for many pundits daily. Estimating the overall index in the next 10 or 20 years can be challenging but useful.

9. **Be a risk manager first:** Robust risk management is embedded in the process of many successful investors. Successful investing is all about avoiding drawdowns, and risk management helps one get there. Risk and return are the two sides of the same coin, but the obsession is always with return rather than managing risk. Instead of starting with a question on "how attractive a stock is", it is better to flip the question to "What can go wrong

here?". There are plenty of risk management lessons that are worth reading to see how a lack of focus on risk management can lead to windfall losses.

10. **Befriend Volatility:** If we are in the equity space, start treating volatility as our friend. A deep understanding of what causes volatility and how to identify extraordinary volatility with normal volatility can be a key to investing success.